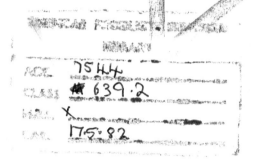
atlas
of the living resources
of the seas

de los recursos
vivos del mar

Prepared by
the FAO Fisheries Department

the
UNIVERSITY
of
GREENWICH

Preparado por
el Departamento de Pesca de la FAO

Food and Agriculture Organization
of the United Nations

Organisation des Nations Unies
pour l'alimentation et l'agriculture

Rome, 1981

Organización de las Naciones Unidas
para la Agricultura y la Alimentación

First edition July 1971[1]
Second edition January 1972[1]
Third edition July 1972
Fourth edition September 1981

Première édition, juillet 1971[1]
Deuxième édition, janvier 1972[1]
Troisième édition, juillet 1972
Quatrième édition, septembre 1981

Primera edición, julio 1971[1]
Segunda edición, enero 1972[1]
Tercera edición, julio 1972
Cuarta edición, septiembre 1981

P-43
ISBN 92-5-001000-1

© FAO 1981

Printed in Italy - Imprimé en Italie - Impreso en Italia

---

[1] Appeared as FAO Fisheries Circular No. 126 and FAO Fisheries Circular No. 126-Rev.1.

[1] A paru comme: FAO, Circulaire des pêches N° 126 et FAO, Circulaire des pêches N° 126-Rév.1.

[1] Aparecida como Circular de Pesca de la FAO N° 126, y Circular de Pesca de la FAO N° 126-Rév.1.

PREPARATION OF MAPS

The revision of the maps in this atlas has been prepared by J.F. de Veen[1] (Rijksinstituut voor Visserijonderzoek, IJmuiden, Netherlands) with the assistance of J.-P. Troadec and G.D. Sharp of the FAO Fisheries Department.

Fiorella Marcon d'Andrea was responsible for cartographic compilation, map and section design, and colour composition, under the supervision of M. Cappucci, Chief of the FAO Graphics Section.

The maps on the end-papers are based on the Briesemeisler elliptical equal-area projection (courtesy of the American Geographical Society, New York).

The FAO field experts who participated in the preparation of the Atlas were as follows: W. Brandhorst (E), R. Buzeta (E), R.W. Ellis (C,L), C.B. Kensler (L), M. Odemar (E), S.L. Okonski (E), S. Olsen (H), F. Poinsard (D), L. Rijavec (E), A.C. Simpson (C), H.J. Squires (L), R.J. Slack-Smith (E), N.P. van Zalinge (K), M. Yesaki (E) and S. Zupanovic (H).

Officers of the FAO Fisheries Department also worked on the preparation of the maps, in particular V. Angelescu, L.K. Boerema, S. Garcia, L.P.D. Gertenbach, J.A. Gulland, A. Isarankura, D. Menasveta, M.N. Mistakidis, M.A. Robinson, G.D. Sharp and S.C. Venema.

The following research workers helped with the preparation of this document by supplying draft maps or basic information:

PRÉPARATION DES CARTES

Les cartes de l'Atlas ont été révisées par M. J.F. de Veen[1] (Rijksinstituut voor Visserijonderzoek, IJmuiden, Pays-Bas) avec le concours de MM. J.-P. Troadec et G.D. Sharp, du Département des pêches de la FAO.

Fiorella Marcon d'Andrea a assumé la responsabilité du travail cartographique, des maquettes des cartes et des profils, ainsi que de la composition des couleurs, sous la direction de M. Cappucci, chef de la Section arts graphiques de la FAO.

Les cartes figurant sur les gardes sont basées sur la projection elliptique équivalente de Briesemeisler (avec l'autorisation de l'American Geographical Society, New York).

MM. W. Brandhorst (E), R. Buzeta (E), R.W. Ellis (C,L), C.B. Kensler (L), M. Odemar (E), S.L. Okonski (E), S. Olsen (H), F. Poinsard (D), L. Rijavec (E), A.C. Simpson (C), H.J. Squires (L), R.J. Slack-Smith (E), N.P. van Zalinge (K), M. Yesaki (E) et S. Zupanovic (H), experts de la FAO sur le terrain, ont également pris une part active à la préparation de cet atlas.

Plusieurs fonctionnaires du Département des pêches de la FAO ont participé à la préparation des cartes, en particulier: M.M. V. Angelescu, L.K. Boerema, S. Garcia, L.P.D. Gertenbach, J.A. Gulland, A. Isarankura, D. Menasveta, M.N. Mistakidis, M.A. Robinson, G.D. Sharp et S.C. Venema.

Les chercheurs suivants ont contribué à la préparation de ce document en fournissant des projets de cartes ou des informations de base:

PREPARACION DE LOS MAPAS

La revisión de los mapas de este Atlas ha sido preparada por J.F. de Veen[1] (Rijksinstituut voor Visserijonderzoek, IJmuiden, Países Bajos), con ayuda de J.-P. Troadec y G.D. Sharp, del Departamento de Pesca de la FAO.

Fiorella Marcon d'Andrea ha realizado la compilación cartográfica, diseño de mapas y secciones, así como la composición del color, bajo la dirección de M. Cappucci, Jefe de la Sección de Gráficos de la FAO.

Los mapas que figuran en las guardas se basan en la proyección elíptica equivalente de Briesemeisler (cortesía de la American Geographical Society, New York).

También colaboraron en la preparación de este Atlas los siguientes expertos de la FAO sobre el terreno: W. Brandhorst (E), R. Buzeta (E), R.W. Ellis (C,L), C.B. Kensler (L), M. Odemar (E), S.L. Okonski (E), S. Olsen (H), F. Poinsard (D), L. Rijavec (E), A.C. Simpson (C), H.J. Squires (L), R.J. Slack-Smith (E), N.P. van Zalinge (K), M. Yesaki (L) y S. Zupanovic (H).

Funcionarios del Departamento de Pesca de la FAO participaron en la preparación de los mapas, en particular V. Angelescu, L.K. Boerema, S. Garcia, L.P.D. Gertenbach, J.A. Gulland, A. Isarankura, D. Menasveta, M.N. Mistakidis, M.A. Robinson, G.D. Sharp y S.C. Venema.

Los siguientes investigadores han contribuido a la preparación de este documento, facilitando proyectos de mapas o informaciones de base:

R.S. Bailey, Marine Laboratory, Aberdeen, Scotland	B[2]	J. Møller Christensen, Danmarks Fisheri- og Havundersøgelser, Charlottenlund, Denmark	B	F. Domain, Centre océanologique de Bretagne, Brest, France	D
A. Ben-Tuvia, Sea Fisheries Research Station, Haifa, Israel	G	A. Corten, Rijksinstituut voor Visserijonderzoek, IJmuiden, Netherlands	2.9	P.Y. Dremière, Centre de recherches, Institut scientifique et technique des pêches maritimes, France	D
M. Blackburn, Friday Harbor, Washington, USA	L	N. Daan, Rijksinstituut voor Visserijonderzoek, IJmuiden, Netherlands	2.2	J. Elwertowski, Sea Fisheries Institute, Gdynia, Poland	D
R.W. Blacker, Fisheries Laboratory, Lowestoft, England	2.2,B	J. Dardignac, Centre de recherches, Institut scientifique et technique des pêches maritimes, La Rochelle, France	B	A. Franklin, Fisheries Laboratory, Burnham-on-Crouch, England	B

Contd-Suite-Cont.

---

[1] It was with deep regret that news was received of the death of Mr de Veen on 21 April 1980 while the Atlas was being prepared for publication. Grateful acknowledgement is made of the time, patience and skill he gave to this revision, which was the last major achievement of his scientific career.

[2] The letters denote the regions covered by the contributors (see list of maps, page *vii*).

---

[1] C'est avec un profond regret que nous avons appris le décès de M. de Veen, survenu le 21 avril 1980, alors que l'Atlas était en préparation. Nous lui rendons hommage pour la patience et la compétence dont il a fait preuve pour cette révision, ainsi que pour le temps qu'il a bien voulu consacrer à cette tâche, l'une des dernières grandes réalisations de sa carrière scientifique.

[2] Les lettres indiquent les régions étudiées par les chercheurs (voir la liste des cartes, page *vii*).

---

[1] Es con gran pesar que se ha recibido la noticia del fallecimiento del Sr. de Veen, acaecido el 21 de abril de 1980, mientras se estaba preparando el Atlas para su publicación. Se reconoce con agradecimiento el tiempo, la paciencia y la habilidad dedicados por el Sr. de Veen a esta revisión, que constituye sin duda el último mayor logro de su carrera científica.

[2] Las letras indican las regiones estudiadas por los autores (véase la lista de los mapas, página *vii*).

R. Gambell, International Whaling Commission, Cambridge, England   2.18

Y. Ghēno, 11 rue des Roses, Fontenay-aux-Roses, France   F

D. de G. Griffith, Fisheries Division, Dublin, Eire   B

J.R.G. Hislop, Marine Laboratory, Aberdeen, Scotland   B

I. Ikeda, Far Seas Fisheries Research Laboratory, Orido, Japan   I,D

W.E. Johnson, Pacific Biological Station, Nanaimo, B.C., Canada   2.12

R.E. Kearney, South Pacific Commission, Nouméa, New Caledonia   K,H,M

S. Kikawa, Far Seas Fisheries Research Laboratory, Orido, Japan   2.12-2.17

W.L. Klawe, Inter-American Tropical Tuna Commission, La Jolla, California, USA   H

E.F. Klima, Office of Living Resources, National Oceanic and Atmospheric Administration, Rockville, Md, USA   C

S. Kume, Far Seas Fisheries Research Laboratory, Orido, Japan   2.12-2.17

M.G. Larrañeta, Laboratorio de Vigo, Vigo, España   G

Loh-Lee Low, N.W. and Alaska Fisheries Center, Seattle, Washington, USA   J

M. Masutti, Laboratorio Oceanográfico de Baleares, Mallorca, España   G

H.J. Montesinos, Centro de Investigaciones Pesqueras, Cumaná, Venezuela   C

R.A. Neal, Gulf Fisheries Center, Galveston, Texas, USA   2.1

G. Newman, Department of Fisheries, Sea Point, South Africa   D,F

W.R. Rathjen, National Marine Fisheries Service, Gloucester, Mass., USA   C

G. Saetersdal, Institute of Marine Research, Bergen, Norway   B

A. Saville, Marine Laboratory, Aberdeen, Scotland   B

C. Shingu, Far Seas Fisheries Research Laboratory, Orido, Japan   2.12-2.17

B.R. Smith, Kanudi Fishery Research Station, Konedobu, Papua New Guinea   K

Y. Takahashi, Far Seas Fisheries Research Laboratory, Orido, Japan   2.3

S. Ueyanagi, Far Seas Fisheries Research Laboratory, Orido, Japan   2.12-2.17

A. Wysokinski, Sea Fisheries Institute, Swinoujšcie, Poland   F

FOREWORD

The first edition of FAO's *Atlas of the Living Resources of the Seas* was issued in 1971, just prior to the first session of the Third United Nations Conference on the Law of the Sea, as part of FAO's technical contribution to the preparatory work for the Conference. The activities of that Conference have resulted in a major revolution in the conditions under which marine fisheries operate. Most coastal countries have now declared, or are in the process of declaring, zones of extended jurisdiction over fisheries, mostly to a distance of 200 miles from their coasts.

Some 99 percent of the world's marine fish catch is currently taken in waters within 200 miles of the shore. The extension of jurisdiction gives states a historic opportunity for obtaining increased benefits from the resources off their coasts, and also a greater responsibility to ensure that these resources are wisely used for the benefit of present and future generations. If countries are to take full advantage of these opportunities and fulfil their responsibilities they must have adequate information about the resources. For example, with the introduction of extended areas of jurisdiction it is increasingly important to know about the migrations of fish across the new man-made boundaries.

In addition to these new demands for information, the years since 1971 have seen considerable additions to our knowledge of the resources, partly due to the development of new and improved methods of study, such as by surveys of pelagic stocks of fish with acoustic equipment. Many of these improvements in knowledge and methods have been achieved with the support of FAO, particularly its field programme.

These new needs and information have necessitated a complete revision and updating of the Atlas. A number of new maps have been introduced, including several with more detail on migrations, and most of the others have been extensively revised. In this work FAO has received the willing collaboration of many scientists in all parts of the world, whose help is gratefully acknowledged.

AVANT-PROPOS

La première édition de l'*Atlas des ressources biologiques des mers* a été publiée par la FAO en 1971, peu avant la première session de la troisième Conférence des Nations Unies sur le droit de la mer, dans le cadre de la contribution technique de l'Organisation aux travaux préparatoires de la Conférence. Les activités de cette conférence ont révolutionné les conditions d'exploitation des pêches maritimes. La plupart des pays côtiers ont maintenant déclaré, ou sont sur le point de déclarer, l'extension de leur juridiction sur les pêches dans des zones s'étendant généralement à 200 milles de leurs côtes.

Quelque 99 pour cent des captures mondiales de poisson sont actuellement effectuées dans les eaux situées à moins de 200 milles du rivage. L'extension de la juridiction fournit aux Etats une occasion historique de tirer plus largement parti des ressources qui se trouvent au large de leurs côtes, tout en leur conférant la responsabilité accrue de veiller à ce que ces ressources soient utilisées à bon escient dans l'intérêt des générations présentes et futures. Pour que les pays profitent pleinement de ces possibilités et assument leurs responsabilités, ils doivent avoir des renseignements adéquats sur les ressources. Par exemple, depuis la création de zones élargies de juridiction, il est de plus en plus important de connaître les migrations des poissons de part et d'autre des limites nouvellement tracées par l'homme.

Outre ces nouveaux besoins d'information, lors des années qui ont suivi 1971 notre connaissance des ressources s'est enrichie d'acquisitions considérables, en partie par suite de la mise au point de méthodes nouvelles et perfectionnées d'étude, telles que les prospections des stocks de poissons pélagiques à l'aide des techniques acoustiques. Ces progrès de la connaissance et des méthodes ont souvent été réalisés grâce à l'aide de la FAO, notamment de son programme de terrain.

Etant donné ces besoins nouveaux et compte tenu de ces nouvelles données, il a fallu revoir totalement l'Atlas, le mettre à jour et le compléter par de nouvelles cartes, dont plusieurs comportent des renseignements plus détaillés sur les migrations, la plupart des autres faisant simplement l'objet d'une ample révision. Dans l'exécution de cette tâche, la FAO a bénéficié dans toutes les parties du monde de la collaboration de maints chercheurs à qui elle tient à exprimer sa reconnaissance.

PROLOGO

La primera edición del *Atlas de los Recursos Vivos del Mar* fue publicada por la FAO en 1971, inmediatamente antes del primer período de sesiones de la Tercera Conferencia de las Naciones Unidas sobre el Derecho del Mar, y representó una de las contribuciones técnicas de nuestra Organización a los trabajos preparatorios de dicha Conferencia. Las actividades de la Conferencia en cuestión han determinado una importante revolución de las condiciones en que operan las pesquerías marítimas. La mayor parte de los estados ribereños han constituido zonas ampliadas de jurisdicción pesquera, o están haciéndolo, en la mayoría de los casos hasta una distancia de 200 millas de sus costas.

El 99 por ciento, aproximadamente, de las capturas mundiales proceden en la actualidad de aguas situadas a menos de 200 millas de la costa. La ampliación de su jurisdicción ofrece a los estados una oportunidad histórica para obtener mayores beneficios de los recursos que se encuentran frente a sus costas y, al mismo tiempo, les impone una mayor responsabilidad: la de asegurar que esos recursos se utilicen con prudencia en beneficio de las generaciones presentes y futuras. Para que los países puedan aprovechar plenamente esas oportunidades y cumplir con sus responsabilidades necesitan disponer de información suficiente sobre los recursos. Por ejemplo, la introducción de zonas ampliadas de jurisdicción hace que sea cada vez más importante disponer de información sobre las migraciones de los peces a través de esas nuevas fronteras trazadas por la mano del hombre.

Pero aparte de esas nuevas necesidades de información, los años transcurridos desde 1971 han visto un continuo y considerable acumularse de nuevos conocimientos sobre los recursos, debido en parte a la introducción de métodos nuevos y mejores de estudio, como los reconocimientos de poblaciones pelágicas con equipo acústico. Muchas de estas mejoras en los conocimientos y en los métodos se han conseguido con ayuda de la FAO, en especial de su programa de campo.

Estas nuevas necesidades e informaciones han hecho necesario revisar completamente y poner al día el Atlas. Se han añadido varios mapas, entre ellos algunos que dan más detalles sobre los movimientos migratorios de los peces, y la mayoría de los ya publicados se han revisado a fondo. Para este trabajo la FAO ha contado con la benévola colaboración de muchos científicos de todas las partes del mundo, cuya ayuda deseamos agradecer.

With the changes in the legal regime of the sea and the increased pressure on the world's fish stocks, this new edition of the Atlas comes at a very opportune time. I therefore have great pleasure in commending it to all potential users in member countries of FAO — administrators, planners, scientists and the fishermen themselves — and believe that it will be found a useful element in FAO's Programme of Assistance in the Development and Management of Fisheries in Exclusive Economic Zones.

E. SAOUMA

Director-General

Compte tenu des modifications apportées au régime juridique des mers et face à la pression croissante qui pèse sur les stocks de poisson de la planète, cette nouvelle édition de l'Atlas paraît à un moment particulièrement opportun. J'ai donc plaisir à la recommander à tous ses utilisateurs éventuels dans les Etats Membres de la FAO — administrateurs, planificateurs, chercheurs et pêcheurs eux-mêmes — et je suis convaincu qu'elle constituera pour eux un utile élément du Programme d'assistance au développement et à la gestion des pêcheries dans les zones économiques exclusives mis sur pied par la FAO.

E. SAOUMA

Directeur général

Dados los cambios que se han producido en el régimen jurídico del mar y la mayor presión a que hoy están sometidas las poblaciones ícticas en todo el mundo, esta nueva edición del Atlas llega en un momento muy oportuno. La recomiendo, pues, a todos los posibles usuarios de los Estados Miembros de la FAO — funcionarios de la administración pública, planificadores, científicos y pescadores — seguro además de que constituirá un útil elemento en el Programa de la FAO de Asistencia para el Desarrollo y la Ordenación de la Explotación Pesquera en las Zonas Económicas Exclusivas.

E. SAOUMA

Director General

CONTENTS   TABLE DES MATIÈRES   INDICE

MAPS   CARTES   MAPAS

D.1 East central Atlantic demersal resources	D.1 Atlantique centre-est - Ressources démersales	D.1 Atlántico centro-oriental - Recursos demersales
D.2 East central Atlantic pelagic resources	D.2 Atlantique centre-est - Ressources pélagiques	D.2 Atlántico centro-oriental - Recursos pelágicos
D.3 East central Atlantic crustacean and cephalopod resources	D.3 Atlantique centre-est - Ressources en crustacés et céphalopodes	D.3 Atlántico centro-oriental - Recursos de crustáceos y cefalópodos
E.1 South West Atlantic demersal resources	E.1 Atlantique sud-ouest - Ressources démersales	E.1 Atlántico sudoccidental - Recursos demersales
E.2 South West Atlantic pelagic resources	E.2 Atlantique sud-ouest - Ressources pélagiques	E.2 Atlántico sudoccidental - Recursos pelágicos
E.3 South West Atlantic crustacean and mollusc resources	E.3 Atlantique sud-ouest - Ressources en crustacés et mollusques	E.3 Atlántico sudoccidental - Recursos de crustáceos y moluscos
F.1 South East Atlantic demersal resources	F.1 Atlantique sud-est - Ressources démersales	F.1 Atlántico sudoriental - Recursos demersales
F.2 South East Atlantic pelagic resources	F.2 Atlantique sud-est - Ressources pélagiques	F.2 Atlántico sudoriental - Recursos pelágicos
F.3 South East Atlantic crustacean resources	F.3 Atlantique sud-est - Ressources en crustacés	F.3 Atlántico sudoriental - Recursos de crustáceos
G.1 Mediterranean Sea demersal resources	G.1 Mer Méditerranée - Ressources démersales	G.1 Mar Mediterráneo - Recursos demersales
G.2 Mediterranean Sea pelagic resources	G.2 Mer Méditerranée - Ressources pélagiques	G.2 Mar Mediterráneo - Recursos pelágicos
G.3 Mediterranean Sea crustacean and mollusc resources	G.3 Mer Méditerranée - Ressources en crustacés et mollusques	G.3 Mar Mediterráneo - Recursos de crustáceos y moluscos
H.1 Indian Ocean demersal resources	H.1 Océan Indien - Ressources démersales	H.1 Océano Indico - Recursos demersales
H.2 Indian Ocean pelagic resources (including tunas)	H.2 Océan Indien - Ressources pélagiques (thons compris)	H.2 Océano Indico - Recursos pelágicos (comprendidos los atunes)
H.3 Indian Ocean crustacean resources	H.3 Océan Indien - Ressources en crustacés	H.3 Océano Indico - Recursos de crustáceos
I.1 North West Pacific demersal resources	I.1 Pacifique nord-ouest - Ressources démersales	I.1 Pacífico nordoccidental - Recursos demersales
I.2 North West Pacific pelagic resources	I.2 Pacifique nord-ouest - Ressources pélagiques	I.2 Pacífico nordoccidental - Recursos pelágicos
I.3 North West Pacific crustacean and cephalopod resources	I.3 Pacifique nord-ouest - Ressources en crustacés et céphalopodes	I.3 Pacífico nordoccidental - Recursos de crustáceos y cefalópodos
J.1 North East Pacific demersal resources	J.1 Pacifique nord-est - Ressources démersales	J.1 Pacífico nordoriental - Recursos demersales
J.2 North East Pacific pelagic resources	J.2 Pacifique nord-est - Ressources pélagiques	J.2 Pacífico nordoriental - Recursos pelágicos
J.3 North East Pacific crustacean and cephalopod resources	J.3 Pacifique nord-est - Ressources en crustacés et céphalopodes	J.3 Pacífico nordoriental - Recursos de crustáceos y cefalópodos

INTRODUCTION

The original 1971 Atlas was prepared at the request of the United Nations Committee on the Peaceful Uses of the Sea-Bed and the Ocean Floor Beyond the Limits of National Jurisdiction. The usefulness of the first Atlas went far beyond the restricted purposes for which it was originally projected and it was decided to make it available to a larger public. The present revision resulted from recognition that there have been substantial changes in legal status regarding marine resources, as well as considerable additions to our knowledge of the resources and their variations in time and space, since the original Atlas was conceived and published. Every effort has been made to provide an up-to-date portrayal of the distribution of the principal living resources of the seas in the hope that this Atlas will be a modern information source for all those interested in problems relating to world-wide ocean resources.

Perhaps the most intriguing differences between the new and old Atlas are in the changes in dominant species abundances and species composition of catches in the major fisheries regions. For example, the changes in Peruvian resources and in the fishing methodology resulting from the decline in the abundance of Peruvian anchoveta since the first Atlas was published point to the need for ever more diligence in monitoring resources, their changes, and the responses within the eco-system which accompany natural and man-induced variations. On the brighter side, the Japanese sardine population, which was at a low point in the 1960s and early 1970s, has made a remarkable come-back. These examples illustrate the true picture of population variation, in the presence of fisheries or otherwise.

Consideration of only these two examples, and our growing but still limited knowledge of the truly dynamic nature of both the physical and biological systems put into perspective the uncertainty regarding the precision and stability of the potential yield figures in the various resource maps. This inevitable degree of uncertainty needs to be recognized before such figures become "fixed" bargaining points, or items of contention.

The potential yield figures represent very rough estimates in most instances, and were produced from the statistics available up through the 1979 fishing year only. Clearly there will be better estimates available for future reference but, like all publications, this one represents only historical perspective due to to the time lapse between the final collating of the statistics, preparation of the figures and their final presentation to the public in Atlas form.

The Atlas comprises three series of maps:

INTRODUCTION

La version originale de l'Atlas a été établie en 1971, à la demande du Comité des utilisations pacifiques du fond des mers et des océans au-delà des limites de la juridiction nationale (Nations Unies). L'utilité du premier Atlas a dépassé les buts limités pour lesquels il avait été initialement conçu, et il a été décidé de le proposer à un plus vaste public. La présente révision tient compte du fait que le statut juridique des ressources marines a subi de profondes modifications et que depuis l'époque où le premier Atlas a été préparé et publié, les connaissances sur les ressources et sur leurs fluctuations dans le temps et dans l'espace se sont considérablement enrichies. Aucun effort n'a été négligé pour fournir un tableau à jour de la distribution des ressources principales biologiques des mers, dans l'espoir que le présent Atlas constituera un outil de travail moderne pour tous ceux qui s'intéressent aux problèmes relatifs aux ressources des océans à l'échelle de la planète.

Les différences les plus curieuses, peut-être, entre le nouvel Atlas et l'ancien ont trait aux modifications des taux d'abondance des espèces dominantes et à la composition par espèces des captures dans les principales régions de pêche. Par exemple, l'évolution des ressources péruviennes et des méthodes de pêche auxquelles il a fallu recourir à la suite de la raréfaction de l'anchoveta péruvienne durant la période considérée, montre qu'il importe plus que jamais de surveiller avec diligence les ressources, leur évolution et les réactions qui, à l'intérieur de l'écosystème, accompagnent des variations naturelles ou provoquées par l'homme. D'un point de vue plus optimiste, la population de sardines japonaises, qui était au plus bas dans les années soixante et au début des années soixante-dix, a fait un retour remarquable. Ces exemples donnent une juste idée de la variation des populations, en présence ou non de pêcheries.

Ces deux exemples à eux seuls, mais aussi une meilleure connaissance, encore limitée cependant, du caractère véritablement dynamique des systèmes aussi bien physiques que biologiques, amènent à s'interroger sur la précision et la stabilité des chiffres relatifs aux rendements potentiels qui figurent sur les diverses cartes des ressources. Il faut admettre cette inévitable marge d'incertitude avant de faire de ces chiffres des éléments « fermes » de discussion ou des points de litige.

Dans la plupart des cas, les estimations des rendements potentiels ne sont que très approximatives et ont été établies à partir des statistiques disponibles jusqu'à la fin de la campagne de pêche de 1979 uniquement. Bien sûr, on disposera par la suite d'estimations plus précises auxquelles se référer, mais, comme toute publication, celle-ci ne représente qu'un moment historique, étant donné le temps qui s'est écoulé entre l'assemblage final des statistiques, l'établissement des données et leur présentation au public sous forme d'atlas.

L'Atlas comprend trois séries de cartes:

INTRODUCCION

El Atlas original de 1971 fue preparado a petición de la Comisión de las Naciones Unidas sobre la utilización con fines pacíficos de los fondos marinos y oceánicos fuera de los límites de la jurisdicción nacional. La utilidad del primer Atlas superó con creces la finalidad restrictiva con que se proyectó originalmente, por lo que se decidió ponerlo a disposición de un público más numeroso. La presente revisión es consecuencia del reconocimiento de los importantes cambios que se han producido en la situación jurídica de los recursos marinos, y del considerable aumento de nuestros conocimientos de los recursos y sus variaciones en el tiempo y espacio, desde que el Atlas original fue concebido y publicado. Se ha hecho todo lo posible para dar una descripción actualizada de la distribución de los principales recursos vivos de los mares, con la esperanza de que este Atlas sea una fuente moderna de información para todos aquellos interesados en problemas relativos a los recursos oceánicos mundiales.

Quizá las diferencias más sorprendentes entre los nuevos y los viejos Atlas sean las variaciones en la abundancia de especies dominantes y la composición de las capturas en las principales regiones pesqueras. Por ejemplo, los cambios experimentados en los recursos del Perú y en la metodología pesquera, derivados de la disminución de la abundancia de la anchoveta peruana desde que se publicó el primer Atlas, ponen de manifiesto la necesidad de observar con más diligencia los recursos, sus cambios y las reacciones en el marco del ecosistema que acompaña las variaciones naturales y artificiales. En otro plano más optimista, las poblaciones de sardina del Japón que, en el decenio de los años sesenta y a principios de los setenta estaban en un punto bajo, han experimentado un notable resurgir. Los ejemplos ilustran el verdadero panorama de la variación de las poblaciones, tanto si hay pesca como si no la hay.

Teniendo en cuenta estos dos ejemplos solamente y nuestro mayor conocimiento, aunque todavía limitado, de la verdadera naturaleza dinámica de los sistemas físicos y biológicos, hay en perspectiva la incertidumbre relativa a la precisión y estabilidad de las cifras de rendimiento potencial en los diversos mapas de recursos. Es necesario admitir este inevitable grado de incertidumbre antes de que dichas cifras se conviertan en puntos « fijos » de negociación o temas de controversia.

Las cifras de rendimiento potencial representan, en la mayoría de los casos, cálculos muy aproximados y se obtuvieron de las estadísticas disponibles hasta fines del año pesquero 1979 solamente. Es evidente que se dispondrá de mejores estimaciones para futuras referencias, pero, como todas las publicaciones, ésta representa sólo la perspectiva histórica, debido al lapso existente entre el cotejo final de las estadísticas, la preparación de las cifras y su presentación final al público en forma de Atlas.

El Atlas comprende tres series de mapas:

1

A first series of 13 maps, numbered from 1.1 to 1.13, illustrates the geographical distribution and present state of exploitation of the resources living in the world's oceans.

A second series of 18 maps, numbered from 2.1 to 2.18, gives some characteristic examples of fish migration.

The third and more detailed series, comprising 42 regional maps, presents in illustrated form the geographical and vertical distribution, as well as the abundance, of the main stocks in each ocean region.

PRODUCTIVITY OF THE SEAS

All the living resources of the seas, like those of the land, are derived ultimately from plants. These require light and nutrients to grow. The need for light confines plant growth to a surface layer no more than a few tens of metres deep. Likewise, the animals that feed on plants are concentrated mainly in the surface layers. In fact, animals are found at all depths because some of them are capable of extensive vertical migration and because both plants and animals tend to sink, especially after death, thus bringing food into the deeper layers.

In addition to light, plants need a constant supply of nutrients in order to develop, so that plant production varies greatly from one ocean region to another in accordance with the factors that control the quantity of nutrients in the surface layer. The geographical distribution of phytoplankton production, as established from the available data, is shown in map 1.1.[1] This map should not be regarded as a faithful portrayal of the average phytoplankton production in each area. Production varies seasonally in each region; as the various areas have not been explored from this point of view with the same intensity or as regularly as is desirable, the available data may have been gathered chiefly at certain comparatively abundant periods of the year. However, despite its inaccuracies, the map illustrates clearly the position of areas of high production; these may be grouped into three categories:

Upwelling areas and divergencies off the western subtropical continental coasts (Peru, California, northwestern and southwestern Africa) and along the equator, where cold, nutrient-rich waters rise to the surface.

Une première série de 13 cartes, numérotées de 1.1 à 1.13, illustre la répartition géographique et l'état actuel d'exploitation des ressources vivant dans l'océan mondial.

Une seconde série de 18 cartes, numérotées de 2.1 à 2.18, donne quelques exemples caractéristiques de migration chez les poissons.

La troisième série, plus détaillée — composée de 42 cartes régionales — présente sous une forme illustrée la répartition géographique et verticale, ainsi que l'abondance des principaux stocks dans chaque région océanique.

PRODUCTIVITÉ DES OCÉANS

Toutes les ressources biologiques des mers, comme celles de la terre, proviennent plus ou moins directement des végétaux. Ceux-ci ont besoin d'énergie lumineuse et de sels nutritifs pour se développer. Ce besoin de lumière limite la présence des végétaux à une couche superficielle ne dépassant pas quelques dizaines de mètres d'épaisseur. Les animaux qui s'en nourrissent sont également surtout concentrés dans les couches superficielles. En fait, comme certains animaux sont capables d'effectuer d'amples migrations verticales et que végétaux et animaux ont tendance à s'enfoncer, notamment après leur mort — ce qui a pour effet d'apporter de la nourriture dans les couches plus profondes — on rencontre des animaux à toutes les profondeurs des océans.

En plus de la lumière, les végétaux ont besoin, pour se développer, d'un apport constant en sels nutritifs. Il en résulte que la production végétale varie grandement d'une région océanique à l'autre, en fonction des facteurs qui régissent la richesse en sels nutritifs de la couche superficielle. La carte 1.1[1] représente la répartition géographique de la production de phytoplancton, telle qu'on peut l'établir à partir des données disponibles. Cette carte ne doit pas être considérée comme une représentation fidèle de la production phytoplanctonique moyenne dans chaque zone. Dans chaque région, cette production varie de façon saisonnière; comme les diverses zones n'ont pas été prospectées à cet égard avec la même intensité, ni avec la régularité souhaitable, les données disponibles peuvent avoir été recueillies principalement à certaines périodes de l'année, plus ou moins riches. Cependant, malgré ses inexactitudes, cette carte illustre bien la localisation des zones de forte production, qui peuvent être regroupées en trois catégories:

Les zones de remontées d'eaux et de divergence, que l'on rencontre au large des côtes subtropicales et occidentales des continents (Pérou, Californie, Afrique nord-occidentale et sud-occidentale) et le long de l'équateur: là des eaux froides, riches en sels nutritifs, remontent continuellement à la surface.

Una primera serie de 13 mapas, numerados de 1.1 a 1.13, ilustra la distribución geográfica y el estado actual de la explotación de los recursos vivos del océano mundial.

Una segunda serie de 18 mapas, numerados de 2.1 a 2.18, da algunos ejemplos característicos de migración en los peces.

La tercera serie, más detallada, compuesta de 42 mapas regionales, presenta en forma ilustrada la distribución geográfica y vertical, así como la abundancia de las principales poblaciones en cada región oceánica.

PRODUCTIVIDAD DE LOS OCEANOS

Todos los recursos biológicos del mar, como los de la tierra, proceden más o menos directamente de las plantas. Para crecer, las plantas necesitan luz y sales nutritivas. La necesidad de luz limita la vegetación a una zona estrecha, de no más de algunas decenas de metros a partir de la superficie. Los animales que se alimentan de ellas están también principalmente concentrados en las capas superficiales. De hecho, como ciertos animales son capaces de efectuar amplias migraciones verticales y como las plantas y también los animales tienden a ir a fondo, especialmente después de la muerte — por lo cual hay alimentos en las capas más profundas —, se encuentran animales en todas las profundidades de los océanos.

Además de la luz, las plantas necesitan, para crecer, una aportación constante de sales nutritivas. Resulta de ello que, en función de los factores que rigen la riqueza de sales nutritivas de la capa superficial, la producción vegetal varía considerablemente de una región oceánica a otra. El mapa 1.1[1] representa esta distribución geográfica de la producción de fitoplancton, según puede establecerse a partir de los datos disponibles. Este mapa no debe considerarse como una representación fiel de la producción fitoplanctónica media de cada zona. En cada región esta producción varía con las estaciones; como las diversas zonas no han sido exploradas a este respecto con la misma intensidad ni con la regularidad que fuera de desear, es posible que los datos disponibles hayan sido colectados principalmente en ciertos períodos del año más o menos ricos. No obstante esas inexactitudes, este mapa ilustra bien la localización de las zonas de gran producción, las cuales pueden reagruparse en tres categorías:

Las zonas de afloramientos situadas frente a las costas subtropicales y occidentales de los continentes (Perú, California, noroeste y sudoeste de Africa) y a lo largo del ecuador, en las cuales afloran continuamente a la superficie aguas frías, ricas en sales nutritivas.

---

[1] After Koblentz, Mishke, Volkovensky & Kabanova, 1969.

[1] D'après: Koblentz, Mishke, Volkovensky & Kabanova, 1969.

[1] Según Koblentz, Mishke, Volkovensky y Kabanova, 1969.

Temperate and sub-Arctic waters of the Southern Ocean, North Atlantic and North Pacific.

Shallow waters over parts of the continental shelves.

Except for seaweeds fixed to the bottom in coastal zones, all the plants in the sea are microscopic. They are fed on by a variety of animals, including some fish, but mainly by small invertebrate animals — the zooplankton. The distribution of zooplankton is depicted in map 1.2,[2] which shows that the areas that are rich in zooplankton are the same as those with high plant production.

The organisms typically constituting zooplankton are too small to be directly exploited by man; with the exception of krill, only species of sufficient size, such as fish, crustaceans, cephalopods and molluscs, which feed on plankton, small fish or other animals which themselves are plankton eaters are currently of economic importance.

The data used in the zooplankton map do not have exactly the same meaning as those in map 1.1. The zooplankton is shown as the amount of material present at any particular time, while the phytoplankton is shown as production, that is, as the amount of living material produced per unit time and area. Both these types of presentation are of interest; at each level of the food chain — and these considerations apply equally to the level of the resources which can be exploited by man — the stock present at a particular moment must be high if its use is to be intensive or economically attractive, while production should be high if such use is to be maintained at a high level.

EXPLOITATION AND UTILIZATION OF RESOURCES

In total, present annual world catches of marine fish and other animals amount to some 65 millions tons. The potential catches, to consider only the types of animals currently harvested, have been estimated at around 100 million tons.

In order to illustrate the magnitude of fishery resources and their present state of exploitation in the oceans and seas of the world, the available data have been grouped by regions in accordance with the breakdown adopted by FAO in the *Yearbook of fishery statistics*. These statistical areas and the identification used are indicated on maps 1.3 and 1.4.

[2] After V.G. Bogorov *et al.*, 1968.

Les eaux tempérées et subarctiques des mers australes, de l'Atlantique nord et du Pacifique nord.

Les eaux peu profondes qui recouvrent certaines parties des plateaux continentaux.

A l'exception des algues fixées sur le fond dans la zone littorale, tous les végétaux marins sont microscopiques; ils servent de nourriture à une grande variété d'animaux, y compris certains poissons; mais ce sont surtout les petits invertébrés constituant le zooplancton qui s'en nourrissent. La distribution du zooplancton est représentée sur la carte 1.2 [2]; cette carte montre que les zones riches se superposent à celles de forte production végétale.

Les organismes *caractéristiques* qui constituent le zooplancton sont de trop petite taille pour être directement exploités par l'homme; *à l'exception du krill*, seules les espèces de taille suffisante, poissons, crustacés, céphalopodes et mollusques qui se nourrissent de plancton, de petits poissons ou d'autres animaux eux-mêmes consommateurs de plancton, présentent actuellement un intérêt économique.

Les données utilisées dans la carte du zooplancton n'ont pas exactement la même signification que celles de la carte 1.1. En effet, alors que le phytoplancton est représenté en termes de production, c'est-à-dire en quantité de matière vivante produite par unité de temps et de surface, le zooplancton est représenté en termes de densité de matière présente à un instant donné. Ces deux formes de présentation ont chacune leur intérêt: à chaque niveau de la chaîne alimentaire — et ces considérations s'appliquent également au niveau des ressources exploitables par l'homme — le stock présent à un instant donné doit être élevé pour que son utilisation soit intense ou économiquement intéressante, et sa production doit être forte pour que cette utilisation puisse se maintenir à un niveau élevé.

EXPLOITATION ET UTILISATION DES RESSOURCES

A l'heure actuelle, les captures mondiales annuelles de poissons et autres animaux marins atteignent un total de quelque 65 millions de tonnes. En ne tenant compte que des espèces exploitées actuellement, on a évalué les captures potentielles à environ 100 millions de tonnes.

Pour décrire sous une forme illustrée l'importance des ressources halieutiques et l'état actuel de leur exploitation dans les océans et mers du monde, les données disponibles ont été regroupées par régions, conformément aux divisions adoptées par la FAO dans l'*Annuaire statistique des pêches*. Ces aires statistiques et le code de lettres utilisé sont indiqués

[2] D'après: V.G. Bogorov *et al.*, 1968.

Las aguas templadas y subárticas del océano austral, del Atlántico Norte y del Pacífico Norte.

Las aguas someras de algunas zonas de la plataforma continental.

Con excepción de las algas fijas en el fondo en la zona del litoral, todos los vegetales marinos son microscópicos y sirven de alimento a una gran variedad de animales, incluidos ciertos peces; pero los que más se nutren de ellos son los pequeños invertebrados que constituyen el zooplancton. La distribución del zooplancton está representada en el mapa 1.2 [2], en el que se demuestra que las zonas ricas se superponen a las zonas de fuerte producción vegetal.

Los organismos que constituyen típicamente el zooplancton son demasiado pequeños para que el hombre pueda explotarlos directamente; excepción hecha del krill, sólo las especies de tamaño suficiente, como los peces, crustáceos, cefalópodos y moluscos, que se alimentan de plancton, pequeños peces u otros animales que asimismo ingieren plancton, tienen normalmente importancia económica.

Los datos utilizados en el mapa del zooplancton no tienen exactamente la misma significación que los del mapa 1.1. En efecto, mientras que el fitoplancton se representa en términos de producción, es decir, en cantidad de materia viva producida por unidades de tiempo y superficie, el zooplancton se representa en términos de densidad de materia presente en un momento dado. Cada una de estas dos formas de presentación tiene su interés: a cada nivel de la cadena alimentaria — y estas consideraciones se aplican igualmente al nivel de los recursos explotables por el hombre — la población presente en un momento dado debe ser alta para que su utilización pueda ser intensa o económicamente interesante, y su producción debe ser abundante para que su utilización pueda mantenerse a un nivel elevado.

EXPLOTACION Y UTILIZACION DE LOS RECURSOS

En el momento actual las capturas mundiales anuales de peces y otros animales marinos alcanzan un total de unos 65 millones de toneladas. Teniendo solamente en cuenta las especies explotadas actualmente, se ha evaluado que las capturas potenciales son alrededor de 100 millones de toneladas.

Para describir en forma ilustrada la importancia de los recursos pesqueros y el estado actual de su explotación en los océanos y mares del mundo, los datos disponibles se han reagrupado por regiones, en conformidad con las divisiones adoptadas por la FAO en el *Anuario estadístico de pesca*. Estas áreas estadísticas y el código de letras utilizado se

[2] Según V.G. Bogorov *et al.*, 1968.

The maps show the size of world resources and catches for each statistical area but take no account of how resources and catches are distributed within each area. In each region are shown the estimates of the total potential harvest (outer circle) and that part of the maximum that is at present being taken (inner circle). The total potential as defined here is the optimum catch that can be obtained on a continuing basis by the rational exploitation of accessible stocks with existing technology. For each region, the catches and potentials have been divided into four main groups: bottom-living or demersal fish (cod, sole, etc.), pelagic fish (sardine, herring, tuna, anchovy, etc.), crustaceans (e.g., shrimp, crab, lobster) and cephalopods (e.g., octopus, squid). Since the commercial value differs widely between groups — one ton of shrimps is worth several tons of fish used to manufacture meal — these estimates have been given in terms of both weight (map 1.3) and commercial value (map 1.4).

The present distribution of catches throughout the world is given schematically in a series of maps showing the position and size of current catches:

demersal fish (map 1.6)

coastal pelagic fish (map 1.7)

tuna and tuna-like fishes (map 1.8)

crustaceans (map 1.9).

Although for many resources the potentials have not yet been estimated, or at least have been estimated only very roughly, an attempt has been made to depict on a world map the distribution of the main stocks and their present state of exploitation. On the following maps (1.10, 1.11 and 1.12), as yet unexploited or little exploited stocks are distinguished from those already exploited from which a substantial increase in production can be expected as a result of increased fishing, and from those already intensively or even overexploited. It is observed that a fair number of the major fishery resources are already heavily fished but that other fish stocks from which catches can be further increased generally exist in the same areas. If the present situation is compared with what it was in the past, an increase is observed in the number of stocks which are fully exploited and which therefore need suitable conservation and management measures. The maps also show that the need for regulatory measures applies both to ocean resources and to resources above the continental shelves. Responsible advisory bodies and commissions are shown in map 1.5.

The state of exploitation of whale stocks is given in map 1.13. Sperm whales are treated separately from the baleen

sur les cartes 1.3 et 1.4. Ces cartes montrent l'importance des ressources et des captures globales par aire statistique, sans tenir compte de la distribution géographique des ressources et des prises au sein de chaque aire. L'estimation de la récolte potentielle totale (cercle externe) et la proportion de ce maximum actuellement capturé (cercle interne) sont données pour chaque région. Le potentiel total, tel qu'il est défini dans le présent document, représente la capture optimale que l'on peut réaliser de façon continue en exploitant rationnellement les stocks accessibles avec les moyens technologiques disponibles actuellement. Pour chaque région, les captures et les potentiels ont été ventilés en quatre grandes rubriques: poissons de fond ou démersaux (morue, sole, etc.), poissons pélagiques (sardine, hareng, thon, anchois, etc.), crustacés (crevette, crabe, langouste, etc.) et céphalopodes (poulpe, seiche, encornet, etc.). Comme la valeur marchande des espèces pêchées diffère largement d'une rubrique à l'autre — celle d'une tonne de crevettes équivaut à celle de plusieurs tonnes de poisson utilisé pour la fabrication de farine — ces estimations sont données en poids (carte 1.3) et en valeur marchande (carte 1.4).

La distribution actuelle des captures dans le monde est schématisée dans une série de cartes représentant la localisation et l'importance des captures actuelles de:

poissons de fond ou démersaux (carte 1.6)

poissons pélagiques côtiers (carte 1.7)

thons et des espèces voisines (carte 1.8)

crustacés (carte 1.9).

Bien que pour de nombreuses ressources les potentiels ne soient pas encore estimés, ou du moins ne le soient que très approximativement, on a tenté de représenter sur une carte mondiale la répartition des principaux stocks et l'état actuel de leur exploitation. Sur les cartes suivantes (1.10, 1.11 et 1.12), les stocks encore inexploités ou faiblement exploités sont distingués de ceux déjà exploités dont on peut attendre par un accroissement de la pêche un accroissement substantiel de la production et de ceux déjà intensément exploités, voire surexploités. On constate que bon nombre des ressources halieutiques principales sont déjà fortement pêchées, mais qu'il existe généralement dans les mêmes zones d'autres stocks de poissons à partir desquels on peut encore accroître les captures. Si l'on compare la situation actuelle à ce qu'elle était dans le passé, on constate que le nombre de stocks pleinement exploités, et qui de ce fait nécessitent des mesures de conservation et d'aménagement appropriées, augmente. A la vue de ces cartes, il apparaît également que le besoin de mesures de réglementation s'applique autant aux ressources océaniques qu'à celles qui se trouvent au-dessus des plateaux continentaux. La carte 1.5 indique les organes consultatifs et commissions responsables.

La carte 1.13 montre l'état d'exploitation des stocks de baleines. Les cachalots sont traités séparément des balei-

indican en los mapas 1.3 y 1.4. Demuestran estos mapas la importancia de los recursos y de las capturas globales por área estadística, haciendo abstracción de la distribución geográfica de los recursos y de las capturas en el interior de cada área. En cada región se dan las estimaciones de la captura potencial total (círculo exterior) y se indica la proporción que actualmente se captura (parte interior sombreada). Por potencial total se entiende aquí la captura máxima posible con carácter continuo de aquellas poblaciones que es posible explotar con la tecnología actualmente existente. En cada región las capturas y los potenciales se han dividido en cuatro grupos principales: peces de fondo o demersales (bacalao, platija, etc.), especies pelágicas (sardina, arenque, atún, anchoa, etc.), crustáceos (camarones, cangrejos, langostas, etc.) y cefalópodos (pulpos, calamares, etc.). Como el valor comercial de las especies pescadas difiere considerablemente de un grupo a otro — el de una tonelada de camarones equivale al de varias toneladas de pescado utilizado para la fabricación de harina —, estas estimaciones se dan en peso (mapa 1.3), y en valor comercial (mapa 1.4).

La distribución actual de las capturas en el mundo se presenta esquemáticamente en una serie de mapas que representan la localización y la importancia de las capturas actuales:

peces de fondo o demersales (mapa 1.6)

peces pelágicos costeros (mapa 1.7)

atunes y especies afines (mapa 1.8)

crustáceos (mapa 1.9).

Aunque aún no se ha estimado el potencial de muchos recursos o, por lo menos, se ha estimado sólo muy aproximadamente, se ha intentado representar en un mapa mundial la distribución de las principales poblaciones y su actual estado de explotación. En los siguientes mapas (1.10, 1.11 y 1.12) se distinguen las poblaciones todavía sin explotar o poco explotadas de aquellas ya explotadas (de las cuales cabe esperar un importante aumento de la producción como consecuencia de haber aumentado la pesca), así como de aquellas ya intensivamente explotadas o incluso explotadas en exceso. Se observa que buen número de los principales recursos pesqueros ya están muy explotados, pero que otras poblaciones ícticas, cuyas capturas pueden aumentar todavía, existen generalmente en las mismas zonas. Si se compara la actual situación con la del pasado, se observa un aumento del número de las poblaciones que están plenamente explotadas y que, en consecuencia, necesitan medidas apropiadas de conservación y reglamentación. Los mapas también muestran que es necesario aplicar medidas reglamentarias, tanto en los recursos oceánicos como en los situados por encima de las plataformas continentales. En el mapa 1.5 figuran los órganos y comisiones asesores responsables.

El estado de explotación de las poblaciones de ballenas figura en el mapa 1.13. Los cachalotes se tratan por separado

whales. The estimated percentage of the virgin, unexploited stocks which at present exists is given for each stock where known.

Another factor that is particularly evident in world fisheries is the activity of long-range vessels from non-local countries. The role of these long-range fleets is, of course, of prime importance in the fishing of ocean resources, especially tuna and whale. It is evident that the long-range fleets concentrate their activities in the richest areas. There are several reasons for this, such as the geographical distribution of the demand for fish which is very different from the distribution of the fish themselves; the variation of consumer preferences from country to country; and differences in the technological capabilities of countries. Sometimes there is direct competition between long-range and local vessels for the same stock of fish. At other times they exploit different species, so that their activities may be independent or may interact to the advantage or disadvantage of one or the other fleet; for instance, one fleet may harvest large fish which are predators on the smaller fish harvested by the other fleet.

Two facts are becoming increasingly obvious. On the one hand, the rapid increase in world catches has been achieved largely through the activities of long-range vessels, and in the short term the present high levels of world catches can be assured only by their continuing activities. On the other hand, the rational management of the resources in order to maintain catches at a high level requires increasingly close cooperation between countries on the formulation and implementation of appropriate regulatory measures. This need becomes all the more acute as fewer and fewer underexploited stocks remain available. It may be expected that in the long term there will be a development of short- or medium-range fishing fleets which will make long-range fishing less important for the maintenance of a high total world catch.

MOVEMENTS AND MIGRATIONS

Some stocks have fairly large areas of distribution or migrate considerable distances. The exploitation of such stocks in a particular region of their areas of distribution may therefore affect abundance and catches over a much wider ground. Other species, however, are less mobile and their exploitation will produce only localized effects on resources. The development of fisheries in a given region, for example in the coastal waters of a particular country, will be affected

noptères. Lorsque l'information était disponible, la taille de chaque stock a été indiquée en pourcentage du stock vierge.

Un autre facteur particulièrement évident dans les pêcheries mondiales est l'activité des navires à grande autonomie originaires de pays éloignés des lieux de pêche. Le rôle de ces flottilles à grand rayon d'action est naturellement primordial dans la pêche des ressources océaniques, thons et baleines en particulier. On constate que l'activité des flottilles à grand rayon d'action est surtout concentrée dans les zones les plus riches. Le développement de ces flottilles s'explique par plusieurs raisons: la répartition géographique de la demande en poisson, très différente de celle des ressources elles-mêmes; les préférences des consommateurs qui varient d'un pays à l'autre; enfin les disparités entre les possibilités technologiques des pays. Parfois les navires à grande autonomie et les navires locaux se font directement concurrence pour la pêche des mêmes stocks. Dans d'autres cas, ils exploitent des espèces différentes, et alors leurs activités restent indépendantes ou peuvent interférer à l'avantage ou au détriment de l'un ou l'autre type de flottilles: par exemple, une flottille peut exploiter de grands poissons prédateurs de poissons plus petits, eux-mêmes pêchés par l'autre flottille.

Deux faits sont de plus en plus évidents: d'une part, l'accroissement rapide des captures mondiales a été obtenu, dans une large mesure, grâce à l'activité des flottilles à long rayon d'action et, à court terme, le niveau élevé actuel des captures mondiales ne peut être maintenu que par la poursuite de leur activité; d'autre part, l'aménagement rationnel des ressources pour maintenir les captures à un niveau élevé nécessite une coopération de plus en plus étroite entre les nations afin d'élaborer et d'appliquer les mesures de réglementation appropriées. Ce besoin devient d'autant plus nécessaire que de moins en moins de stocks sous-exploités restent disponibles. A long terme, on peut s'attendre également à ce que les flottilles à faible ou moyen rayon d'action se développent, ce qui réduirait le rôle de la pêche lointaine pour le maintien des captures mondiales à un niveau élevé.

DÉPLACEMENTS ET MIGRATIONS

Certains stocks ont des aires de répartition relativement vastes ou effectuent des migrations de grande amplitude. L'exploitation de tels stocks dans une région particulière de leurs aires de répartition peut donc se répercuter sur l'abondance et les captures dans une zone beaucoup plus vaste. D'autres espèces au contraire sont plus sédentaires et leur exploitation n'entraînera sur les ressources que des effets localisés. Le développement des pêcheries dans une région

de las ballenas. El porcentaje estimado de las poblaciones vírgenes, sin explotar, que existen actualmente, figura para cada población cuando se conoce.

Otro factor que es particularmente evidente en las pesquerías mundiales es la actividad de embarcaciones de gran radio de acción procedentes de países alejados de los lugares de pesca. Estas flotas de gran radio de acción desempeñan naturalmente un papel primordial en la pesca de los recursos oceánicos, y en particular de atunes y ballenas. Es evidente que la actividad de las flotas de gran radio de acción se concentra sobre todo en las zonas más ricas. Esto se explica por varias razones: la distribución geográfica de la demanda de pescado, que es muy distinta de la distribución de los recursos; las preferencias de los consumidores, que varían de un país a otro, y las diferencias en las posibilidades tecnológicas entre los países. A veces existe una competencia directa entre los barcos de gran radio de acción y las embarcacines locales en la captura de una misma población de peces. Otras veces ambas flotas explotan especies diferentes, de forma que sus actividades pueden ser independientes o repercutir mutuamente en beneficio o perjuicio de una o de la otra; por ejemplo, una flota puede capturar peces de gran tamaño que son depredadores de los peces de menor tamaño capturados por la otra.

Dos hechos resultan cada vez más evidentes. Por una parte, el rápido aumento de las capturas mundiales se ha conseguido, en gran medida, gracias a la intervención de flotas de gran radio de acción y, a breve plazo, sólo es posible mantener las capturas mundiales al elevado nivel actual si dichos barcos prosiguen sus actividades. Por otra parte, la ordenación racional de los recursos para mantener las capturas a un alto nivel exige una cooperación cada vez más estrecha entre las naciones para elaborar y aplicar medidas apropiadas de reglamentación. Esta necesidad resulta tanto más aguda cuanto que es cada vez menor el número de las poblaciones subexplotadas todavía disponibles. Es de esperar, además, que a la larga se produzca un aumento de las flotas de radio de acción reducido y medio, lo cual hará que las flotas de gran radio de acción sean menos importantes para mantener la captura mundial a un nivel elevado.

DESPLAZAMIENTOS Y MIGRACIONES

Algunas poblaciones tienen áreas de distribución relativamente vastas o efectúan migraciones de gran amplitud. La explotación de tales poblaciones en una región particular de sus áreas de distribución puede, pues, repercutir en la abundancia y las capturas en una zona mucho más vasta. Otras especies, en cambio, son más sedentarias y su explotación sólo tendrá efectos localizados sobre los recursos. El desarrollo de la pesca en una región determinada, por

insofar as these stocks migrate and are exploited in the outlying regions.

It has not been possible to depict the migrations and movements of stocks on regional maps for two main reasons: for many resources, there is little or no knowledge of the movements of the stocks; when known, the movements, which are often complex, cannot easily be described in these regional maps.

For this reason, some examples of the best known and most characteristic migrations have been portrayed in a special series of maps numbered from 2.1 to 2.18.

All the animals in the sea are mobile for at least part of their lives, but the degree of mobility varies considerably from one species to another and also between different stages of life. The least mobile, like the shellfish — oysters, mussels, clams, etc. — have, however, a free phase at the beginning of their life cycle when the larvae drift in the water currents with the other members of the plankton community. This mobility during larval life is essential for the dissemination of the species and the natural repopulation of areas where a species may have become scarce for some reason. After their plankton phase, the larvae reach the bottom and there the adults either become permanently fixed (e.g. mussels) or are capable of only very short movements of the order of a few metres (e.g. abalones). A very few species (e.g. scallops) are active enough to leave the bottom for a moment when making short jumps to avoid enemies.

A more extensive group of animals consists of those which, while more active, still do not wander far. Each individual is restricted to a local range of at most a few miles in extent. This group includes most of the fauna of coral reefs, as well as animals found on hard bottoms and many bottom crustaceans. Some, such as the spiny lobster of Western Australia, are probably quite local after they reach a harvestable size, but in their early stages are carried by the currents for sometimes hundreds of miles in the open ocean. Yet adult bottom crustaceans are not invariably home-loving; tagging experiments have shown that the edible crab (*Cancer pagurus*) found in north European waters may cover several tens of miles, sometimes even more than a hundred miles.

The third and biggest group, which contains the majority of animals supporting large commercial fisheries, is composed of those which make movements of some tens or hundreds of miles. Some species found in particular envi-

donnée, par exemple dans les eaux côtières d'une nation particulière, sera affecté dans la mesure où ces stocks migrent et sont exploités dans les régions périphériques.

Les migrations et déplacements des stocks n'ont pu être représentés sur les cartes régionales pour deux raisons principales: pour de nombreuses ressources, les mouvements des stocks sont peu ou mal connus; lorsqu'ils le sont, ces cartes régionales se prêtent mal à une description de mouvements souvent complexes.

Quelques exemples de migrations, choisis parmi les mieux connus et les plus caractéristiques, ont été présentés dans une série particulière de cartes, numérotées de 2.1 à 2.18.

Tous les animaux marins sont mobiles, au moins pendant une partie de leur existence, mais le degré de mobilité varie considérablement d'une espèce à l'autre, ainsi qu'aux divers stades de leur existence. Les moins mobiles, comme les coquillages —huîtres, moules, palourdes, etc. —ont cependant au début de leur cycle de vie une phase libre durant laquelle les larves dérivent au gré des courants, mêlées aux autres membres de la communauté planctonique. Cette mobilité pendant la vie larvaire est essentielle pour la dissémination des espèces et le repeuplement naturel des zones où une espèce aurait pu, pour une raison ou pour une autre, se raréfier. A la fin de leur phase planctonique, les larves gagnent le fond, et là, les adultes, ou bien comme les moules se fixent définitivement, ou bien comme les ormeaux n'effectuent ensuite que des déplacements restreints de l'ordre de quelques mètres. Un très petit nombre d'espèces, comme les coquilles Saint-Jacques, sont suffisamment mobiles (par exemple pour échapper à leurs ennemis) pour pouvoir quitter temporairement le fond en effectuant de petits bonds.

Un second groupe plus vaste est constitué d'animaux qui, bien qu'étant plus mobiles, restent cantonnés dans des territoires d'étendue très limitée. Les déplacements de chaque individu sont restreints à un périmètre de quelques milles au plus. Ce groupe comprend la majorité des espèces de la faune des récifs coralliens, certains poissons que l'on trouve sur les fonds durs et beaucoup de crustacés de fond. Certains de ceux-ci, comme la langouste d'Australie occidentale, se déplacent peu lorsqu'ils ont atteint une taille exploitable, mais aux premiers stades de leur cycle de vie ils sont entraînés par les courants, parfois très loin en haute mer jusqu'à des centaines de milles. Pourtant ce caractère casanier des crustacés de fond adultes n'est pas une règle absolue: des expériences de marquage ont montré que le tourteau (*Cancer pagurus*) des mers nord-européennes pouvait parcourir des distances de plusieurs dizaines de milles, dépassant même parfois 100 milles.

Dans un troisième groupe plus important figure la majorité des espèces exploitées par les grandes pêcheries commerciales; ces animaux effectuent des déplacements de quelques dizaines à plusieurs centaines de milles. Certaines

ejemplo en las aguas costeras de una determinada nación, resultará afectado en la medida en que esas poblaciones emigran y son explotadas en las regiones periféricas.

Las migraciones y desplazamientos de las poblaciones no han podido representarse en los mapas regionales, por dos razones principales: en el caso de muchos recursos, los movimientos de las poblaciones se conocen poco o mal; cuando se conocen tales movimientos, que son con frencuencia bastante complejos, las cartas regionales se prestan mal a su descripción.

Por este motivo, algunos ejemplos de migraciones, escogidos entre los más conocidos y más característicos, se han presentado en una serie especial de mapas numerados del 2.1 al 2.18.

Todos los animales marinos son móviles, al menos durante parte de su vida, pero el grado de movilidad varía considerablemente de una especie a otra, y también en las diversas fases del ciclo vital. Los menos móviles, como los moluscos — ostras, mejillones, almejas, etc. — tienen, al comienzo de su ciclo vital, una fase libre durante la cual las larvas son arrastradas por las corrientes junto con los otros miembros de la comunidad planctónica. Esta movilidad durante la vida larval es esencial para la diseminación de las especies y la repoblación natural de las zonas donde una especie haya podido resultar rara, por una razón u otra. Al cabo de esa fase planctónica las larvas se asientan en el fondo, y allí los adultos, o se fijan definitivamente, como los mejillones, o efectúan desplazamientos limitados del orden de unos metros, como la oreja de mar. Sólo un número muy pequeño de especies, como las vieiras, son suficientemente móviles para abandonar temporalmente el fondo dando pequeños saltos y escapar así de sus enemigos.

Un segundo grupo más amplio está constituido por animales que, siendo más móviles, permanecen, sin embargo, en territorios de extensión muy limitada. Los desplazamientos de cada individuo se limitan a un perímetro de unas cuantas millas, cuando más. Figuran en este grupo la mayor parte de las especies de la fauna de los arrecifes coralinos, ciertos peces que se encuentran en los fondos duros y muchos crustáceos de fondo. Algunos de estos últimos, como la langosta de Australia occidental, se desplazan poco una vez que alcanzan un tamaño aprovechable, pero en los primeros estadios de su ciclo biológico son arrastrados por las corrientes, a veces muy en alta mar, hasta cientos de millas. Sin embargo, este carácter sedentario de los crustáceos adultos de fondo no es una regla absoluta: experimentos de marcado han demostrado que el cangrejo buey (*Cancer pagurus*) de los mares del norte de Europa puede recorrer distancias de varias decenas de millas e incluso a veces de más de 100 millas.

En un tercer grupo, el más importante, figura la mayor parte de las especies explotadas por las grandes pesquerías comerciales; estos animales efectúan desplazamientos que varían de algunas decenas a varios centenares de millas.

ronments have highly localized habitats between which there is very little exchange of populations, at least adult. In the Gulf of Guinea, for example, a species of croaker (*Pseudotolithus elongatus*) lives exclusively in the low-salinity waters found at the mouths of rivers; populations are composed of a succession of small stocks isolated from one another. In other species, movements may be of well-defined migrations, often associated with different stages of their life cycle (eggs and larvae, juveniles, young and adults) and occurring at definite seasons and under specific environmental conditions. Some tropical shrimps are spawned offshore in relatively deep water (in depths of 100 metres or more), the eggs and then the successive larval stages are carried away by the currents and the postlarvae settle in the waters near the coasts or in brackish-water lagoons where they assume their adult form. After a few months in these coastal areas, the juveniles migrate in a body out to sea where they settle on the continental shelf (map 2.1). The total movements, in the case of the pink shrimp of Florida (*Penaeus duorarum*), may be several hundred miles.

Fish very often make similar inshore-offshore movements. For example, in summer several species of bottom fish, especially sea bream, approach the northwest coast of Africa, where they mass for spawning. Migration patterns are complex in some species; adult plaice of the western North Sea move into the Southern Bight between England and the Low Countries to spawn in the late winter, and disperse back to their main fishing grounds in the central North Sea around the Dogger Bank in summer. The young plaice found in the coastal areas from Belgium to Denmark also migrate, gradually settling in the southern and central North Sea.

Of trawled species, hake represents one of those that make the longest migrations along coasts. The concentrations of Patagonian hake found on the Argentine continental shelf in the summer at latitude 47°S and even further south move along the Argentine coast during the autumn to reach the Uruguayan shelf in winter and perhaps even the southern areas of the Brazilian shelf. In spring, they retrace their steps. Similar migration patterns, sometimes up to a thousand nautical miles long, are known in most other hake species off western Europe, southern and northwest Africa, the Chilean coast and the American and Canadian Atlantic and Pacific coasts.

espèces que l'on trouve dans des milieux particuliers ont des habitats très localisés, entre lesquels les mélanges de populations, au moins adultes, sont très réduits. Ainsi dans le golfe de Guinée, une espèce d'ombrine, le bossu (*Pseudotolithus elongatus*), vit uniquement dans les eaux dessalées que l'on rencontre aux embouchures des fleuves; les populations se composent d'une succession de petits stocks isolés les uns des autres. Chez d'autres espèces, les déplacements peuvent prendre la forme de migrations bien définies, souvent associées aux divers stades du cycle de vie (œufs et larves, juvéniles, jeunes et adultes) et se produisant à des saisons et dans des conditions de milieu bien déterminées. Nombre de crevettes tropicales pondent leurs œufs au large à des niveaux relativement profonds (jusqu'à 100 mètres et même davantage), les œufs puis les différents stades larvaires successifs sont emportés par les courants, les postlarves colonisent les eaux très côtières ou les lagunes d'eaux saumâtres où elles prennent leur forme adulte; après quelques mois passés dans ces zones littorales, les juvéniles migrent massivement vers le large où ils colonisent le plateau continental (carte 2.1). L'ensemble de ces migrations peut, dans le cas de la grosse crevette rose de Floride (*Penaeus duorarum*), représenter plusieurs centaines de milles.

Les poissons effectuent très souvent des déplacements analogues entre les zones côtières peu profondes et les eaux hauturières. Par exemple, au large des côtes nord-occidentales de l'Afrique, plusieurs espèces de poissons de fond, de sparidés en particulier, se rapprochent de la côte en été et se concentrent pour y pondre. Chez certaines espèces les schémas de migration sont complexes: ainsi les plies adultes qui vivent dans la partie occidentale de la mer du Nord gagnent à la fin de l'hiver le secteur méridional, entre l'Angleterre et les Pays-Bas, pour y frayer. Après la ponte, au cours de l'été, les adultes remontent vers les principaux lieux de pêche situés dans la partie centrale de la mer du Nord autour du Dogger Bank. Les jeunes plies que l'on rencontre dans les zones littorales, de la Belgique au Danemark, migrent également vers le nord, colonisant progressivement les régions méridionale et centrale de la mer du Nord.

Le merlu représente, parmi les espèces pêchées au chalut, l'une de celles qui réalisent les plus longues migrations le long des côtes. Par exemple, les concentrations de merlu de Patagonie que l'on trouve en été sur le plateau continental argentin à la hauteur de la latitude 47° S, et même plus au sud, remontent au cours de l'automne le long des côtes argentines pour atteindre en hiver le plateau uruguayen et peut-être même les zones méridionales du plateau brésilien. Au cours du printemps, elles parcourent le chemin inverse. Des schémas de migration similaires, atteignant parfois 1 000 milles marins, sont connus chez la plupart des autres espèces de merlu, au large de l'Europe occidentale, de l'Afrique australe et nord-occidentale, au large des côtes chiliennes et dans l'Atlantique et le Pacifique devant les côtes américaines et canadiennes.

Ciertas especies que se encuentran en medios particulares tienen hábitats muy localizados, en los cuales son muy reducidas las mezclas de poblaciones, por lo menos las adultas. Así, en el Golfo de Guinea, una especie de corvina (*Pseudotolithus elongatus*) vive únicamente en las aguas de baja salinidad que se encuentran en las desembocaduras de los ríos; las poblaciones se componen de una sucesión de pequeñas poblaciones aisladas unas de otras. En otras especies, los desplazamientos pueden revestir la forma de migraciones bien definidas, con frecuencia asociadas a los diversos estadios del ciclo biológico (huevos y larvas, formas juveniles, jóvenes y adultos), que se producen en estaciones y en condiciones del medio bien determinadas. Muchas especies tropicales de camarones desovan frente a las costas en aguas relativamente profundas (hasta 100 metros e incluso más), y luego los huevos y las diferentes fases larvarias sucesivas son arrastrados por las corrientes y las formas poslarvarias colonizan las aguas costeras o las lagunas de agua salobre donde adquieren su forma adulta. Después de pasar unos meses en esas zonas costeras, los especímenes juveniles emigran en masa a alta mar, donde colonizan la plataforma continental (mapa 2.1). El conjunto de estas migraciones puede, como en el caso del camarón rosado de Florida (*Penaeus duorarum*), representar varios centenares de millas.

Los peces efectúan a menudo desplazamientos análogos entre las zonas costeras poco profundas y las aguas de alta mar. Por ejemplo, frente a las costas nordoccidentales de Africa, varias especies de peces de fondo y en particular de espáridos, se acercan a la costa en el verano y se concentran para desovar. En algunas especies los esquemas de migración son complejos; por ejemplo, las sollas europeas adultas que viven en la parte occidental del Mar del Norte alcanzan a fines de invierno el sector meridional, entre Inglaterra y los Países Bajos, para desovar. Después del desove, durante el verano, los adultos acuden a los principales lugares de pesca que están situados en la parte central del Mar del Norte, alrededor del Dogger Bank. Las sollas jóvenes que se encuentran en las zonas litorales desde Bélgica hasta Dinamarca emigran igualmente hacia el norte colonizando progresivamente las regiones meridional y central del Mar del Norte.

La merluza representa, entre las especies que se pescan con red de arrastre, una de las que realizan las migraciones más extensas a lo largo de la costa. Por ejemplo, las concentraciones de merluza de Patagonia que se encuentran en verano sobre la plataforma continental de la Argentina a una latitud de 47°S, e incluso más al sur, migran durante el otoño a lo largo de las costas argentinas para alcanzar en el invierno la plataforma uruguaya y quizá incluso las zonas meridionales de la plataforma brasileña. Durante la primavera hacen el camino inverso. Se conocen esquemas semejantes de migración en la mayor parte de las demás especies de merluza, que alcanzan a veces las 1 000 millas marinas frente a las costas de Europa occidental, Africa meridional y nordoccidental, a lo largo de las costas chilenas, y en el Atlántico y el Pacífico frente a las costas americanas y canadienses.

In the foregoing examples, the movements of stocks were confined to the continental shelf. Several species of fish, especially among the coastal pelagic species, periodically move out into the ocean. Off Peru, the anchoveta disperses along the coast above the continental shelf but may move offshore 50 miles or more over very deep water. In the waters off the northwest African coast, concentrations of adult round sardinella migrate as one or two independent stocks from Sierra Leone to south of the Western Sahara, usually accompanying the seasonal movement of the front separating the warm tropical waters from the colder waters of the Canaries. Generally speaking, schools take up their abode over the continental shelf and move toward the coast seasonally, but occasionally dense layers have been detected, and sometimes successfully fished, beyond the continental slope over depths of 500 to 2 500 metres. Some species of demersal fish may also be found in large numbers in deep waters off continental shelves, such as the northern redfish between Greenland and Labrador (see map A.1). Other examples of migrations of comparable extent are given for the Atlanto-Scandian herring (map 2.10), the South West Atlantic anchoita (map 2.6) and the North Atlantic cod (map 2.2).

Finally, there are some animals which make very long movements across whole oceans. The albacore, like most tuna, moves within each of the three major oceans: the same group of fish may be exploited at different seasons off Japan and California (map 2.13); in the Atlantic, several albacore tagged off the United States have been caught in the Bay of Biscay. The southern bluefin tuna may cross the whole Indian Ocean from the southwest region of the Pacific to the South Atlantic (map 2.16). The bigeye tuna (map 2.14) and the yellowfin tuna also undertake migrations of lesser extent in each ocean. The salmon (map 2.12), in addition to its ocean migrations, goes very great distances up rivers and streams to spawn. Whales and similar species are also great migrants: large baleen whales exploited around the Antarctic continent during the southern summer move during the winter up to the equator, where they reproduce (map 2.18).

For all except the most localized stocks, i.e., the first and second abovementioned groups, the area of distribution is very large. Furthermore, the fish in their movements pay no respect to present or potential man-made boundaries. A plaice in the North Sea may, at different times in a year, be over the parts of the continental shelf claimed by four or five European states; a round sardinella in the Atlantic may move through the waters off the coasts of several west African countries and sometimes reach the waters outside the continental shelf. Tuna, whales and other wide-ranging fish

Dans les exemples précédemment décrits, les mouvements des stocks étaient confinés à l'intérieur des limites du plateau continental. Plusieurs espèces de poissons, en particulier parmi les espèces pélagiques côtières, débordent périodiquement dans les zones océaniques. Au large du Pérou, l'anchoveta est répartie le long des côtes au-dessus du plateau continental, mais peut se déplacer vers le large jusqu'à 50 milles ou plus, au-dessus de fonds très importants. Au large des côtes nord-occidentales de l'Afrique, les concentrations de sardinelles rondes adultes migrent, en un ou deux stocks indépendants, de la Sierra Leone au sud du Sahara occidental, accompagnant le plus souvent le mouvement saisonnier du front qui sépare les eaux chaudes tropicales des eaux canariennes plus froides. En général, les bancs sont localisés au-dessus du plateau continental, se rapprochant de façon saisonnière de la côte, mais occasionnellement des couches denses ont été détectées, et parfois pêchées avec succès, au-delà du talus continental, au-dessus des fonds de 500 à 2 500 mètres. Certaines espèces de poissons démersaux peuvent aussi se rencontrer en grandes quantités en pleine eau au-delà des plateaux continentaux: c'est le cas pour le sébaste nordique entre le Groenland et le Labrador (voir carte A.1). D'autres exemples de migrations d'une étendue comparable sont donnés pour le hareng atlantico-scandinave (carte 2.10), l'anchoita de l'Atlantique sud-ouest (carte 2.6) et la morue de l'Atlantique nord (carte 2.2).

Enfin, il existe certains animaux qui effectuent de très longs parcours à travers des océans entiers. Le germon par exemple, comme la plupart des thonidés, se déplace à travers chacun des trois océans: le même groupe de poissons peut être exploité à des saisons différentes au large du Japon et de la Californie (carte 2.13); dans l'Atlantique, plusieurs germons marqués au large des Etats-Unis ont été recapturés dans le golfe de Gascogne. Le thon rouge du sud peut se déplacer, à travers tout l'océan Indien, de la région sud-occidentale du Pacifique jusqu'à l'Atlantique sud (carte 2.16). Le thon obèse (carte 2.14) et le thon à nageoires jaunes réalisent également dans chaque océan des migrations plus limitées. Le saumon (carte 2.12), outre les migrations océaniques qu'il effectue, remonte sur de très grandes distances les rivières et les fleuves pour frayer. Les baleines et espèces voisines sont un autre exemple de grands migrateurs: les grands baleinoptères, qui sont exploités autour du continent antarctique pendant l'été austral, remontent au cours de l'hiver jusqu'au niveau de l'équateur, où ils se reproduisent (carte 2.18).

Excepté pour les stocks les plus sédentaires, c'est-à-dire ceux du premier et du deuxième groupe, l'aire de répartition des stocks halieutiques est très étendue. Ces aires, et les déplacements des poissons à l'intérieur de celles-ci, sont totalement indépendantes des frontières présentes ou futures tracées par l'homme. Dans la mer du Nord, une plie peut au cours des différentes périodes de l'année fréquenter des portions du plateau continental revendiquées par quatre ou cinq pays européens; dans l'Atlantique, une sardinelle ronde peut se déplacer au-dessus du plateau continental au large

En los ejemplos que acaban de describirse, los movimientos de las poblaciones quedaban circunscritos al interior de los límites de la plataforma continental. Varias especies de peces, particularmente entre las especies pelágicas costeras, pasan periódicamente a las zonas oceánicas. Frente al Perú, la anchoveta se distribuye a lo largo de la costa sobre la plataforma continental, pero puede desplazarse hacia alta mar hasta 50 millas o más por encima de fondos de gran profundidad. En las costas nordoccidentales de Africa, las concentraciones de alachas adultas migran, en una o dos poblaciones independientes, de Sierra Leona al sur del Sahara occidental, acompañando las más de las veces el movimiento estacional del frente que separa las aguas cálidas tropicales de las aguas canarias, que son más frías. En general, los cardúmenes están localizados encima de la plataforma continental y estacionalmente se acercan a la costa, pero de cuando en cuando se han localizado capas densas, que a veces se han pescado con éxito, más allá del talud continental, por encima de fondos de 500 a 2 500 metros. También pueden encontrarse ciertas especies de peces demersales en grandes cantidades en mar abierto, más allá de las plataformas continentales; tal ocurre con la gallineta nórdica entre Groenlandia y el Labrador (véase el mapa A.1). Se dan otros ejemplos de migraciones de amplitud comparable para el arenque atlántico-escandinavo (mapa 2.10), la anchoíta del Atlántico sudoccidental (mapa 2.6) y el bacalao del Atlántico Norte (mapa 2.2).

Existen finalmente ciertos animales que recorren grandes distancias atravesando océanos enteros. El atún blanco, por ejemplo, como la mayor parte de las especies de atunes, se desplaza a través de cada uno de los tres océanos: el mismo grupo de peces puede explotarse en diferentes estaciones frente a las costas del Japón y de California (mapa 2.13). En el Atlántico se ha capturado, en el Golfo de Vizcaya, varios bonitos que habían sido marcados frente al litoral de los Estados Unidos. El atún rojo del sur puede cruzar todo el Océano Indico, desde la región sudoccidental del Pacífico hasta el Atlántico meridional (mapa 2.16). El patudo (mapa 2.14) y el rabil realizan igualmente en cada océano migraciones de menor amplitud. El salmón (mapa 2.12), además de sus migraciones oceánicas, sube los ríos recorriendo grandes distancias para desovar. Las ballenas y especies afines son otro ejemplo de grandes emigrantes: las grandes ballenas de barba, que se explotan alrededor del continente antártico durante el verano austral, llegan durante el invierno hasta el ecuador, donde se reproducen (mapa 2.18).

Excepción hecha de las poblaciones más sedentarias, es decir, de las del primero y del segundo grupos arriba mencionados, las áreas de distribución de las poblaciones pesqueras son muy extensas. Estas áreas y los desplazamientos de los peces dentro de ellas son totalmente independientes de las fronteras presentes o futuras trazadas por el hombre. En el Mar del Norte, una solla puede, durante diferentes períodos del año, frecuentar sectores de la plataforma continental reivindicados por cuatro o cinco países europeos; en el Atlántico, una alacha puede desplazarse por encima de la

may even migrate across the much more extensive boundaries of regional fishery bodies; as has been noted, the bluefin tuna may move from one ocean to the other.

In any planning of regulatory measures to conserve or manage a stock of fish, it is essential to consider the movement and migration potential of the stock. To be effective, such measures must be applied to the whole stock throughout its entire range. Restrictions on the amount or sizes caught in one area will have a limited effect if the same animals are still caught when they move to another area. Rational management of the stock as a whole may however require specific limitations of fishing in some parts of the range because the fish there are small, or in poor condition, or because the various grounds contain mixtures of different groups which require different management regimes.

TOPOGRAPHY AND NOMENCLATURE

The maps and vertical sections shown in inset have been so designed as to need no particular explanation. The substance of the necessary information is given, sometimes schematically, in the various legends accompanying the maps. For the sake of uniformity, a number of conventions have been adopted but absolute standardization has not been possible as the available information varies considerably from one region or resource to another.

Topography

Only the 200-metre bathymetric line (i.e., about 100 fathoms) is shown on the maps as an indication of the offshore extension of the continental shelf on and above which the largest part of the fish resource is concentrated. In view of the map scale, this line must be considered approximate.

In the vertical sections the horizontal scale is shown in nautical miles. Some of the maps also carry a bar scale in nautical miles and sometimes in kilometres.

Mercator's projection is used in all cases except the North Atlantic, the Antarctic, the South West Atlantic and the South East Pacific. In the first of these cases (the North

de plusieurs pays ouest-africains et même gagner périodiquement des eaux situées en dehors du plateau continental. Les thons, les baleines et autres grands migrateurs peuvent même franchir les limites des aires de compétence beaucoup plus étendues des organismes régionaux en matière de pêche; nous avons vu que le thon rouge du sud pouvait passer d'un océan à l'autre.

Lorsque l'on envisage d'appliquer des mesures de réglementation destinées à aménager ou à conserver un stock de poissons, il est indispensable de tenir compte des possibilités de déplacement et de migration de ce stock. Pour être efficaces, ces mesures doivent être appliquées au stock dans son ensemble, sur toute l'étendue de son aire de répartition. Des restrictions apportées aux quantités pêchées ou aux dimensions des individus capturés dans une région n'auront qu'un effet limité si l'on continue à les pêcher librement lorsqu'ils gagnent d'autres régions. L'aménagement rationnel de l'exploitation d'un stock dans son ensemble peut cependant nécessiter que l'on applique à la pêche dans certaines zones de son habitat des limitations particulières, soit parce que les individus y sont trop petits ou en mauvaise condition, soit parce que les différents lieux de pêche sont habités par des individus appartenant à des groupes différents auxquels il convient d'appliquer des modalités d'aménagement particulières.

TOPOGRAPHIE ET NOMENCLATURE

Les cartes et les coupes verticales figurant en cartouche ont été conçues de façon qu'aucun texte explicatif particulier ne soit nécessaire à leur compréhension. Pour cela l'essentiel des indications nécessaires est donné, parfois schématiquement, dans les diverses légendes accompagnant les cartes. Un certain nombre de conventions ont été adoptées pour l'homogénéité de la présentation, mais une standardisation absolue n'a pu être appliquée, car les renseignements disponibles varient considérablement d'une région ou d'une ressource à l'autre.

Topographie

Seule l'isobathe 200 mètres figure sur les cartes: son tracé donne une indication de l'extension vers le large du plateau continental au-dessus duquel est concentrée la plus grande partie des ressources halieutiques des océans. Vu l'échelle des cartes, ce tracé doit être considéré comme approximatif.

Dans les coupes verticales, l'échelle horizontale est indiquée en milles marins. Certaines cartes comportent aussi une échelle linéaire en milles marins (et parfois aussi en kilomètres).

On utilise dans tous les cas la projection de Mercator, sauf pour l'Atlantique nord, l'Antarctique, l'Atlantique sud-ouest et le Pacifique sud-est. Pour l'Atlantique nord, on utilise la

plataforma continental a través de las aguas de varios países oesteafricanos e incluso periódicamente alcanzar aguas situadas fuera de la plataforma continental. Los atunes, las ballenas y otros grandes emigrantes pueden incluso atravesar los límites geográficos de competencia, mucho más extensos, de los organismos regionales en materia de pesca; ya hemos visto que el atún del sur podía pasar de un océano a otro.

Cuando se prevé la aplicación de medidas reglamentarias destinadas a ordenar o a conservar una población de peces, es indispensable tener en cuenta las posibilidades de desplazamiento y migración de esa población. Para ser eficaces, esas medidas deben aplicarse a la población en su conjunto y en toda la extensión de su área de distribución. La imposición de restricciones a las capturas y a las tallas de los individuos capturados en una región tendrá un efecto limitado si se les sigue pescando libremente cuando llegan a otras regiones. La ordenación racional de la explotación de una población en su conjunto puede, sin embargo, exigir la aplicación de limitaciones particulares a la pesca en ciertas zonas de su hábitat, sea porque los individuos son demasiado pequeños o se hallan en condiciones desfavorables, sea porque los diferentes lugares de pesca estén habitados por individuos pertenecientes a grupos diferentes, a los cuales conviene aplicar modalidades particulares de ordenación.

TOPOGRAFIA Y NOMENCLATURA

Los mapas y las secciones verticales en recuadros se han concebido de manera que para entenderlas no sea necesario ningún texto explicativo particular. Por ello, en los diversos textos que acompañan a los mapas se da lo más esencial de las indicaciones necesarias, a veces esquemáticamente. En gracia a la homogeneidad de la presentación, se han adoptado cierto número de convenciones, pero no ha podido aplicarse una normalización absoluta toda vez que las informaciones disponibles varían considerablemente de una región o un recurso a otro.

Topografía

En los mapas sólo figura la isobata de 200 metros: su trazado da una indicación de la extensión de la plataforma continental sobre la cual se concentran la mayor parte de los recursos pesqueros de los océanos. Vista la escala de los mapas, este trazado debe considerarse como aproximado.

En las secciones verticales, la escala horizontal se indica en millas marinas. Algunos mapas llevan también una escala en millas marinas, y a veces en kilómetros.

La proyección cartográfica utilizada es la de Mercator en todos los casos, salvo en los siguientes: para el Atlántico Norte, la Antártida, el Atlántico sudoccidental y el Pacífico

Atlantic), the projection is an azimuthal equal-area projection prepared by the Woods Hole Oceanographic Institute.

Nomenclature of species and stocks

In order to identify species and stocks, use has been made as far as possible of the common names, in particular, those appearing in FAO documents such as the *Yearbook of fishery statistics*. When, as far as is known, there is no sufficiently explicit common name in English, French or Spanish, the local name of common use in the area where the stock is exploited has been given. In some cases, when there is no common name (for instance, for a resource not yet exploited) or when it has to be clearly indicated, the scientific name is used or added. Difficulties of identification due on the one hand to the use of common names whose meaning often varies from one region to another, and on the other to the fairly frequent absence of synonyms in the three languages are, however, relatively few because the maps are trilingual and show the English, French and Spanish names side by side.

An alphabetical index of over 700 common and scientific names of species and stocks is to be found at the end of the volume.

SIZE AND DISTRIBUTION OF RESOURCES

More detailed information on the geographical distribution of the principal resources, their distance from the coast, their vertical distribution and the order of magnitude of potential yields is given in the series of regional maps numbered from A.1 to P.1. The boundaries of the areas are those used by FAO for the compilation of regional statistics, as published in the *Yearbook of fishery statistics;* these boundaries are outlined on world maps 1.3 and 1.4 together with the area identification code (letters).

For each of the statistical areas considered, the Atlas contains at least one map for each major type of resource: demersal fish, pelagic fish and crustaceans. However, for the Mediterranean, Western central Pacific and South West Pacific, demersal fish and crustaceans appear on the same map. Molluscs are not considered in this Atlas except for the North East Atlantic. These resources are mostly under the control of riparian countries (habitat very near to the coast, absence of migration in adults); in addition, because several species are cultivated, potentials are not limited to natural production.

For each regional map, one or more vertical sections at right angles to the coast are given in inset. They indicate the distance of stocks from the coast and the depth distribution

projection azimutale équivalente établie par le Woods Hole Oceanographic Institute.

Nomenclature des espèces et des stocks

Pour identifier les espèces et les stocks, on a utilisé autant que possible les noms communs, en particulier ceux qui figurent dans des documents FAO comme l'*Annuaire statistique des pêches*. En l'absence, à notre connaissance, de nom commun suffisamment explicite en anglais, espagnol ou français, le nom local, couramment en usage dans la zone où le stock est exploité, est alors donné. Dans certains cas, en l'absence de nom commun (par exemple pour une ressource encore inexploitée), ou lorsqu'il est nécessaire de le préciser, le nom scientifique a été utilisé ou ajouté. Les imprécisions provenant, d'une part, de l'emploi de noms communs dont la signification varie souvent d'une région à une autre et, d'autre part, de l'absence assez fréquente de synonymes dans les trois langues sont toutefois réduites par le fait que, les cartes étant trilingues, les noms en anglais, français et espagnol figurent côte à côte sur les documents.

On trouvera à la fin du volume un index alphabétique groupant plus de 700 noms communs et noms scientifiques d'espèces et de stocks.

IMPORTANCE ET DISTRIBUTION DES RESSOURCES

Des renseignements plus détaillés concernant la distribution géographique des principales ressources, leur distance par rapport à la côte, leur répartition verticale et l'ordre de grandeur des captures potentielles sont donnés dans la série des cartes régionales numérotées de A.1 à P.1. Les limites des zones sont celles qu'utilise la FAO pour présenter ses statistiques par régions dans l'*Annuaire statistique des pêches;* le tracé de ces limites figure sur les cartes mondiales 1.3 et 1.4 ainsi que le code (lettres) d'identification des zones.

Pour chacune des zones statistiques ainsi retenues, l'Atlas comprend au moins une carte par grand type de ressources: poissons démersaux, poissons pélagiques et crustacés. Toutefois, pour la Méditerranée, le Pacifique centre-ouest et le Pacifique sud-ouest, poissons démersaux et crustacés figurent sur la même carte. Excepté pour l'Atlantique nord-est, les coquillages n'ont pas été pris en considération dans cet atlas. En effet, ces ressources se trouvent en majorité sous le contrôle des pays riverains (habitat très côtier, absence de migrations chez les adultes); d'autre part, du fait de l'élevage dont font l'objet plusieurs espèces, les potentiels ne sont pas limités à la production naturelle.

Pour chaque carte régionale, une ou plusieurs coupes verticales, perpendiculaires à la côte, sont présentées en cartouche. Elles précisent la distance des stocks par rapport à

sudoriental. Para el Atlántico Norte se utilizó la proyección acimutal equivalente preparada por el Woods Hole Oceanographic Institute.

Nomenclatura de las especies y de las poblaciones

Para identificar las especies y las poblaciones se ha utilizado, en la medida de lo posible, los nombres comunes, en particular los que figuran en documentos de la FAO como el *Anuario estadístico de pesca*. Mientras no haya un nombre común suficientemente explícito en español, francés o inglés, se da el nombre local utilizado corrientemente en la zona donde se explota la población. En algunos casos, en ausencia de un nombre común (por ejemplo para un recurso todavía no explotado) o cuando es necesario precisarlo, se ha utilizado o añadido el nombre científico. Las dificultades para la identificación, debidas, por una parte, al empleo de nombres comunes cuya significación varía con frecuencia de una región a otra y, por otra, a la ausencia bastante frecuente de sinónimos en los tres idiomas, son, sin embargo, relativamente pocas pues los mapas son trilingües y los nombres en inglés, francés y español figuran uno junto a otro.

Al final del volumen se encuentra un índice alfabético que reúne más de 700 nombres comunes y científicos de especies y de poblaciones de peces.

IMPORTANCIA Y DISTRIBUCION DE LOS RECURSOS

En la serie de mapas regionales enumerados de A.1 a P.1 se dan informaciones más detalladas relativas a la distribución geográfica de los principales recursos, a su distancia de la costa, a su distribución vertical y al orden de magnitud de los potenciales de captura. Los límites de las zonas son los que utiliza la FAO para presentar sus estadísticas por regiones en el *Anuario estadístico de pesca;* el trazado de estos límites figura en los mapas mundiales 1.3 y 1.4 así como en el código (letras) de identificación de las zonas.

Para cada una de las zonas estadísticas examinadas, el Atlas comprende por lo menos un mapa por tipo principal de recursos: peces demersales, peces pelágicos y crustáceos. No obstante, para el Mediterráneo y el Pacífico centro-occidental y el Pacífico sudoccidental, figuran en el mismo mapa los peces demersales y los crustáceos. Excepción hecha del Atlántico nordoriental, no se han tomado en consideración en este Atlas los mariscos. Estos recursos están en su mayor parte bajo el control de los países ribereños (hábitat muy costero, ausencia de migraciones en los adultos); por otra parte, dado que se practica la cría de varias especies, los potenciales no se limitan a la producción natural.

En cada mapa regional se presentan en recuadro una o varias secciones verticales perpendiculares a la costa. Estas secciones indican la distancia de las poblaciones respecto

of the resources. Some sections refer to a specific point on the coast. In that case, the distance from the coast is given on the horizontal axis in nautical miles. The other sections are valid for a fairly extensive region parallel with the coast; then the distance from the coast is not given as it obviously depends on the width of the continental shelf, which may vary widely from one point to another. As the fish are usually distributed according to depth of water rather than distance from coast, the horizontal distribution of the stocks at a point may be deduced by reference to hydrographical charts giving the profile of the continental shelf at that point.

Distribution of resources

In the light of the available information, the complexity of migration patterns and the degree of interpenetration between neighbouring stocks, the horizontal and vertical distribution is described on the regional maps and vertical sections in one of the following three ways:

1. By drawing, for each stock or resource distinguished, the average boundaries of their areas of concentration (e.g. maps A.1, A.3 and B.2). In a few cases it has also been possible to show the distribution limits. This is the type of presentation usually adopted for the vertical sections.

2. By indicating, from the position of the names identifying each stock, the central location of these stocks (e.g. maps A.2 and C.2). In this case, the boundaries of the areas of concentration are not given.

3. When a species is scattered in small localized patches over a large area, a number of symbols indicate the locations of the main grounds (see, for instance, map F.3).

When possible, substantial seasonal variations in the distribution of stocks have also been mentioned either on the regional maps or on the sections. However, although such variations can sometimes be wide in some stocks, migrations parallel to the coast have not been described in this series of documents.

It should also be noted that for typographical reasons the regional maps do not always permit the exact determination of the distance of resources from the coast. This is the case, for example, when the position of the stocks is depicted by the placing of their names. It is then necessary to refer to the vertical sections which supply this type of information to a correct scale.

la côte et décrivent la répartition en profondeur des ressources. Certains de ces groupes se rapportent à un point précis du littoral; dans ce cas la distance par rapport à la côte est indiquée en milles marins sur l'axe des abscisses. Les autres coupes sont valables pour une région plus ou moins large, parallèle à la côte; dans ce cas, la distance à la côte n'est pas indiquée, car elle dépend évidemment de la largeur du plateau continental, laquelle peut varier très largement d'un point à un autre. Comme en général le poisson se répartit en fonction de la profondeur plutôt qu'en fonction de la distance de la côte, la répartition horizontale des stocks en un point peut se déduire en se reportant à des cartes marines afin de préciser le profil du plateau continental en ce point.

Répartition des ressources

En fonction des renseignements disponibles, de la complexité des schémas de migration et du degré d'interpénétration entre les stocks voisins, la distribution horizontale et verticale a été décrite en utilisant, sur les cartes régionales et les coupes verticales, l'un des trois types de représentation suivants:

1. En traçant, pour chaque stock ou ressource que l'on a distingué, les limites moyennes de leurs zones de concentration (par exemple, cartes A.1, A.3 et B.2). Dans un petit nombre de cas, il a été possible de faire figurer également les limites de distribution. C'est le type de présentation qui a été adopté le plus souvent pour les coupes verticales.

2. En indiquant, par la position des noms identifiant chaque stock, la localisation centrale de ceux-ci (par exemple, cartes A.2 et C.2). Dans ce cas, les limites des zones de concentration ne sont pas précisées.

3. Enfin lorsqu'une espèce est disséminée sur une aire très vaste en petites concentrations localisées, en indiquant par des symboles l'emplacement des principales zones de pêche (voir, par exemple, carte F.3).

Lorsque cela était possible, les variations saisonnières importantes qui existent dans la distribution des stocks ont également été mentionnées, soit sur les cartes régionales, soit sur les coupes. Mais, bien que celles-ci puissent être parfois très étendues chez plusieurs stocks, les migrations parallèles à la côte n'ont pas été décrites dans cette série de documents.

Il faut noter enfin que, pour des raisons typographiques, les cartes régionales ne permettent pas toujours de localiser avec exactitude la distance des ressources par rapport à la côte. Ceci est le cas en particulier lorsque la position des stocks est représentée par l'emplacement de leurs noms. Il est alors nécessaire de se reporter aux coupes verticales qui fournissent, avec une échelle correcte, ce type de renseignements.

a la costa y describen la distribución en profundidad de los recursos. Algunas de esas secciones se refieren a un punto preciso del litoral; en ese caso, la distancia de la costa se indica en millas marinas en el eje de las abscisas. Las otras secciones son válidas para una región más o menos amplia, paralela a la costa; en este caso no se indica la distancia de la costa puesto que ésta depende evidentemente de la amplitud de la plataforma continental, la cual puede variar considerablemente de un punto a otro. Como generalmente los peces se distribuyen en función de la profundidad más bien que en función de la distancia de la costa, la distribución horizontal de las poblaciones en un punto puede deducirse refiriéndose a los mapas marinos donde se indica el perfil de la plataforma continental en este punto.

Distribución de los recursos

En función de las informaciones disponibles, de la complejidad de los esquemas de migración y del grado de interpenetración entre las poblaciones vecinas, se ha descrito la distribución horizontal y vertical utilizando en los mapas regionales y en las secciones verticales uno de los tres tipos siguientes de representación:

1. Trazando, para cada población o recurso que se ha identificado, los límites medios de sus zonas de concentración (por ejemplo, mapas A.1, A.3 y B.2). En un pequeño número de casos ha sido posible indicar asimismo los límites de distribución. Este tipo de presentación es el que se ha adoptado con más frecuencia para las secciones verticales.

2. Indicando, por la posición de los nombres que identifican a cada población, la localización central de éstas (por ejemplo, mapas A.2 y C.2). En este caso no se precisan los límites de las zonas de concentración.

3. Cuando una especie está diseminada en un área muy vasta en forma de pequeñas concentraciones localizadas, se ha indicado por símbolos el emplazamiento de las principales zonas de pesca (véase, por ejemplo, el mapa F.3).

Cuando ha sido posible, se han mencionado también las variaciones estacionales importantes existentes en la distribución de las poblaciones, sea en los mapas regionales, sea en las secciones. Ahora bien, aunque esas variaciones sean a veces muy extensas en varias poblaciones, no se han descrito en esta serie de documentos las migraciones paralelas a la costa.

Es de señalar, por último, que por razones tipográficas los mapas regionales no permiten siempre localizar con exactitud la distancia de los recursos a la costa. Tal es sobre todo el caso cuando la posición de las poblaciones está representada por el emplazamiento de sus nombres. Es entonces necesario referirse a las secciones verticales que facilitan, con una escala correcta, ese tipo de informaciones.

Size of resources

For each map, the total estimated potential yield (in weight) is given for the area and resources considered. When available data are sufficient, potentials are also supplied, at least roughly, for the various resources shown on a map (e.g. map A.1). The order of magnitude of these individual potentials is indicated.

In some cases, catches have also been shown for resources which are currently fully exploited (e.g. map A.1).

VALUE OF ESTIMATES

The values of potential yield, in weight or monetary terms, should be interpreted as the best estimates now available. Their accuracy varies greatly according to regions and resources. Although they can be regarded as reasonably accurate, future refinements may well result in quite appreciable corrections in some cases.

The same applies to the approximate limits shown for the area and depth distribution of resources. The limits indicated represent average annual limits — at some seasons of the year the area of distribution of a particular stock may be larger or smaller than here depicted, or may even have shifted. The information supplied in this Atlas is based on the experience and inferences of scientific experts on the fish and fisheries of each region, but none would claim that the distribution patterns are precise in detail.

Importance des ressources

Pour chaque carte, l'estimation des captures totales potentielles (en poids), pour la zone et les ressources considérées, est donnée. Lorsque les données disponibles sont suffisantes, les potentiels sont également fournis, au moins approximativement, pour les diverses ressources représentées sur une carte (par exemple, A.1). L'ordre de grandeur de ces potentiels individuels est indiqué.

Dans certains cas, les captures ont également été indiquées pour les ressources qui sont actuellement pleinement exploitées (carte A.1, par exemple).

VALEUR DES ESTIMATIONS

Les estimations de la production potentielle, en poids comme en valeur, doivent être comprises comme représentant les meilleures estimations dont on dispose actuellement. Leur précision varie beaucoup suivant les régions et les ressources. Bien qu'on puisse les considérer comme relativement exactes, les améliorations qui leur seront apportées pourraient donner lieu dans certains cas à des corrections substantielles.

Il en est de même des limites approximatives indiquées pour la répartition en surface et en profondeur des ressources. Ces tracés correspondent à des limites annuelles moyennes: à certaines saisons de l'année, l'aire de distribution d'un stock donné peut être plus ou moins étendue ou même décentrée par rapport à celle qui est représentée. Bien que toutes les informations fournies dans cet atlas soient basées sur l'expérience et les déductions de chercheurs spécialistes des poissons et des pêches dans chaque région, on ne saurait tenir pour précis jusque dans les détails les schémas de distribution décrits.

Importancia de los recursos

Para cada mapa se da el potencial de captura total estimado (en peso) para la zona y los recursos considerados. Cuando los datos disponibles son suficientes, se indican también los potenciales, al menos aproximadamente, para los diversos recursos representados en el mapa (por ejemplo, mapa A.1) y se da el orden de magnitud de esos potenciales individuales.

En algunos casos se han indicado también las capturas de los recursos que actualmente se explotan plenamente (mapa A.1, por ejemplo).

VALOR DE LAS ESTIMACIONES

Debe entenderse que las cifras de producción potencial, en peso y en valor, representan las mejores estimaciones de las cuales se dispone actualmente. Su precisión varía mucho según las regiones y los recursos. Aunque pueden considerarse relativamente exactas, las mejoras que se introduzcan en ellas podrían traducirse en ciertos casos en correcciones apreciables.

Lo mismo cabe decir de los límites aproximados que se indican para la distribución de los recursos en superficie y en profundidad. Estos trazados corresponden a límites anuales medios: en determinadas estaciones del año, el área de distribución de una población dada puede ser más o menos extensa e incluso estar descentrada con respecto a la que se representa. Aunque todas las informaciones facilitadas en este Atlas se basan en la experiencia y las deducciones de investigadores especialistas en ictiología y pesca de cada región, los sistemas de distribución descritos no pueden considerarse como precisos en lo que se refiere a los detalles.

REFERENCES FOR FURTHER INFORMATION

FAO. *FAO species identification sheets for fishery purposes. Mediterranean*
1973   *and Black Sea*, ed. by W. Fischer. Rome. 2 vols.
FAO. *FAO species identification sheets for fishery purposes. Eastern India*
1974   *and Western Central Pacific*, ed. by W. Fischer. Rome. 4 vols.
FAO. *FAO species identification sheets for fishery purposes. Western Central*
1978   *Atlantic*, ed. by W. Fischer. Rome. 7 vols.
FAO. *The fish resources of the Western Central Pacific Islands*, by Richard
1978   N. Uchida. Rome. FAO Fisheries Circular No. 712.
FAO. *Review of the state of world fishery resources*, by J.A. Gulland. Rome.
1978   FAO Fisheries Circular No. 710.
FAO. *Les ressources halieutiques de l'Atlantique centre-est*. Première partie.
1979   *Les ressources du golfe de Guinée de l'Angola à la Mauritanie*, par
        J.-P. Troadec et S. Garcia. Rome. FAO document technique sur
        les pêches N° 186.1.
FAO/UNITED NATIONS ENVIRONMENT PROGRAMME. *The living marine re-*
1977   *sources of the Southeast Atlantic*, by Garth Newman. Rome. FAO
        Fisheries Technical Paper No. 178.

OUVRAGES A CONSULTER
POUR INFORMATION COMPLÉMENTAIRE

FAO. *Fiches FAO d'identification des espèces pour les besoins de la pêche.*
1973   *Méditerranée et Mer Noire*, édit. par W. Fischer. Rome. 2 vols.
FAO. *FAO species identification sheets for fishery purposes. Eastern India*
1974   *and Western Central Pacific*, ed. by W. Fischer. Rome. 4 vols.
FAO. *Examen de l'état des ressources ichtyologiques mondiales*, par J.A.
1978   Gulland. Rome. COFI/78/Inf. 4.
FAO. *FAO species identification sheets for fishery purposes. Western Central*
1978   *Atlantic*, ed. by W. Fischer. Rome. 7 vols.
FAO. *The fish resources of the Western Central Pacific Islands*, by Richard
1978   N. Uchida. Rome. FAO Fisheries Circular No. 712.
FAO. *Les ressources halieutiques de l'Atlantique centre-est*. Première partie.
1979   *Les ressources du golfe de Guinée de l'Angola à la Mauritanie*, par
        J.-P. Troadec et S. Garcia. Rome. FAO document technique sur
        les pêches N° 186.1.
FAO/PROGRAMME DES NATIONS UNIES POUR L'ENVIRONNEMENT. *Les res-*
1977   *sources vivantes de l'Atlantique sud-est*, par Garth Newman.
        Rome. FAO document technique sur les pêches N° 178.

REFERENCIAS PARA OBTENER MAS INFORMACION

FAO. *FAO species identification sheets for fishery purposes. Mediterranean*
1973   *and Black Sea*, ed. by W. Fischer. Rome. 2 vols.
FAO. *FAO species identification sheets for fishery purposes. Eastern India*
1974   *and Western Central Pacific*, ed. by W. Fischer. Rome. 4 vols.
FAO. *Examen de la situación de los recursos pesqueros mundiales*, por J.A.
1978   Gulland. Roma. COFI/78/Inf. 4.
FAO. *FAO species identification sheets for fishery purposes. Western Central*
1978   *Atlantic*, ed. by W. Fischer. Rome. 7 vols.
FAO. *The fish resources of the Western Central Pacific Islands*, by Richard
1978   N. Uchida. Rome. FAO Fisheries Circular No. 712.
FAO. *Les ressources halieutiques de l'Atlantique centre-est*. Première partie.
1979   *Les ressources du golfe de Guinée de l'Angola à la Mauritanie*, par
        J.-P. Troadec et S. Garcia. Rome. FAO document technique sur
        les pêches N° 186.1.
FAO/PROGRAMA DE LAS NACIONES UNIDAS PARA EL MEDIO AMBIENTE.
1979   *Los recursos vivos del Atlántico sudoriental*, por Garth Newman.
        Roma. Documentos Técnicos de Pesca N° 178.

DISTRIBUTION OF DEMERSAL CATCHES (1979)
RÉPARTITION DES CAPTURES DÉMERSALES (1979)
DISTRIBUCION DE LAS CAPTURAS DE PECES DEMERSALES (1979)

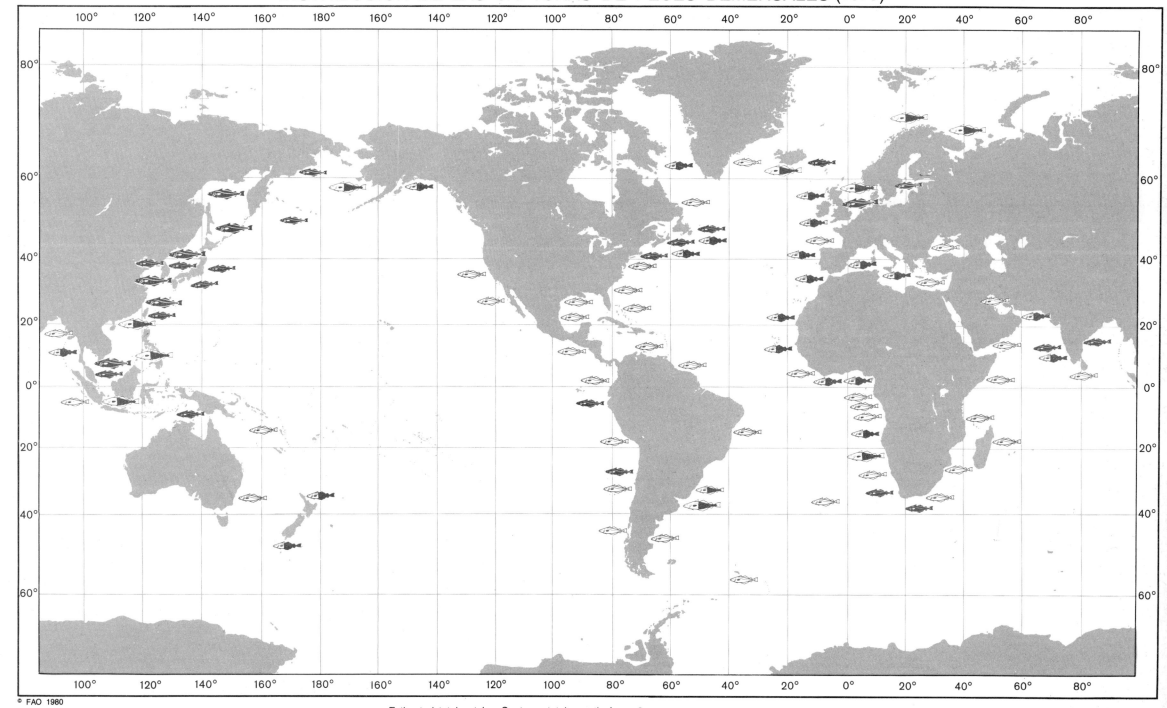

© FAO 1980

Estimated total catch – Captures totales estimées – Capturas totales estimadas
21 000 000 t

>1 000 000 t

250 000 - 1 000 000 t

50 000 - 250 000 t

25 000 - 50 000 t

<25 000 t

DISTRIBUTION OF COASTAL PELAGIC CATCHES (1979)
RÉPARTITION DES CAPTURES PÉLAGIQUES CÔTIÈRES (1979)
DISTRIBUCION DE LAS CAPTURAS PELAGICAS COSTERAS (1979)

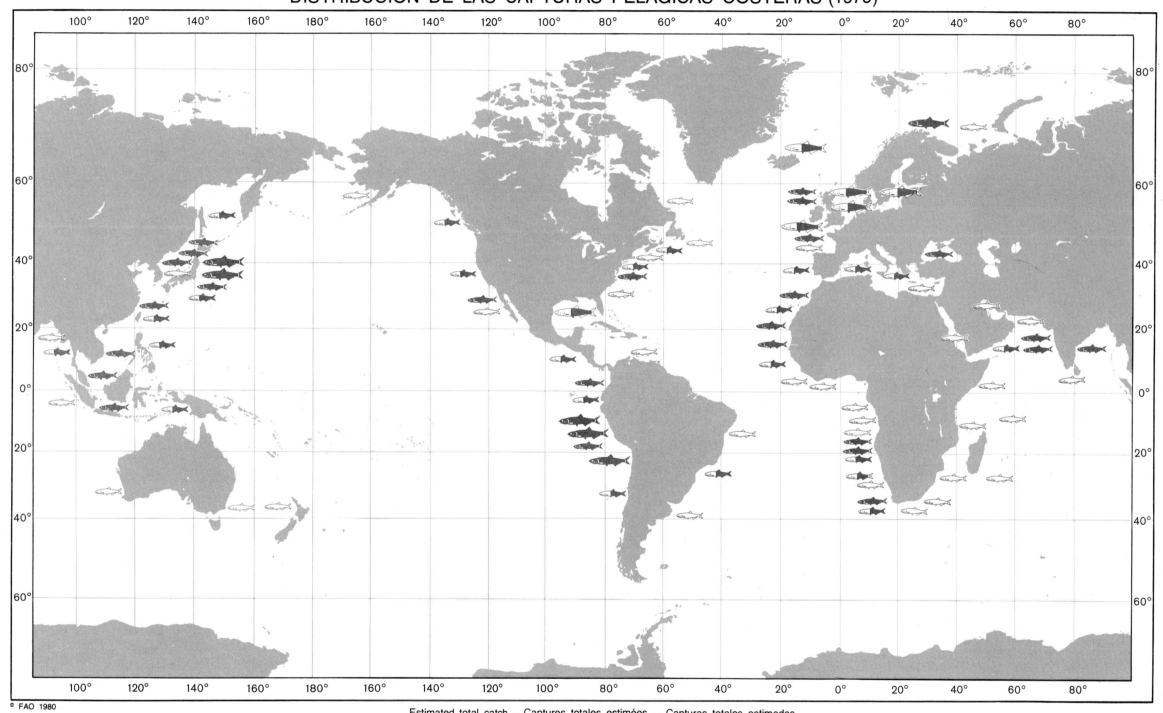

© FAO 1980

Estimated total catch – Captures totales estimées – Capturas totales estimadas
32 000 000 t

>1 000 000 t
500 000-1 000 000 t
200 000- 500 000 t
50 000- 200 000 t
<50 000 t

DISTRIBUTION OF CATCHES OF TUNAS AND TUNA-LIKE FISHES (1977)
DISTRIBUTION DES CAPTURES DE THONS ET DES ESPÈCES VOISINES (1977)
DISTRIBUCION DE LAS CAPTURAS DE ATUNES Y ESPECIES AFINES (1977)

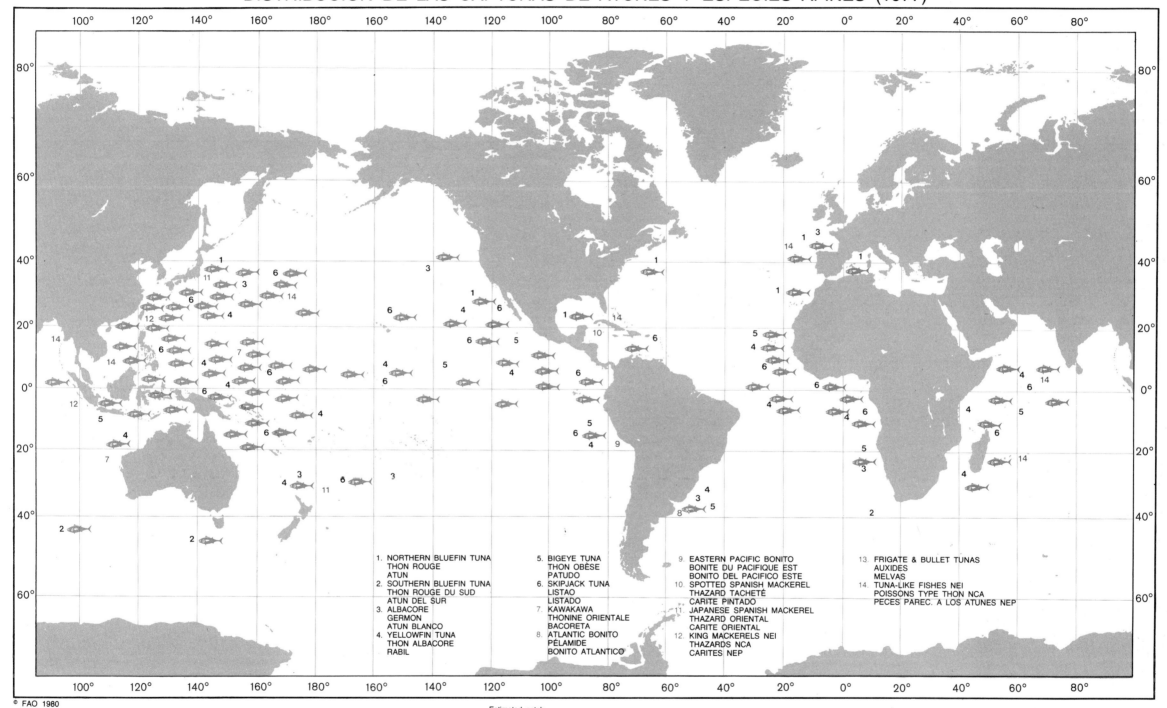

1. NORTHERN BLUEFIN TUNA
   THON ROUGE
   ATUN
2. SOUTHERN BLUEFIN TUNA
   THON ROUGE DU SUD
   ATUN DEL SUR
3. ALBACORE
   GERMON
   ATUN BLANCO
4. YELLOWFIN TUNA
   THON ALBACORE
   RABIL
5. BIGEYE TUNA
   THON OBÈSE
   PATUDO
6. SKIPJACK TUNA
   LISTAO
   LISTADO
7. KAWAKAWA
   THONINE ORIENTALE
   BACORETA
8. ATLANTIC BONITO
   PÉLAMIDE
   BONITO ATLANTICO
9. EASTERN PACIFIC BONITO
   BONITE DU PACIFIQUE EST
   BONITO DEL PACIFICO ESTE
10. SPOTTED SPANISH MACKEREL
    THAZARD TACHETÉ
    CARITE PINTADO
11. JAPANESE SPANISH MACKEREL
    THAZARD ORIENTAL
    CARITE ORIENTAL
12. KING MACKERELS NEI
    THAZARDS NCA
    CARITES NEP
13. FRIGATE & BULLET TUNAS
    AUXIDES
    MELVAS
14. TUNA-LIKE FISHES NEI
    POISSONS TYPE THON NCA
    PECES PAREC. A LOS ATUNES NEP

© FAO 1980

Estimated catch
Captures estimées   **25 000 t**
Capturas estimadas

DISTRIBUTION OF CRUSTACEANS CATCHES (1979)
RÉPARTITION DES CAPTURES DE CRUSTACÉS (1979)
DISTRIBUCION DE LAS CAPTURAS DE CRUSTACEOS (1979)

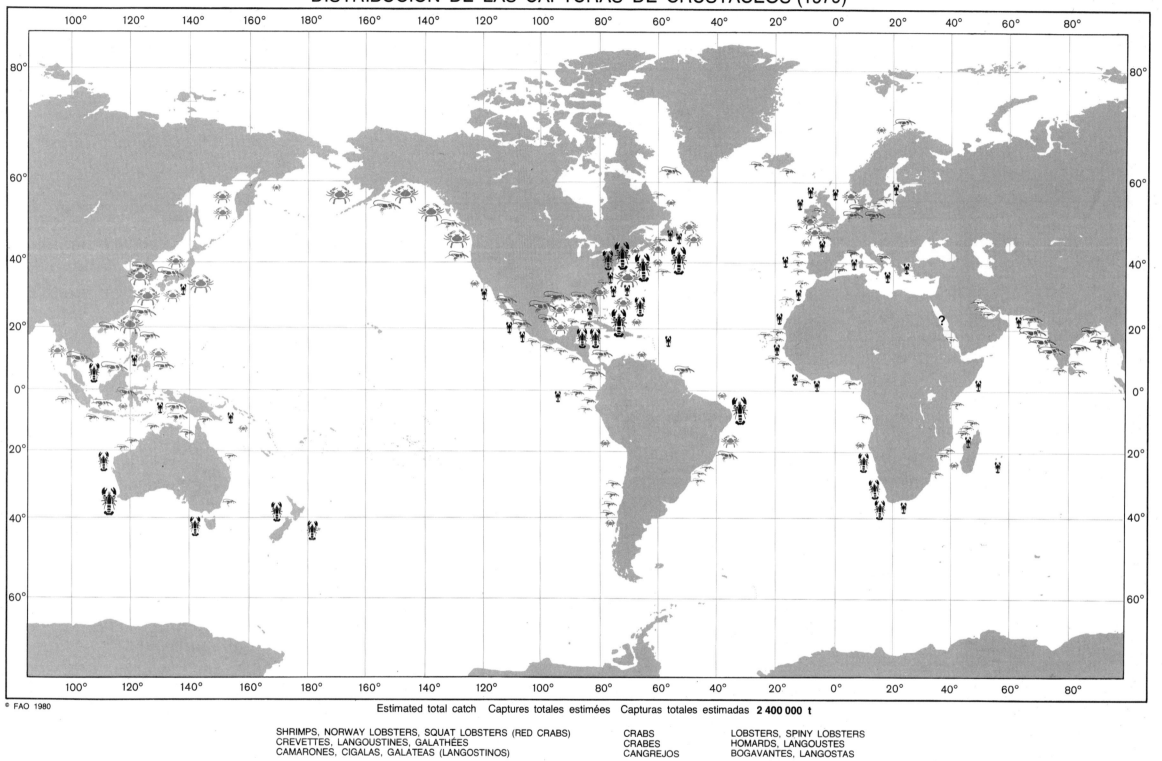

© FAO 1980

Estimated total catch   Captures totales estimées   Capturas totales estimadas **2 400 000 t**

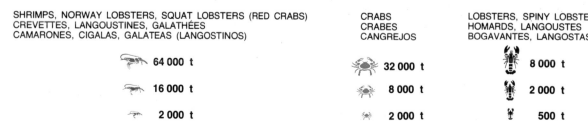

SHRIMPS, NORWAY LOBSTERS, SQUAT LOBSTERS (RED CRABS)
CREVETTES, LANGOUSTINES, GALATHÉES
CAMARONES, CIGALAS, GALATEAS (LANGOSTINOS)

CRABS
CRABES
CANGREJOS

LOBSTERS, SPINY LOBSTERS
HOMARDS, LANGOUSTES
BOGAVANTES, LANGOSTAS

64 000 t	32 000 t	8 000 t
16 000 t	8 000 t	2 000 t
2 000 t	2 000 t	500 t

STATE OF EXPLOITATION OF THE MAJOR STOCKS OF DEMERSAL AND PELAGIC RESOURCES
ÉTAT D'EXPLOITATION DES PRINCIPALES RESSOURCES DÉMERSALES ET PÉLAGIQUES
ESTADO DE EXPLOTACION DE LOS MAYORES RECURSOS DEMERSALES Y PELAGICOS

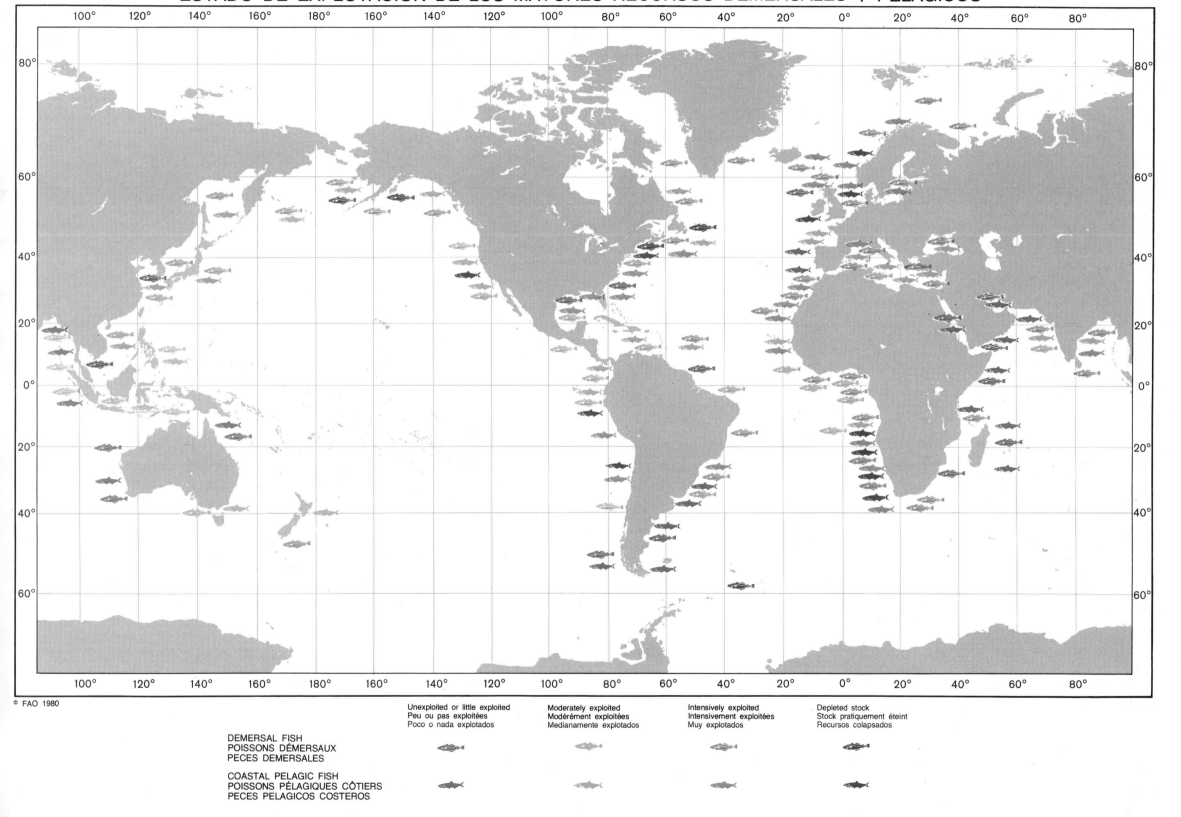

© FAO 1980

	Unexploited or little exploited / Peu ou pas exploitées / Poco o nada explotados	Moderately exploited / Modérément exploitées / Medianamente explotados	Intensively exploited / Intensivement exploitées / Muy explotados	Depleted stock / Stock pratiquement éteint / Recursos colapsados
DEMERSAL FISH / POISSONS DÉMERSAUX / PECES DEMERSALES				
COASTAL PELAGIC FISH / POISSONS PÉLAGIQUES CÔTIERS / PECES PELAGICOS COSTEROS				

STATE OF EXPLOITATION OF THE MAJOR TUNA AND CEPHALOPOD STOCKS
ÉTAT D'EXPLOITATION DES PRINCIPAUX STOCKS DE THONS ET DE CÉPHALOPODES
ESTADO DE EXPLOTACION DE LOS EFECTIVOS DE POBLACIONES DE ATUNES Y CEFALOPODOS

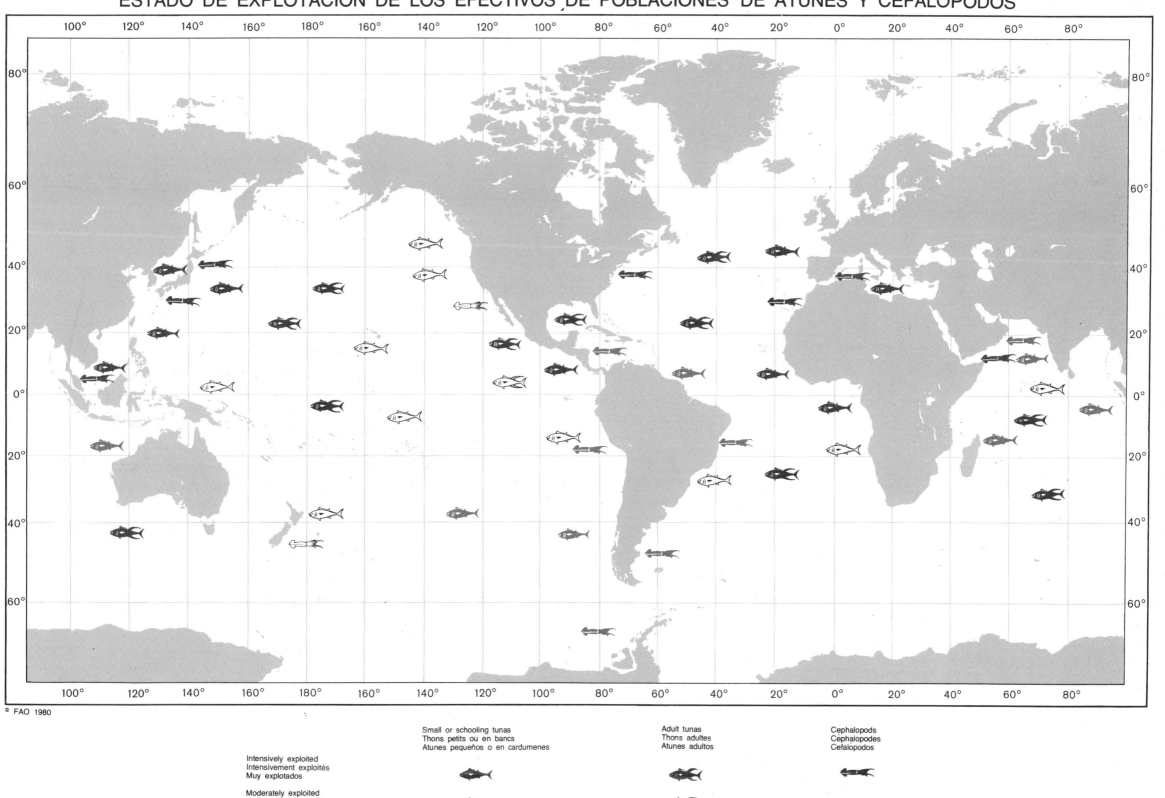

© FAO 1980

	Small or schooling tunas Thons petits ou en bancs Atunes pequeños o en cardumenes	Adult tunas Thons adultes Atunes adultos	Cephalopods Céphalopodes Cefalopodos
Intensively exploited Intensivement exploités Muy explotados			
Moderately exploited Modérément exploités Medianamente explotados			
Unexploited or little exploited Peu ou pas exploités Poco o nada explotados			

STATE OF EXPLOITATION OF THE MAJOR STOCKS OF CRUSTACEANS RESOURCES
ÉTAT D'EXPLOITATION DES PRINCIPALES RESSOURCES DE CRUSTACÉS
ESTADO DE EXPLOTACION DE LOS MAYORES RECURSOS DE CRUSTACEOS

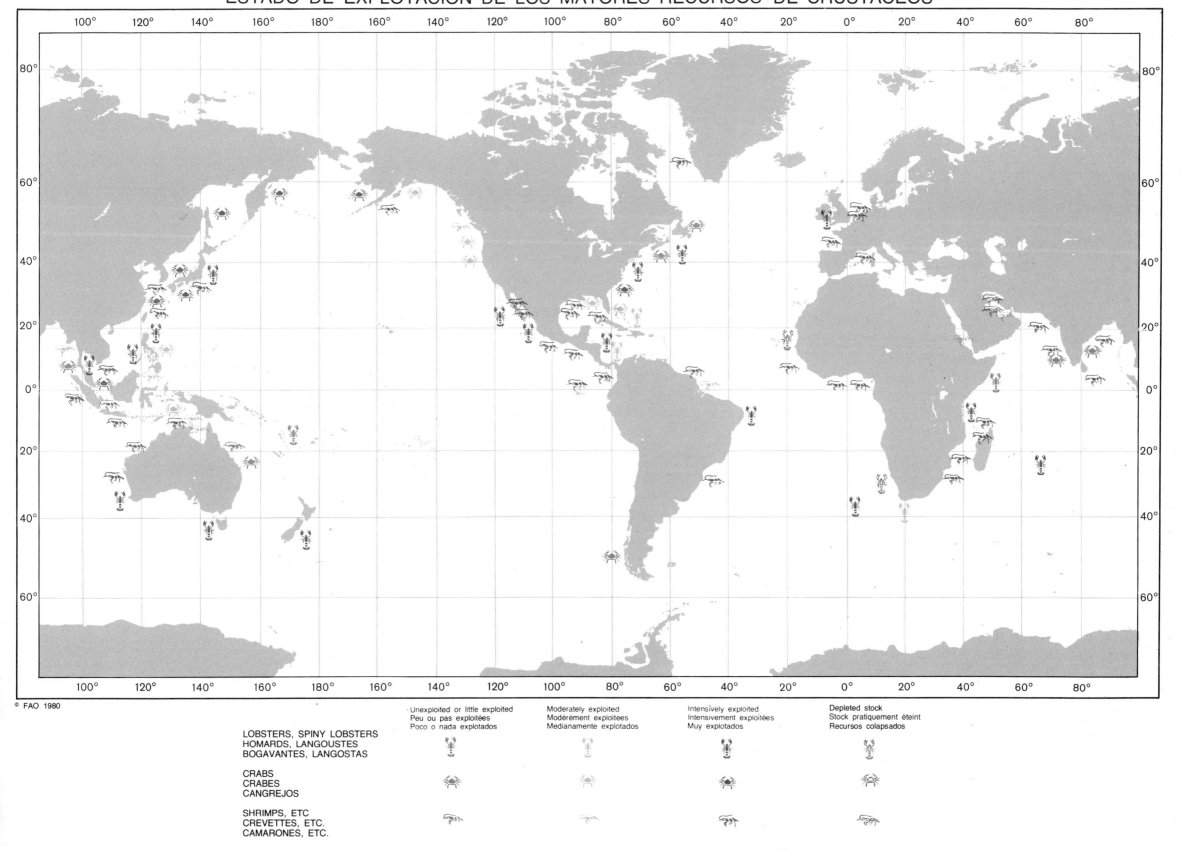

© FAO 1980

	Unexploited or little exploited Peu ou pas exploitées Poco o nada explotados	Moderately exploited Modérèment exploitées Medianamente explotados	Intensively exploited Intensivement exploitées Muy explotados	Depleted stock Stock pratiquement éteint Recursos colapsados
LOBSTERS, SPINY LOBSTERS HOMARDS, LANGOUSTES BOGAVANTES, LANGOSTAS				
CRABS CRABES CANGREJOS				
SHRIMPS, ETC CREVETTES, ETC. CAMARONES, ETC.				

STATE OF EXPLOITATION OF THE WHALE STOCKS (1979)
ÉTAT D'EXPLOITATION DES STOCKS DE BALEINES (1979)
ESTADO DE EXPLOTACION DE LOS EFECTIVOS DE POBLACIONES DE BALLENAS (1979)

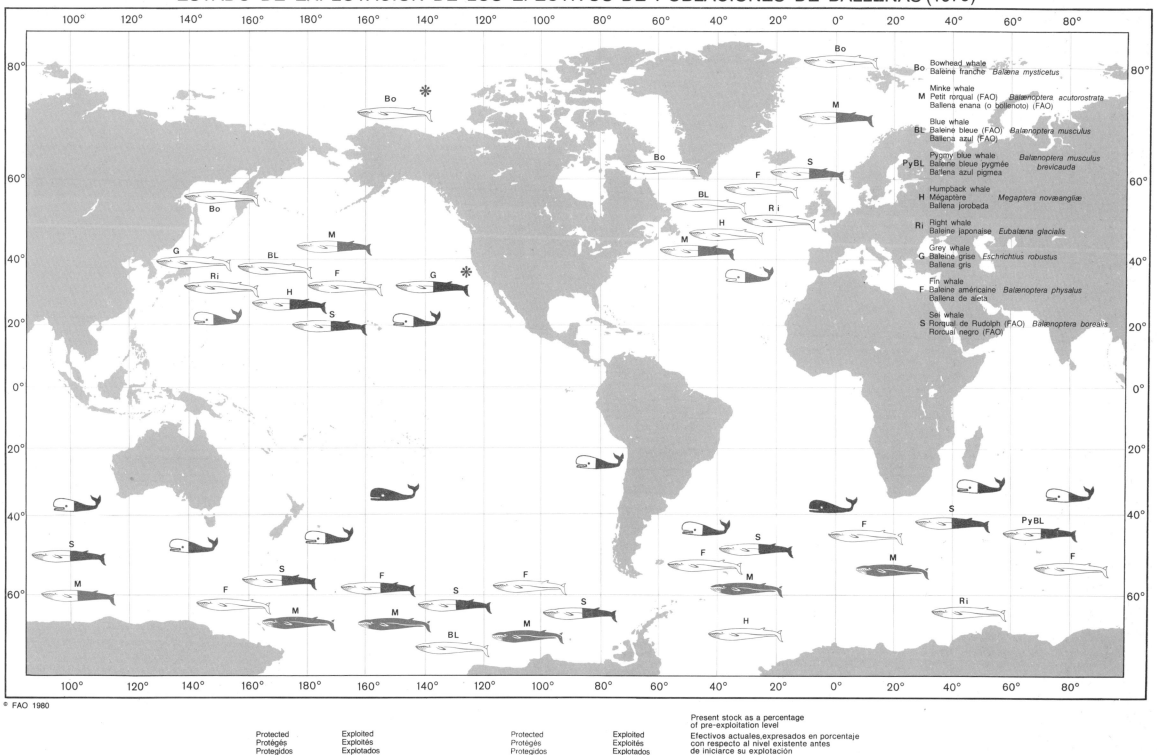

Bo Bowhead whale
    Baleine franche *Balæna mysticetus*

M   Minke whale
    Petit rorqual (FAO) *Balænoptera acutorostrata*
    Ballena enana (o bollenoto) (FAO)

BL Blue whale
    Baleine bleue (FAO) *Balænoptera musculus*
    Ballena azul (FAO)

PyBL Pygmy blue whale
    Baleine bleue pygmée *Balænoptera musculus*
    Ballena azul pigmea *brevicauda*

H   Humpback whale
    Mégaptère *Megaptera novæangliæ*
    Ballena jorobada

Ri Right whale
    Baleine japonaise *Eubalæna glacialis*

G   Grey whale
    Baleine grise *Eschrichtius robustus*
    Ballena gris

F   Fin whale
    Baleine américaine *Balænoptera physalus*
    Ballena de aleta

S   Sei whale
    Rorqual de Rudolph (FAO) *Balænoptera borealis*
    Rorcual negro (FAO)

© FAO 1980

Protected   Exploited
Protégés   Exploités
Protegidos   Explotados

Spermwhale
Cachalot
Cachalote

Protected   Exploited
Protégés   Exploités
Protegidos   Explotados

Baleen whales
Baleines à fanons
Ballenas de barba

Present stock as a percentage
of pre-exploitation level
Efectivos actuales,expresados en porcentaje
con respecto al nivel existente antes
de iniciarce su explotación
Stock actuel exprimé en pourcentage par
rapport à son niveau avant exploitation

> 75%

25 - 75%

< 25%

* Aboriginal hunting only
   Seulement chasse indigène
   Caza por los indigenas solamente

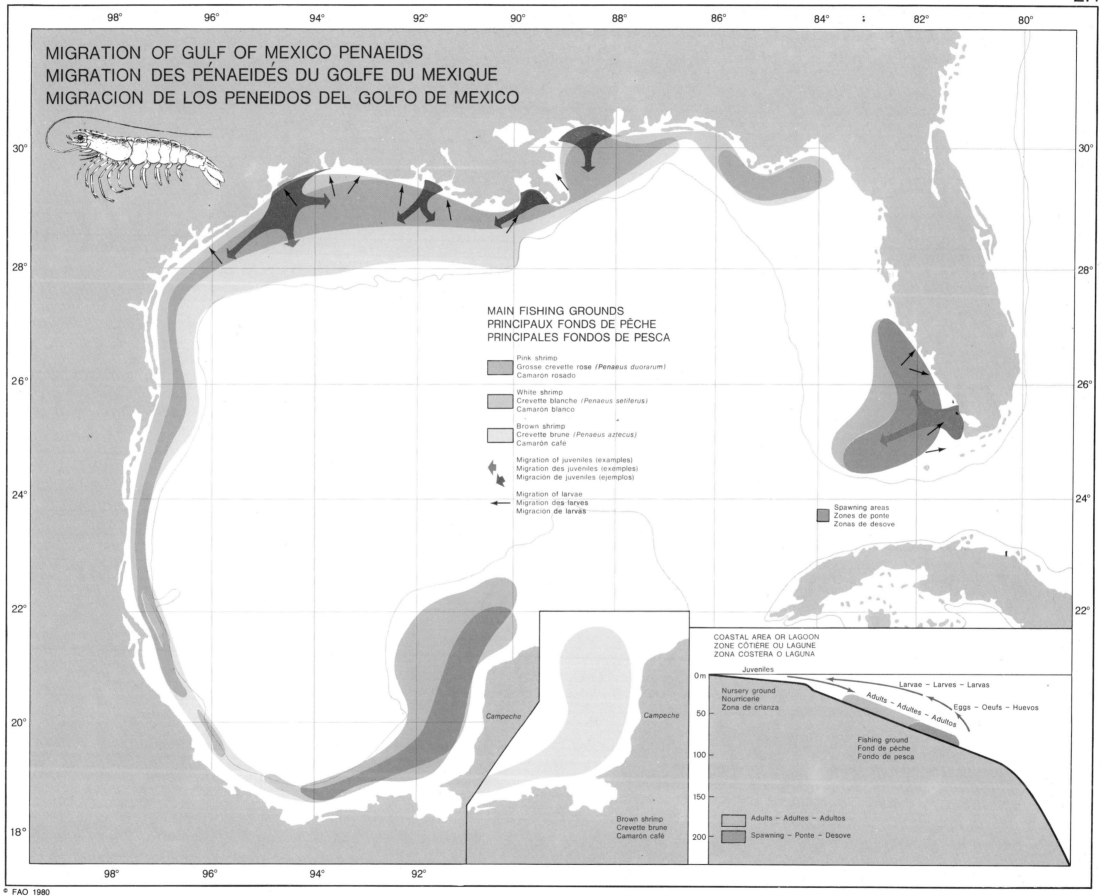

MIGRATION OF GULF OF MEXICO PENAEIDS
MIGRATION DES PÉNAEIDÉS DU GOLFE DU MEXIQUE
MIGRACION DE LOS PENEIDOS DEL GOLFO DE MEXICO

MAIN FISHING GROUNDS
PRINCIPAUX FONDS DE PÊCHE
PRINCIPALES FONDOS DE PESCA

Pink shrimp
Grosse crevette rose *(Penaeus duorarum)*
Camarón rosado

White shrimp
Crevette blanche *(Penaeus setiferus)*
Camarón blanco

Brown shrimp
Crevette brune *(Penaeus aztecus)*
Camarón café

Migration of juveniles (examples)
Migration des juvéniles (exemples)
Migración de juveniles (ejemplos)

Migration of larvae
Migration des larves
Migración de larvas

Spawning areas
Zones de ponte
Zonas de desove

Campeche

Campeche

Brown shrimp
Crevette brune
Camarón café

COASTAL AREA OR LAGOON
ZONE CÔTIÈRE OU LAGUNE
ZONA COSTERA O LAGUNA

Juveniles

Larvae – Larves – Larvas

Nursery ground
Nourricerie
Zona de crianza

Adults – Adultes – Adultos

Eggs – Oeufs – Huevos

Fishing ground
Fond de pêche
Fondo de pesca

0 m
50
100
150
200

Adults – Adultes – Adultos

Spawning – Ponte – Desove

© FAO 1980

2.1

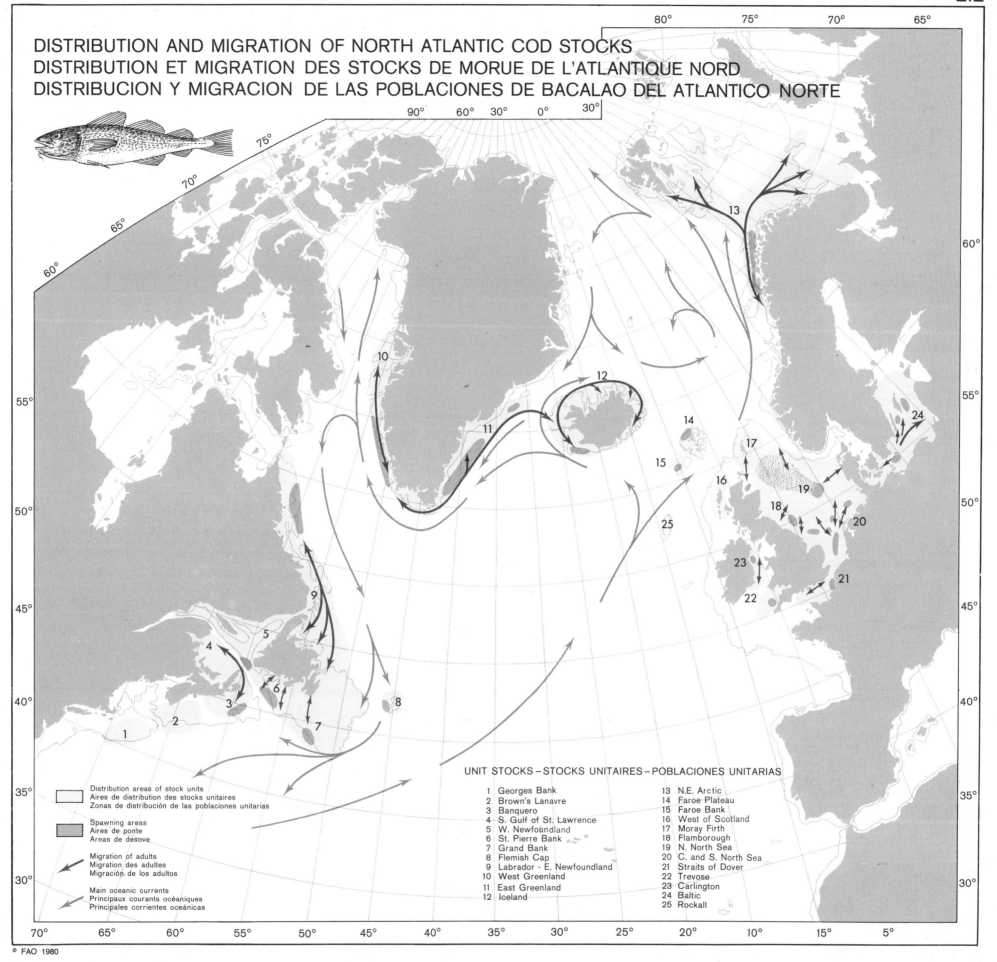

DISTRIBUTION AND MIGRATION OF NORTH ATLANTIC COD STOCKS
DISTRIBUTION ET MIGRATION DES STOCKS DE MORUE DE L'ATLANTIQUE NORD
DISTRIBUCION Y MIGRACION DE LAS POBLACIONES DE BACALAO DEL ATLANTICO NORTE

Distribution areas of stock units
Aires de distribution des stocks unitaires
Zonas de distribución de las poblaciones unitarias

Spawning areas
Aires de ponte
Areas de desove

Migration of adults
Migration des adultes
Migración de los adultos

Main oceanic currents
Principaux courants océaniques
Principales corrientes océanicas

UNIT STOCKS – STOCKS UNITAIRES – POBLACIONES UNITARIAS

1	Georges Bank	
2	Brown's Lanavre	
3	Banquero	
4	S. Gulf of St. Lawrence	
5	W. Newfoundland	
6	St. Pierre Bank	
7	Grand Bank	
8	Flemish Cap	
9	Labrador - E. Newfoundland	
10	West Greenland	
11	East Greenland	
12	Iceland	

13	N.E. Arctic
14	Faroe Plateau
15	Faroe Bank
16	West of Scotland
17	Moray Firth
18	Flamborough
19	N. North Sea
20	C. and S. North Sea
21	Straits of Dover
22	Trevose
23	Carlington
24	Baltic
25	Rockall

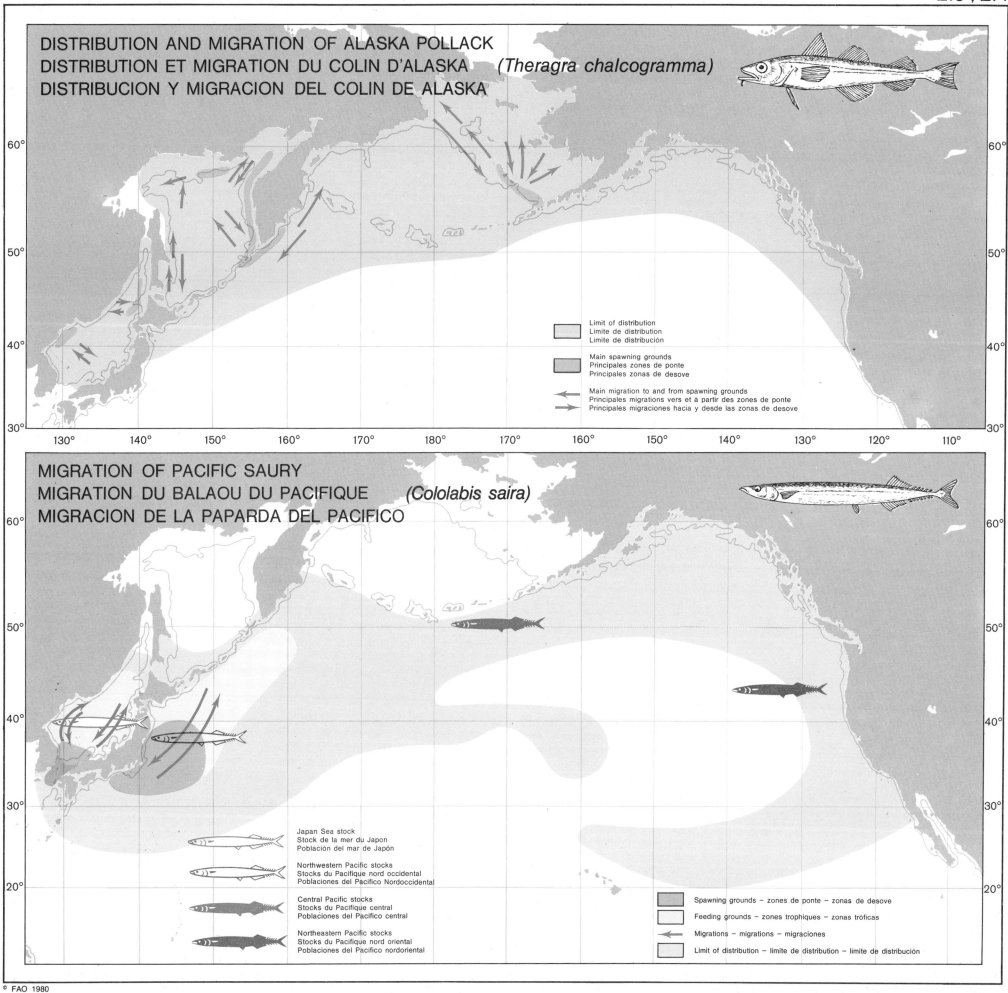

DISTRIBUTION AND MIGRATION OF ALASKA POLLACK
DISTRIBUTION ET MIGRATION DU COLIN D'ALASKA   *(Theragra chalcogramma)*
DISTRIBUCION Y MIGRACION DEL COLIN DE ALASKA

Limit of distribution
Limite de distribution
Limite de distribución

Main spawning grounds
Principales zones de ponte
Principales zonas de desove

Main migration to and from spawning grounds
Principales migrations vers et à partir des zones de ponte
Principales migraciones hacia y desde las zonas de desove

MIGRATION OF PACIFIC SAURY
MIGRATION DU BALAOU DU PACIFIQUE   *(Cololabis saira)*
MIGRACION DE LA PAPARDA DEL PACIFICO

Japan Sea stock
Stock de la mer du Japon
Población del mar de Japón

Northwestern Pacific stocks
Stocks du Pacifique nord occidental
Poblaciones del Pacifico Nordoccidental

Central Pacific stocks
Stocks du Pacifique central
Poblaciones del Pacifico central

Northeastern Pacific stocks
Stocks du Pacifique nord oriental
Poblaciones del Pacifico nordoriental

Spawning grounds – zones de ponte – zonas de desove

Feeding grounds – zones trophiques – zonas tróficas

Migrations – migrations – migraciones

Limit of distribution – limite de distribution – limite de distribución

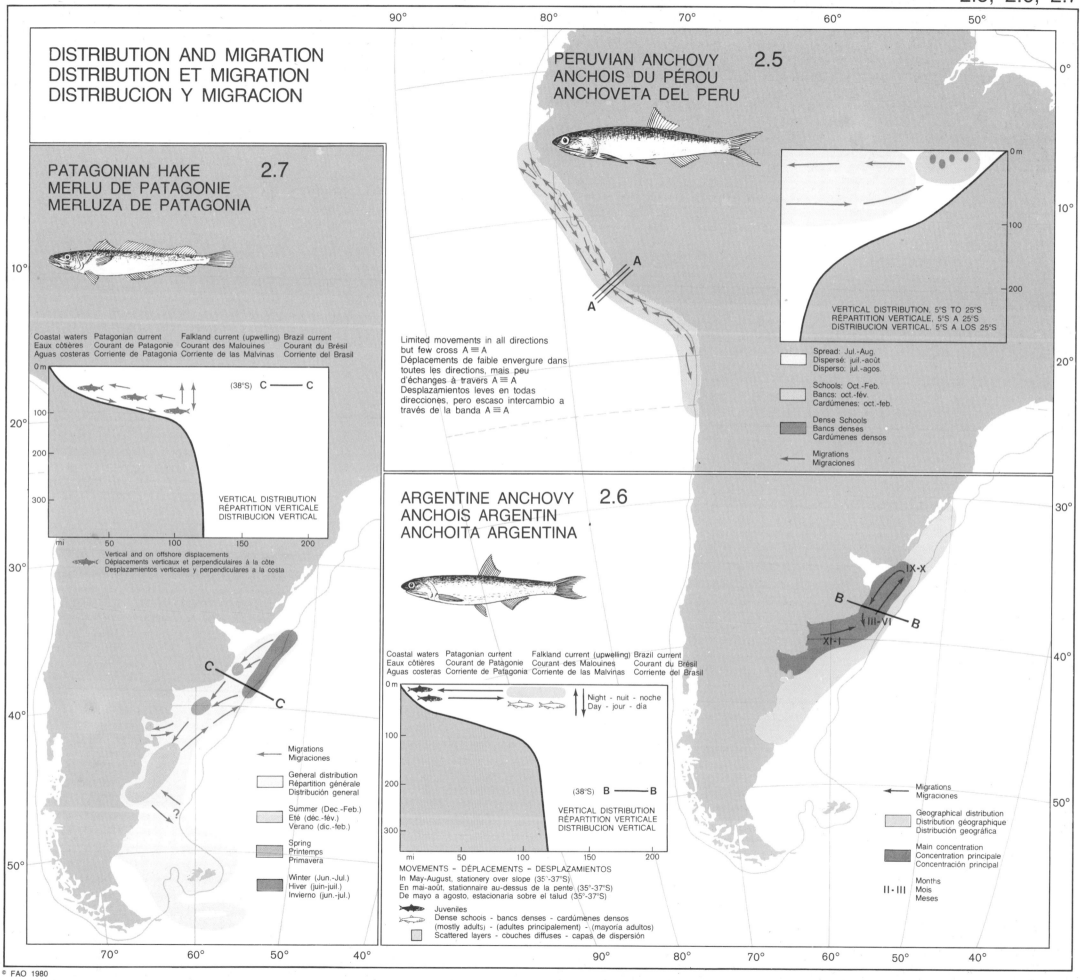

DISTRIBUTION AND MIGRATION
DISTRIBUTION ET MIGRATION
DISTRIBUCION Y MIGRACION

PATAGONIAN HAKE 2.7
MERLU DE PATAGONIE
MERLUZA DE PATAGONIA

Coastal waters	Patagonian current	Falkland current (upwelling)	Brazil current
Eaux côtières	Courant de Patagonie	Courant des Malouines	Courant du Brésil
Aguas costeras	Corriente de Patagonia	Corriente de las Malvinas	Corriente del Brasil

(38°S) C — C

VERTICAL DISTRIBUTION
RÉPARTITION VERTICALE
DISTRIBUCION VERTICAL

Vertical and on offshore displacements
Déplacements verticaux et perpendiculaires à la côte
Desplazamientos verticales y perpendiculares a la costa

Migrations
Migraciones

General distribution
Répartition générale
Distribución general

Summer (Dec.-Feb.)
Eté (déc.-fév.)
Verano (dic.-feb.)

Spring
Printemps
Primavera

Winter (Jun.-Jul.)
Hiver (juin-juil.)
Invierno (jun.-jul.)

PERUVIAN ANCHOVY 2.5
ANCHOIS DU PÉROU
ANCHOVETA DEL PERU

Limited movements in all directions
but few cross A ≡ A
Déplacements de faible envergure dans
toutes les directions, mais peu
d'échanges à travers A ≡ A
Desplazamientos leves en todas
direcciones, pero escaso intercambio a
través de la banda A ≡ A

VERTICAL DISTRIBUTION, 5°S TO 25°S
RÉPARTITION VERTICALE, 5°S A 25°S
DISTRIBUCION VERTICAL, 5°S A LOS 25°S

Spread: Jul.-Aug.
Dispersé: juil.-août
Disperso: jul.-agos.

Schools: Oct.-Feb.
Bancs: oct.-fév.
Cardúmenes: oct.-feb.

Dense Schools
Bancs denses
Cardúmenes densos

Migrations
Migraciones

ARGENTINE ANCHOVY 2.6
ANCHOIS ARGENTIN
ANCHOITA ARGENTINA

Coastal waters	Patagonian current	Falkland current (upwelling)	Brazil current
Eaux côtières	Courant de Patagonie	Courant des Malouines	Courant du Brésil
Aguas costeras	Corriente de Patagonia	Corriente de las Malvinas	Corriente del Brasil

Night - nuit - noche
Day - jour - día

(38°S) B — B

VERTICAL DISTRIBUTION
RÉPARTITION VERTICALE
DISTRIBUCION VERTICAL

MOVEMENTS - DÉPLACEMENTS - DESPLAZAMIENTOS
In May-August, stationery over slope (35°-37°S)
En mai-août, stationnaire au-dessus de la pente (35°-37°S)
De mayo a agosto, estacionaria sobre el talud (35°-37°S)

Juveniles
Dense schools - bancs denses - cardúmenes densos
(mostly adults) - (adultes principalement) - (mayoría adultos)
Scattered layers - couches diffuses - capas de dispersión

Migrations
Migraciones

Geographical distribution
Distribution géographique
Distribución geográfica

Main concentration
Concentration principale
Concentración principal

Months
Mois
Meses

© FAO 1980

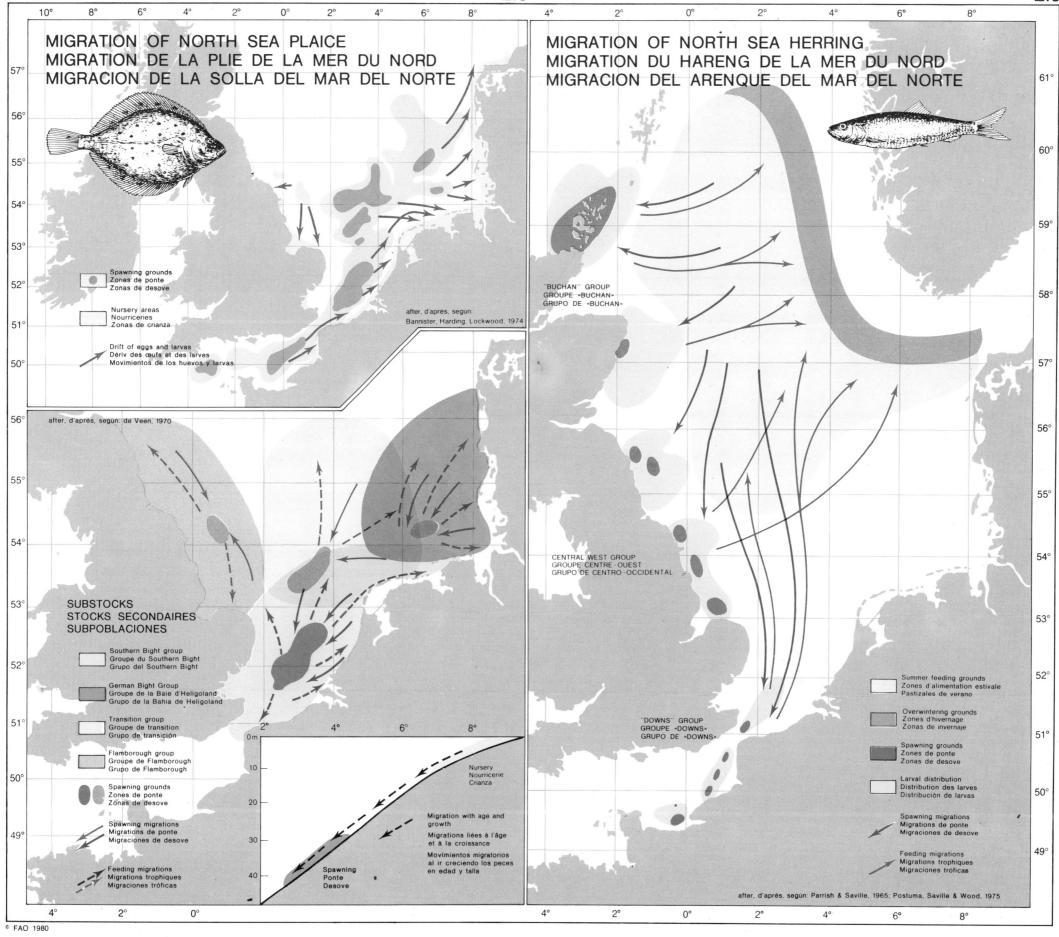

MIGRATION OF NORTH SEA PLAICE
MIGRATION DE LA PLIE DE LA MER DU NORD
MIGRACION DE LA SOLLA DEL MAR DEL NORTE

Spawning grounds
Zones de ponte
Zonas de desove

Nursery areas
Nourriceries
Zonas de crianza

Drift of eggs and larvas
Dériv des œufs et des larves
Movimientos de los huevos y larvas

after, d'après, según:
Bannister, Harding, Lockwood, 1974

after, d'après, según: de Veen, 1970

SUBSTOCKS
STOCKS SECONDAIRES
SUBPOBLACIONES

Southern Bight group
Groupe du Southern Bight
Grupo del Southern Bight

German Bight Group
Groupe de la Baie d'Heligoland
Grupo de la Bahia de Heligoland

Transition group
Groupe de transition
Grupo de transición

Flamborough group
Groupe de Flamborough
Grupo de Flamborough

Spawning grounds
Zones de ponte
Zonas de desove

Spawning migrations
Migrations de ponte
Migraciones de desove

Feeding migrations
Migrations trophiques
Migraciones tróficas

Nursery
Nourricerie
Crianza

Migration with age and growth
Migrations liées à l'âge et à la croissance
Movimientos migratorios al ir creciendo los peces en edad y talla

Spawning
Ponte
Desove

MIGRATION OF NORTH SEA HERRING
MIGRATION DU HARENG DE LA MER DU NORD
MIGRACION DEL ARENQUE DEL MAR DEL NORTE

"BUCHAN" GROUP
GROUPE «BUCHAN»
GRUPO DE «BUCHAN»

CENTRAL WEST GROUP
GROUPE CENTRE-OUEST
GRUPO DE CENTRO-OCCIDENTAL

"DOWNS" GROUP
GROUPE «DOWNS»
GRUPO DE «DOWNS»

Summer feeding grounds
Zones d'alimentation estivale
Pastizales de verano

Overwintering grounds
Zones d'hivernage
Zonas de invernaje

Spawning grounds
Zones de ponte
Zonas de desove

Larval distribution
Distribution des larves
Distribución de larvas

Spawning migrations
Migrations de ponte
Migraciones de desove

Feeding migrations
Migrations trophiques
Migraciones tróficas

after, d'après, según: Parrish & Saville, 1965; Postuma, Saville & Wood, 1975

© FAO 1980

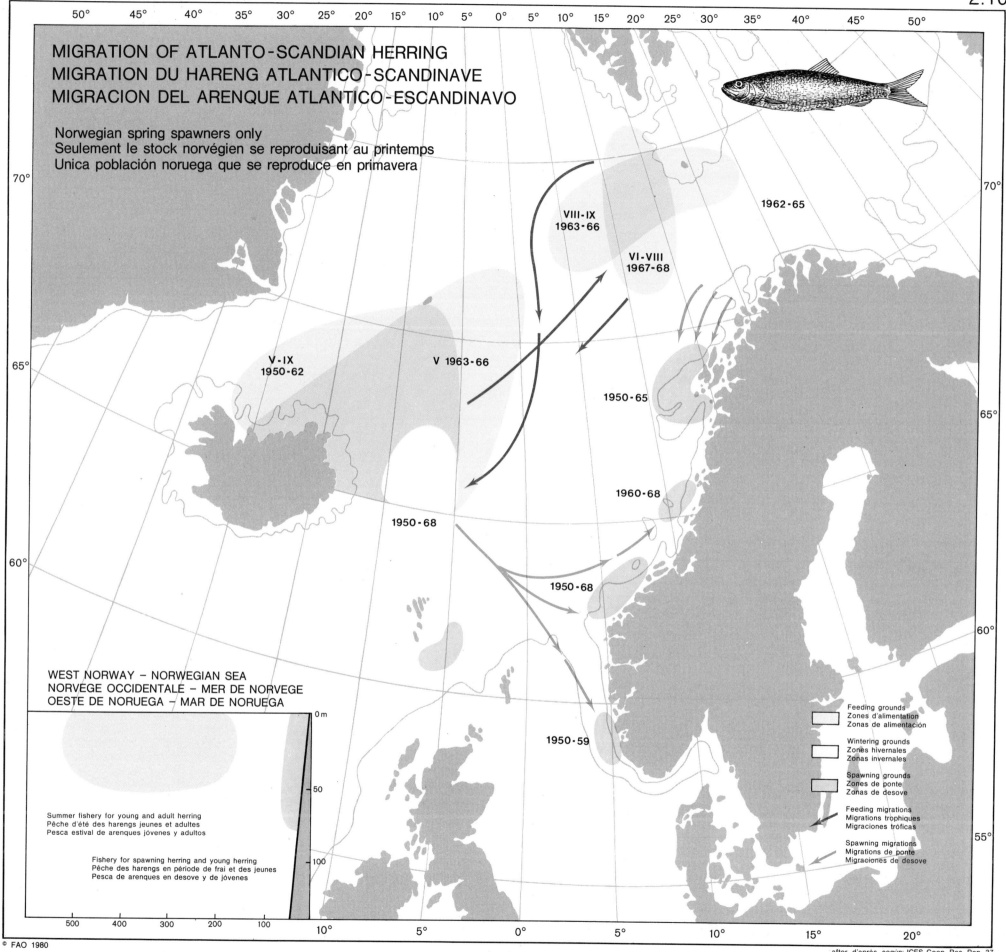

MIGRATION OF ATLANTO-SCANDIAN HERRING
MIGRATION DU HARENG ATLANTICO-SCANDINAVE
MIGRACION DEL ARENQUE ATLANTICO-ESCANDINAVO

Norwegian spring spawners only
Seulement le stock norvégien se reproduisant au printemps
Unica población noruega que se reproduce en primavera

VIII-IX
1963-66

1962-65

VI-VIII
1967-68

V-IX
1950-62

V 1963-66

1950-65

1950-68

1960-68

1950-68

1950-59

WEST NORWAY – NORWEGIAN SEA
NORVEGE OCCIDENTALE – MER DE NORVEGE
OESTE DE NORUEGA – MAR DE NORUEGA

0 m

50

100

Summer fishery for young and adult herring
Pêche d'été des harengs jeunes et adultes
Pesca estival de arenques jóvenes y adultos

Fishery for spawning herring and young herring
Pêche des harengs en période de frai et des jeunes
Pesca de arenques en desove y de jóvenes

500   400   300   200   100

Feeding grounds
Zones d'alimentation
Zonas de alimentación

Wintering grounds
Zones hivernales
Zonas invernales

Spawning grounds
Zones de ponte
Zonas de desove

Feeding migrations
Migrations trophiques
Migraciones tróficas

Spawning migrations
Migrations de ponte
Migraciones de desove

after, d'après, según: ICES Coop. Res. Rep. 37

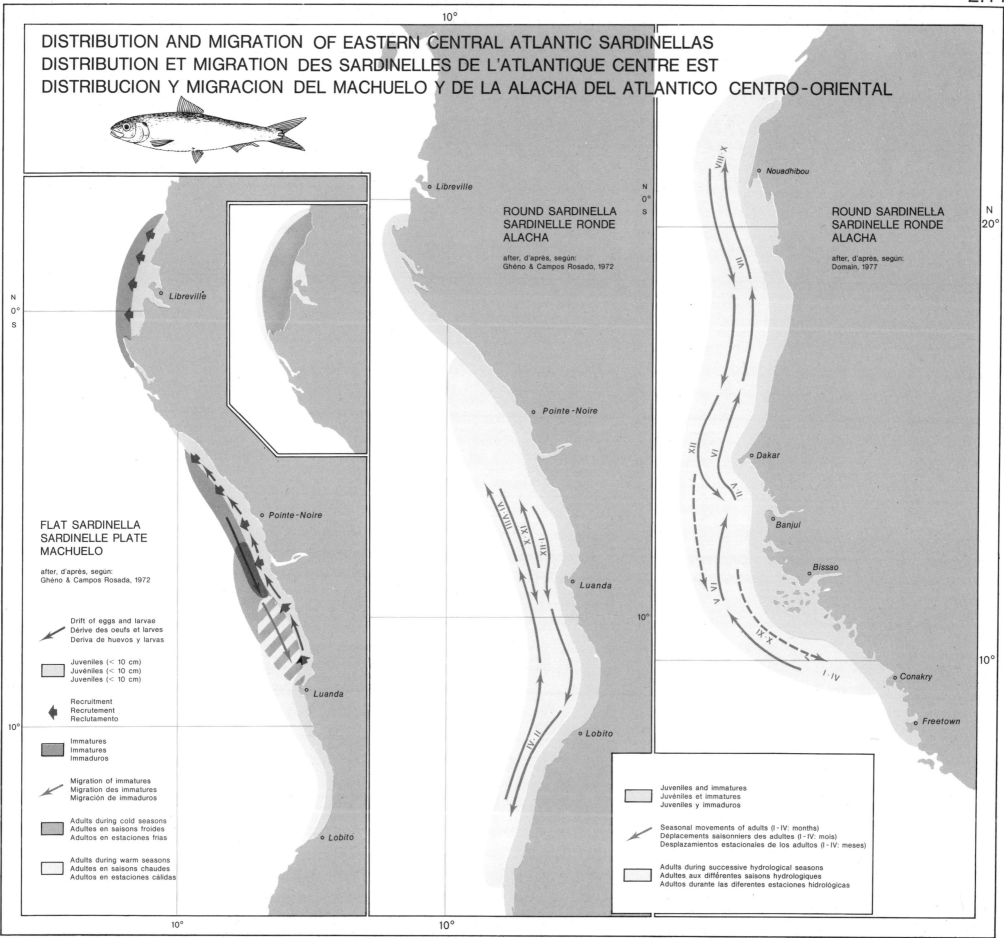

DISTRIBUTION AND MIGRATION OF EASTERN CENTRAL ATLANTIC SARDINELLAS
DISTRIBUTION ET MIGRATION DES SARDINELLES DE L'ATLANTIQUE CENTRE EST
DISTRIBUCION Y MIGRACION DEL MACHUELO Y DE LA ALACHA DEL ATLANTICO CENTRO-ORIENTAL

ROUND SARDINELLA
SARDINELLE RONDE
ALACHA

after, d'après, según:
Ghéno & Campos Rosado, 1972

ROUND SARDINELLA
SARDINELLE RONDE
ALACHA

after, d'après, según:
Domain, 1977

FLAT SARDINELLA
SARDINELLE PLATE
MACHUELO

after, d'après, según:
Ghéno & Campos Rosada, 1972

Drift of eggs and larvae
Dérive des oeufs et larves
Deriva de huevos y larvas

Juveniles (< 10 cm)
Juvéniles (< 10 cm)
Juveniles (< 10 cm)

Recruitment
Recrutement
Reclutamiento

Immatures
Immatures
Immaduros

Migration of immatures
Migration des immatures
Migración de immaduros

Adults during cold seasons
Adultes en saisons froides
Adultos en estaciones frias

Adults during warm seasons
Adultes en saisons chaudes
Adultos en estaciones cálidas

Juveniles and immatures
Juvéniles et immatures
Juveniles y immaduros

Seasonal movements of adults (I - IV: months)
Déplacements saisonniers des adultes (I - IV: mois)
Desplazamientos estacionales de los adultos (I - IV: meses)

Adults during successive hydrological seasons
Adultes aux différentes saisons hydrologiques
Adultos durante las diferentes estaciones hidrológicas

Libreville

Libreville

Pointe-Noire

Luanda

Lobito

Libreville

Pointe-Noire

Luanda

Lobito

Nouadhibou

Dakar

Banjul

Bissao

Conakry

Freetown

© FAO 1980

N.B. For typographical reasons, the scale of distances perpendicular to the coast has been artificially enlarged

N.B. Pour des raisons typographiques, l'échelle des distances perpendiculaires à la côte a été artificiellement agrandie

N.B. Por razones tipográficas se ha ampliado artificialmente la escala de las distancias perpendiculares a la costa

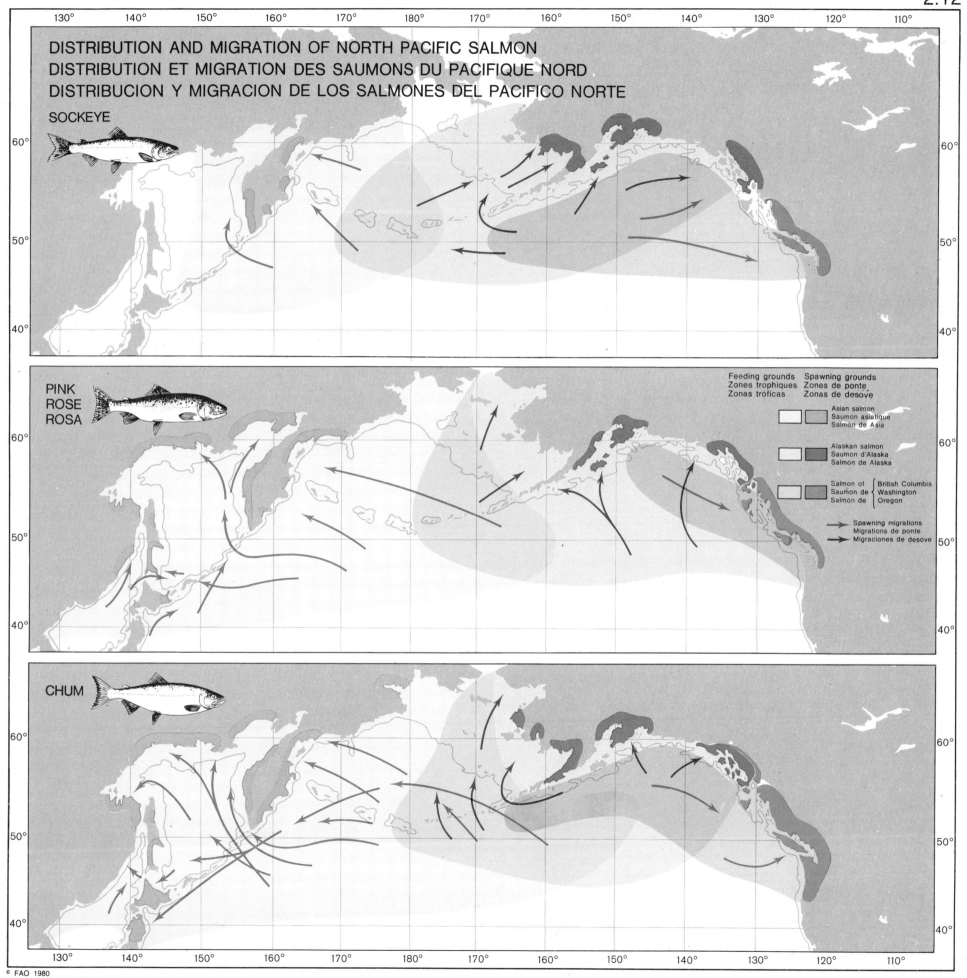

DISTRIBUTION AND MIGRATION OF NORTH PACIFIC SALMON
DISTRIBUTION ET MIGRATION DES SAUMONS DU PACIFIQUE NORD
DISTRIBUCION Y MIGRACION DE LOS SALMONES DEL PACIFICO NORTE

SOCKEYE

PINK
ROSE
ROSA

CHUM

Feeding grounds   Spawning grounds
Zones trophiques   Zones de ponte
Zonas tróficas   Zonas de desove

Asian salmon
Saumon asiatique
Salmón de Asia

Alaskan salmon
Saumon d'Alaska
Salmón de Alaska

Salmon of   { British Columbia
Saumon de { Washington
Salmón de { Oregon

→ Spawning migrations
  Migrations de ponte
  Migraciones de desove

© FAO 1980

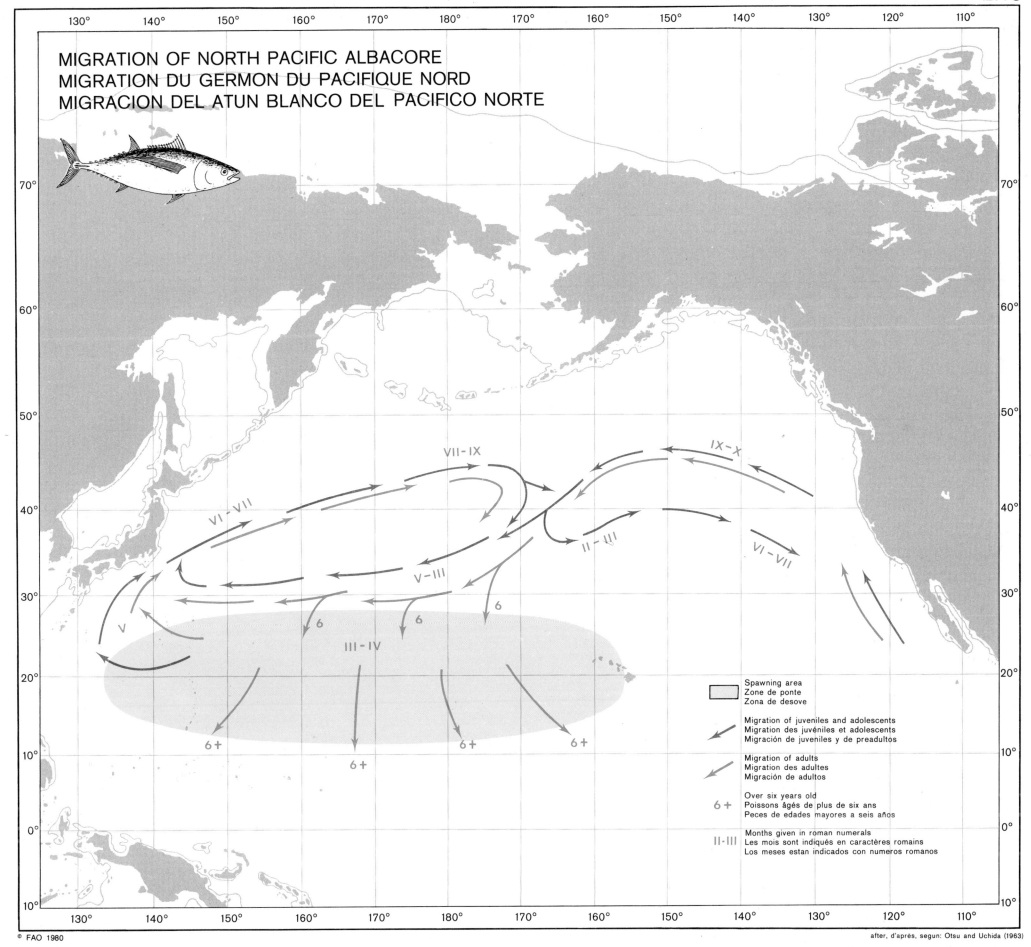

MIGRATION OF NORTH PACIFIC ALBACORE
MIGRATION DU GERMON DU PACIFIQUE NORD
MIGRACION DEL ATUN BLANCO DEL PACIFICO NORTE

Spawning area
Zone de ponte
Zona de desove

Migration of juveniles and adolescents
Migration des juvéniles et adolescents
Migración de juveniles y de preadultos

Migration of adults
Migration des adultes
Migración de adultos

Over six years old
Poissons âgés de plus de six ans
Peces de edades mayores a seis años

Months given in roman numerals
Les mois sont indiqués en caractères romains
Los meses estan indicados con numeros romanos

© FAO 1980

after, d'après, segun: Otsu and Uchida (1963)

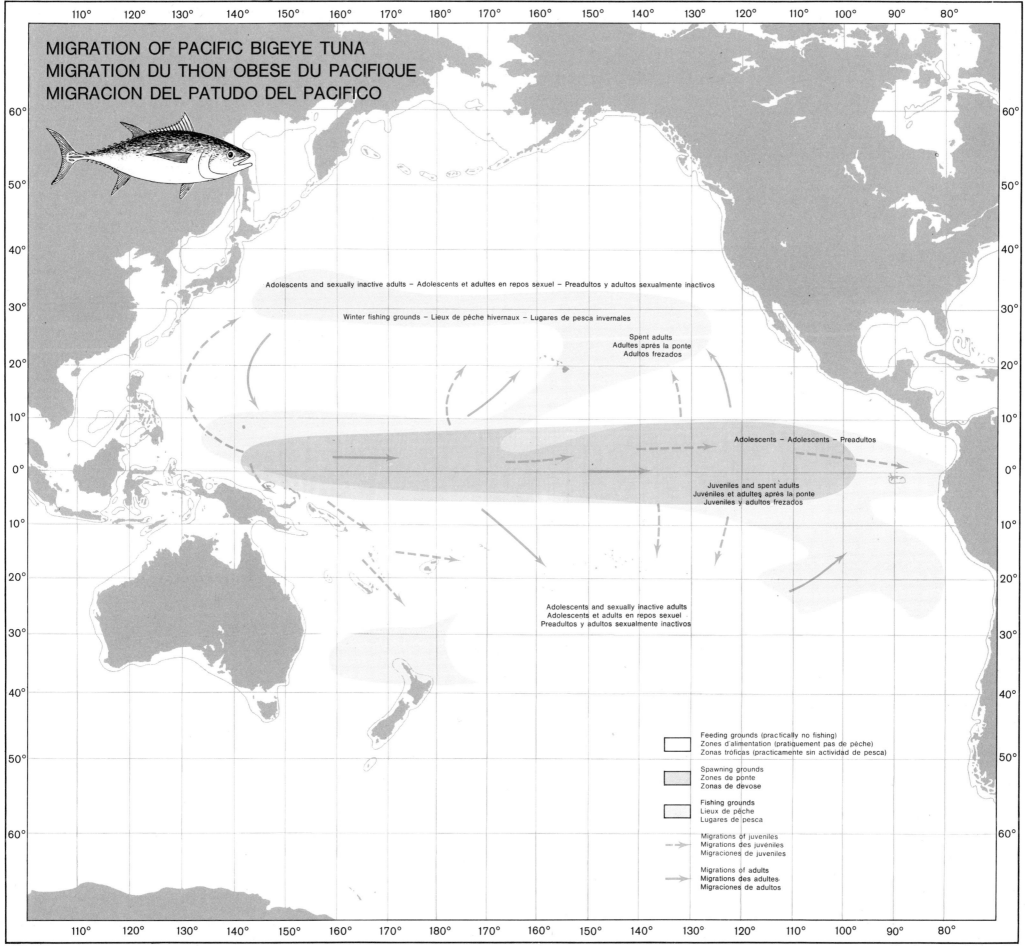

MIGRATION OF PACIFIC BIGEYE TUNA
MIGRATION DU THON OBESE DU PACIFIQUE
MIGRACION DEL PATUDO DEL PACIFICO

Adolescents and sexually inactive adults – Adolescents et adultes en repos sexuel – Preadultos y adultos sexualmente inactivos

Winter fishing grounds – Lieux de pêche hivernaux – Lugares de pesca invernales

Spent adults
Adultes après la ponte
Adultos frezados

Adolescents – Adolescents – Preadultos

Juveniles and spent adults
Juvéniles et adultes après la ponte
Juveniles y adultos frezados

Adolescents and sexually inactive adults
Adolescents et adults en repos sexuel
Preadultos y adultos sexualmente inactivos

Feeding grounds (practically no fishing)
Zones d'alimentation (pratiquement pas de pêche)
Zonas tróficas (practicamente sin actividad de pesca)

Spawning grounds
Zones de ponte
Zonas de devose

Fishing grounds
Lieux de pêche
Lugares de pesca

Migrations of juveniles
Migrations des juvéniles
Migraciones de juveniles

Migrations of adults
Migrations des adultes
Migraciones de adultos

After, d'après, según: Nakamura, 1960

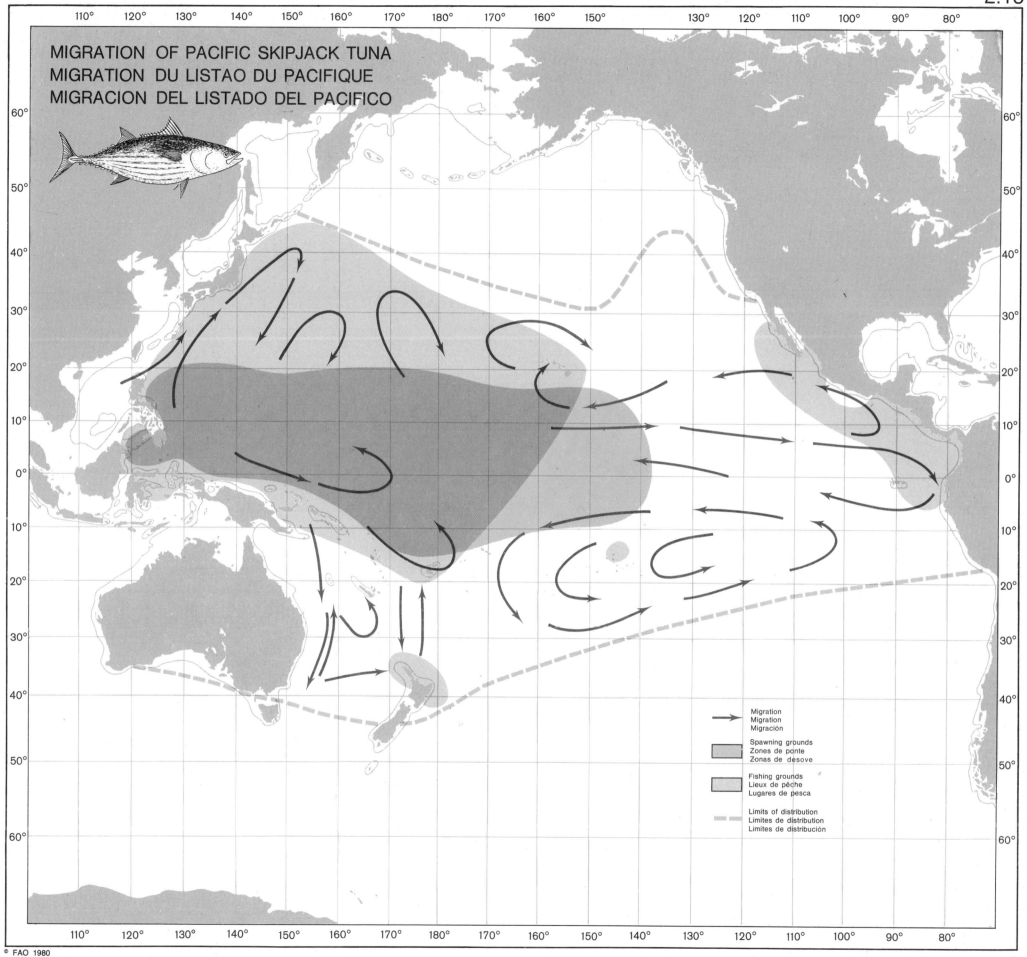

MIGRATION OF PACIFIC SKIPJACK TUNA
MIGRATION DU LISTAO DU PACIFIQUE
MIGRACION DEL LISTADO DEL PACIFICO

Migration
Migration
Migración

Spawning grounds
Zones de ponte
Zonas de desove

Fishing grounds
Lieux de pêche
Lugares de pesca

Limits of distribution
Limites de distribution
Limites de distribución

© FAO 1980

DISTRIBUTION AND MIGRATION OF SOUTHERN BLUEFIN
DISTRIBUTION ET MIGRATION DU THON ROUGE DU SUD
DISTRIBUCION Y MIGRACION DEL ATUN DEL SUR

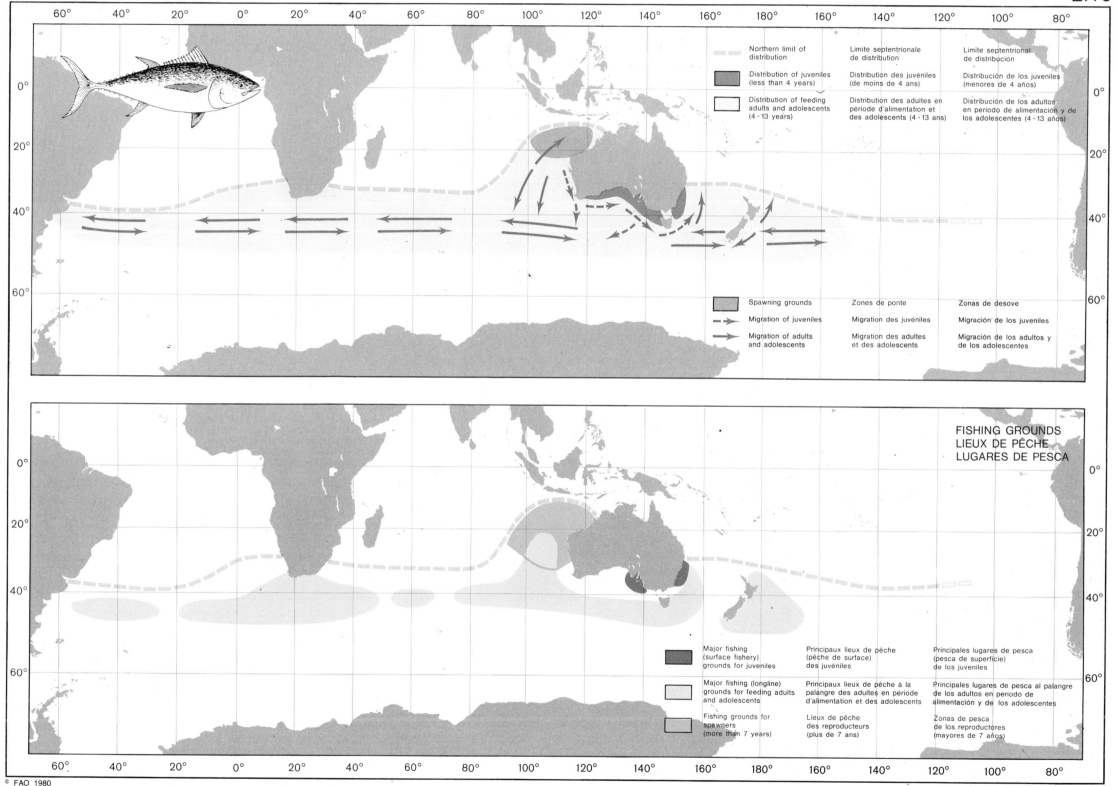

Northern limit of distribution — Limite septentrionale de distribution — Limite septentrional de distribución

Distribution of juveniles (less than 4 years) — Distribution des juvéniles (de moins de 4 ans) — Distribución de los juveniles (menores de 4 años)

Distribution of feeding adults and adolescents (4 - 13 years) — Distribution des adultes en période d'alimentation et des adolescents (4 - 13 ans) — Distribución de los adultos en periodo de alimentación y de los adolescentes (4 - 13 años)

Spawning grounds — Zones de ponte — Zonas de desove

Migration of juveniles — Migration des juvéniles — Migración de los juveniles

Migration of adults and adolescents — Migration des adultes et des adolescents — Migración de los adultos y de los adolescentes

FISHING GROUNDS
LIEUX DE PÊCHE
LUGARES DE PESCA

Major fishing (surface fishery) grounds for juveniles — Principaux lieux de pêche (pêche de surface) des juvéniles — Principales lugares de pesca (pesca de superficie) de los juveniles

Major fishing (longline) grounds for feeding adults and adolescents — Principaux lieux de pêche à la palangre des adultes en période d'alimentation et des adolescents — Principales lugares de pesca al palangre de los adultos en periodo de alimentación y de los adolescentes

Fishing grounds for spawners (more than 7 years) — Lieux de pêche des reproducteurs (plus de 7 ans) — Zonas de pesca de los reproductores (mayores de 7 años)

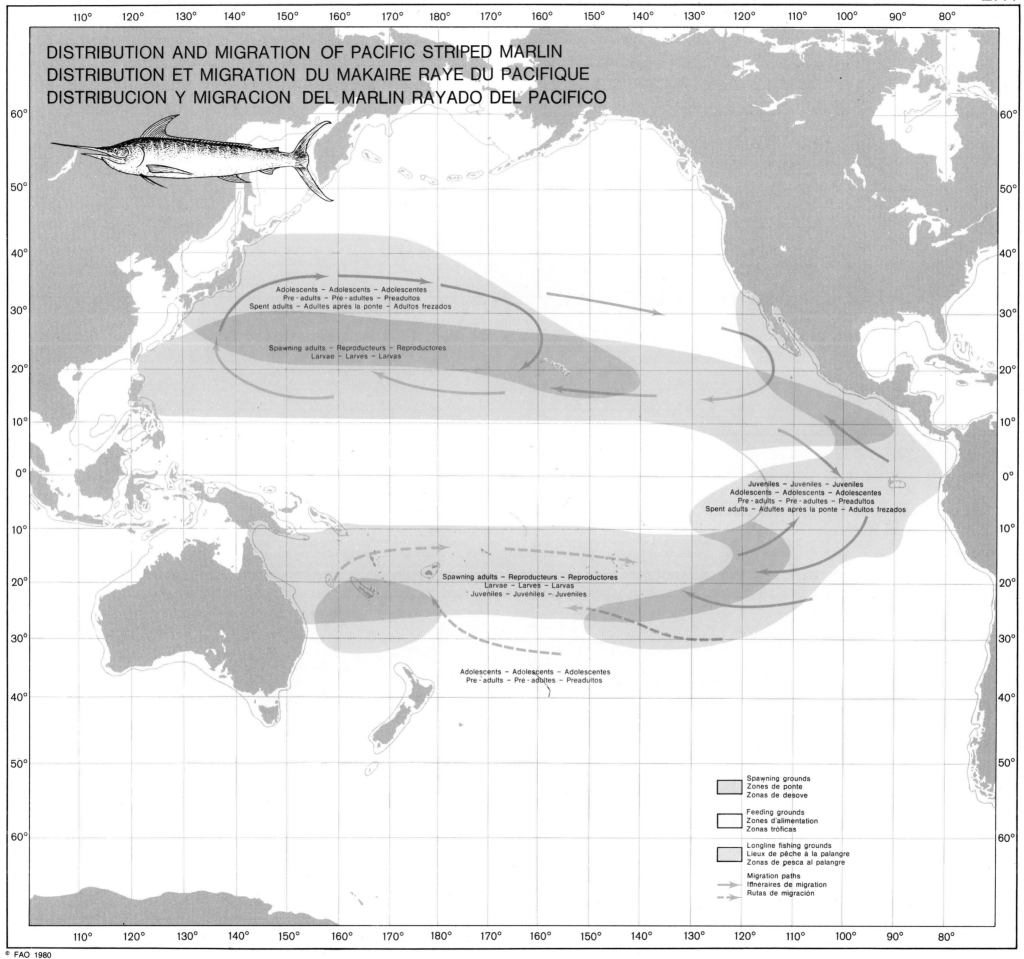

DISTRIBUTION AND MIGRATION OF PACIFIC STRIPED MARLIN
DISTRIBUTION ET MIGRATION DU MAKAIRE RAYE DU PACIFIQUE
DISTRIBUCION Y MIGRACION DEL MARLIN RAYADO DEL PACIFICO

Adolescents – Adolescents – Adolescentes
Pre - adults – Pré - adultes – Preadultos
Spent adults – Adultes après la ponte – Adultos frezados

Spawning adults – Reproducteurs – Reproductores
Larvae – Larves – Larvas

Juveniles – Juvéniles – Juveniles
Adolescents – Adolescents – Adolescentes
Pre - adults – Pré - adultes – Preadultos
Spent adults – Adultes après la ponte – Adultos frezados

Spawning adults – Reproducteurs – Reproductores
Larvae – Larves – Larvas
Juveniles – Juvéniles – Juveniles

Adolescents – Adolescents – Adolescentes
Pre - adults – Pré - adultes – Preadultos

Spawning grounds
Zones de ponte
Zonas de desove

Feeding grounds
Zones d'alimentation
Zonas tróficas

Longline fishing grounds
Lieux de pêche à la palangre
Zonas de pesca al palangre

Migration paths
Itinéraires de migration
Rutas de migración

© FAO 1980

DISTRIBUTION AND MIGRATION OF HUMPBACK
DISTRIBUTION ET MIGRATION DES JUBARTES
DISTRIBUCION Y MIGRACION DE BALLENAS JOROBADAS

FIN WHALE MIGRATION (as shown by recovered whale marks)
MIGRATION DES RORQUALS COMMUNS (déduites d'expériences de marquage)
MIGRACION DE BALLENAS DE ALETA (segun las experiencias de marcado) 2.18

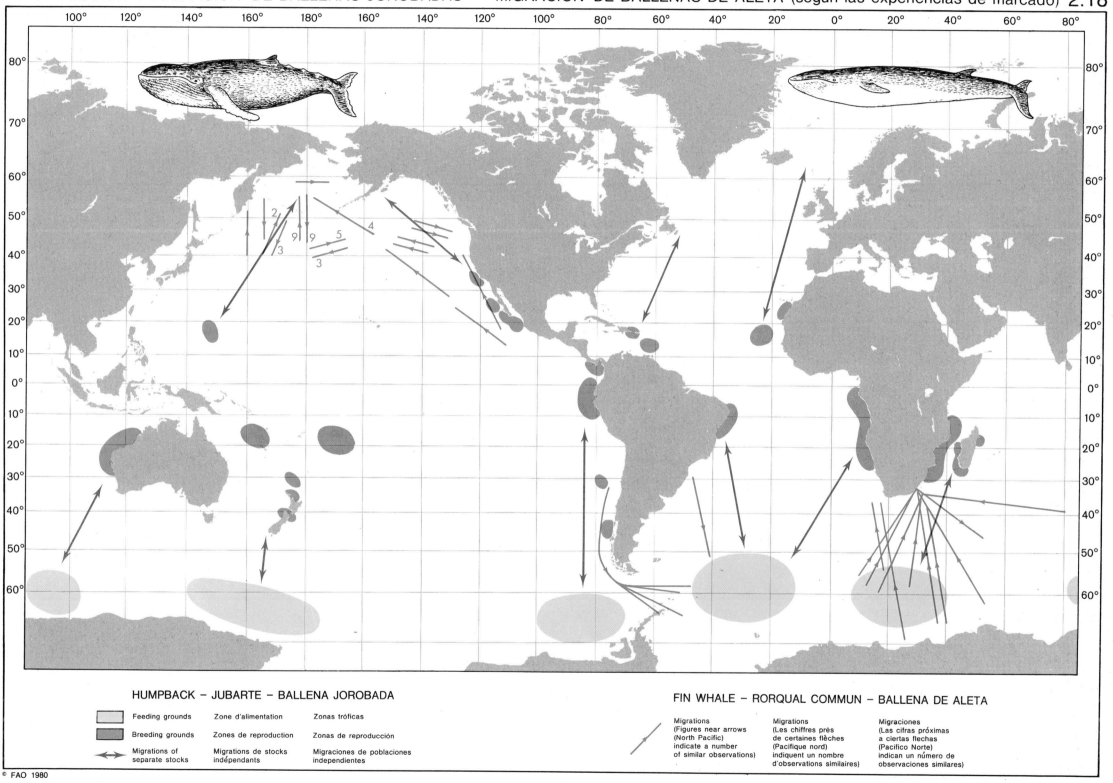

HUMPBACK – JUBARTE – BALLENA JOROBADA

Feeding grounds	Zone d'alimentation	Zonas tróficas
Breeding grounds	Zones de reproduction	Zonas de reproducción
Migrations of separate stocks	Migrations de stocks indépendants	Migraciones de poblaciones independientes

FIN WHALE – RORQUAL COMMUN – BALLENA DE ALETA

Migrations (Figures near arrows (North Pacific) indicate a number of similar observations)	Migrations (Les chiffres près de certaines flèches (Pacifique nord) indiquent un nombre d'observations similaires)	Migraciones (Las cifras próximas a ciertas flechas (Pacifico Norte) indican un número de observaciones similares)

© FAO 1980

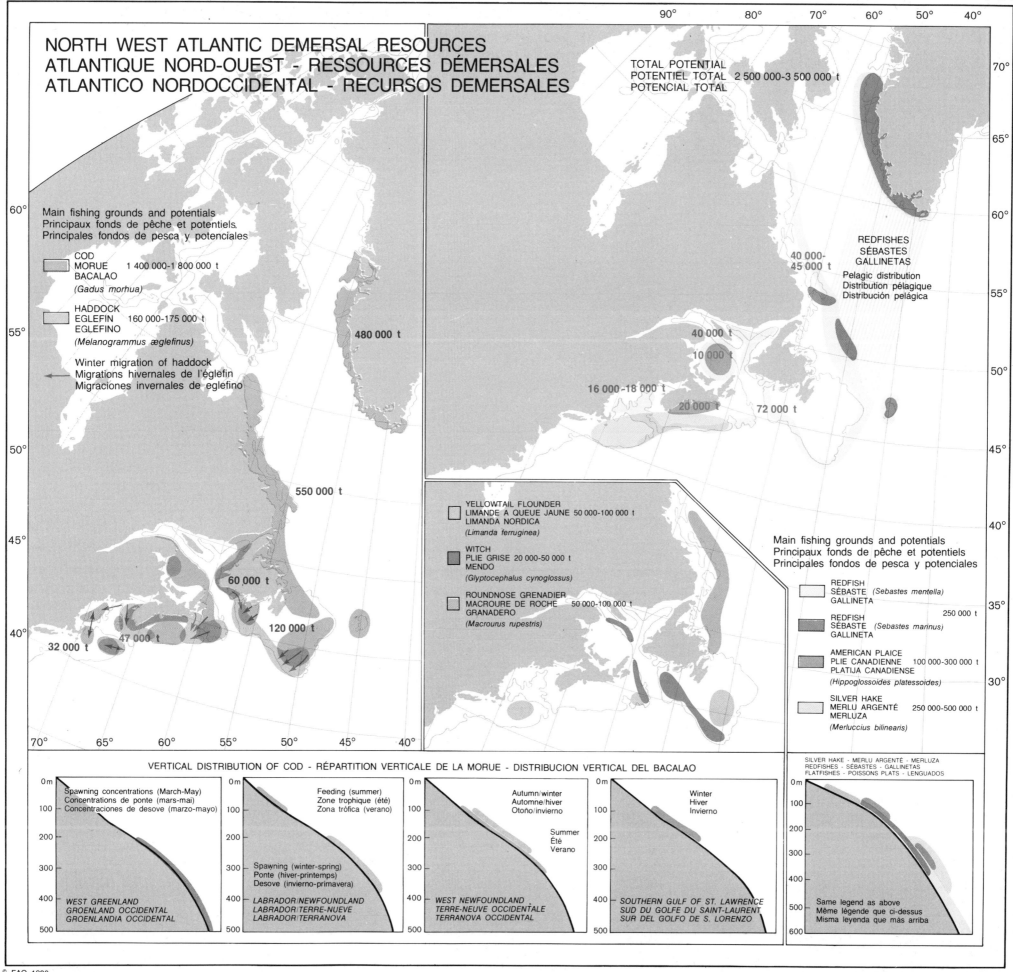

**NORTH WEST ATLANTIC DEMERSAL RESOURCES
ATLANTIQUE NORD-OUEST - RESSOURCES DÉMERSALES
ATLANTICO NORDOCCIDENTAL - RECURSOS DEMERSALES**

TOTAL POTENTIAL
POTENTIEL TOTAL   2 500 000-3 500 000 t
POTENCIAL TOTAL

Main fishing grounds and potentials
Principaux fonds de pêche et potentiels
Principales fondos de pesca y potenciales

COD
MORUE   1 400 000-1 800 000 t
BACALAO
(Gadus morhua)

HADDOCK
EGLEFIN   160 000-175 000 t
EGLEFINO
(Melanogrammus æglefinus)

Winter migration of haddock
Migrations hivernales de l'églefin
Migraciones invernales de eglefino

480 000 t

REDFISHES
SÉBASTES
GALLINETAS
40 000-
45 000 t
Pelagic distribution
Distribution pélagique
Distribución pelágica

40 000 t

10 000 t

16 000-18 000 t

20 000 t   72 000 t

550 000 t

YELLOWTAIL FLOUNDER
LIMANDE A QUEUE JAUNE 50 000-100 000 t
LIMANDA NORDICA
(Limanda ferruginea)

WITCH
PLIE GRISE 20 000-50 000 t
MENDO
(Glyptocephalus cynoglossus)

ROUNDNOSE GRENADIER
MACROURE DE ROCHE   50 000-100 000 t
GRANADERO
(Macrourus rupestris)

60 000 t

120 000 t

47 000 t

32 000 t

Main fishing grounds and potentials
Principaux fonds de pêche et potentiels
Principales fondos de pesca y potenciales

REDFISH
SÉBASTE *(Sebastes mentella)*
GALLINETA

REDFISH
SÉBASTE *(Sebastes marinus)*
GALLINETA   250 000 t

AMERICAN PLAICE
PLIE CANADIENNE   100 000-300 000 t
PLATIJA CANADIENSE
(Hippoglossoides platessoides)

SILVER HAKE
MERLU ARGENTÉ   250 000-500 000 t
MERLUZA
(Merluccius bilinearis)

VERTICAL DISTRIBUTION OF COD - RÉPARTITION VERTICALE DE LA MORUE - DISTRIBUCION VERTICAL DEL BACALAO

Spawning concentrations (March-May)
Concentrations de ponte (mars-mai)
Concentraciones de desove (marzo-mayo)

*WEST GREENLAND
GROENLAND OCCIDENTAL
GROENLANDIA OCCIDENTAL*

Feeding (summer)
Zone trophique (été)
Zona trófica (verano)

Spawning (winter-spring)
Ponte (hiver-printemps)
Desove (invierno-primavera)

*LABRADOR/NEWFOUNDLAND
LABRADOR/TERRE-NEUVE
LABRADOR/TERRANOVA*

Autumn/winter
Automne/hiver
Otoño/invierno

Summer
Été
Verano

*WEST NEWFOUNDLAND
TERRE-NEUVE OCCIDENTALE
TERRANOVA OCCIDENTAL*

Winter
Hiver
Invierno

*SOUTHERN GULF OF ST. LAWRENCE
SUD DU GOLFE DU SAINT-LAURENT
SUR DEL GOLFO DE S. LORENZO*

SILVER HAKE - MERLU ARGENTÉ - MERLUZA
REDFISHES - SÉBASTES - GALLINETAS
FLATFISHES - POISSONS PLATS - LENGUADOS

Same legend as above
Même légende que ci-dessus
Misma leyenda que más arriba

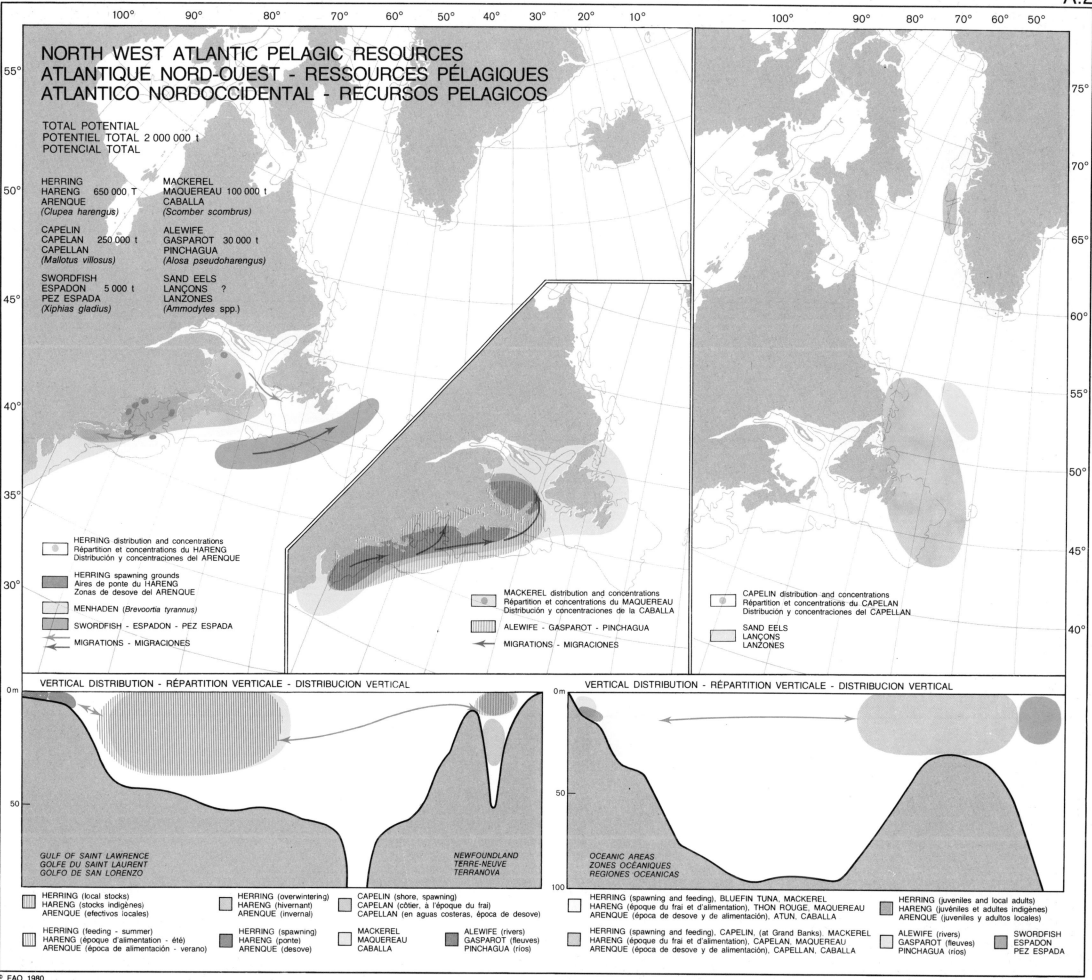

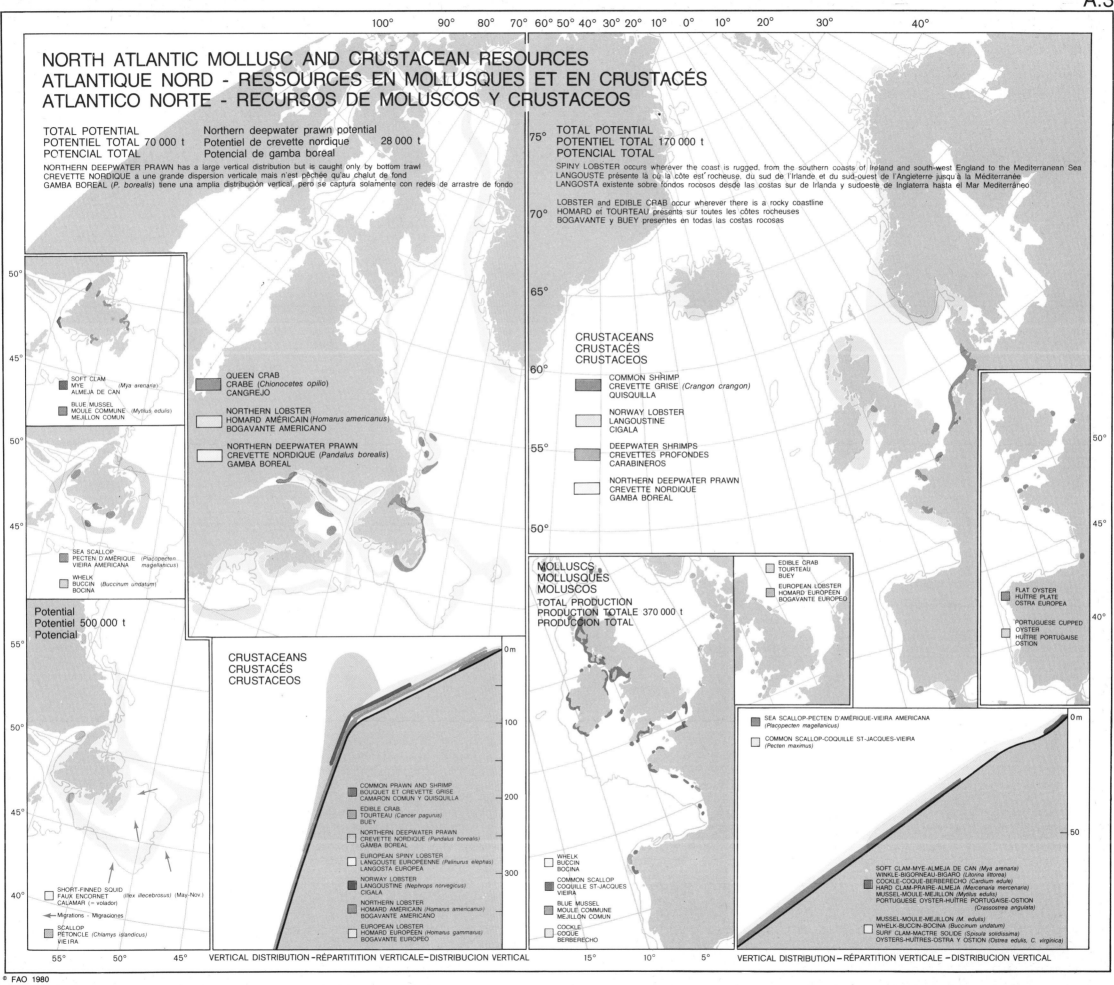

NORTH ATLANTIC MOLLUSC AND CRUSTACEAN RESOURCES
ATLANTIQUE NORD - RESSOURCES EN MOLLUSQUES ET EN CRUSTACÉS
ATLANTICO NORTE - RECURSOS DE MOLUSCOS Y CRUSTACEOS

TOTAL POTENTIAL
POTENTIEL TOTAL 70 000 t
POTENCIAL TOTAL

Northern deepwater prawn potential
Potentiel de crevette nordique   28 000 t
Potencial de gamba boreal

NORTHERN DEEPWATER PRAWN has a large vertical distribution but is caught only by bottom trawl
CREVETTE NORDIQUE a une grande dispersion verticale mais n'est pêchée qu'au chalut de fond
GAMBA BOREAL (P. borealis) tiene una amplia distribución vertical, pero se captura solamente con redes de arrastre de fondo

SOFT CLAM
MYE   (Mya arenaria)
ALMEJA DE CAN

BLUE MUSSEL
MOULE COMMUNE (Mytilus edulis)
MEJILLON COMUN

QUEEN CRAB
CRABE (Chionocetes opilio)
CANGREJO

NORTHERN LOBSTER
HOMARD AMÉRICAIN (Homarus americanus)
BOGAVANTE AMERICANO

NORTHERN DEEPWATER PRAWN
CREVETTE NORDIQUE (Pandalus borealis)
GAMBA BOREAL

TOTAL POTENTIAL
POTENTIEL TOTAL 170 000 t
POTENCIAL TOTAL

SPINY LOBSTER occurs wherever the coast is rugged, from the southern coasts of Ireland and south-west England to the Mediterranean Sea
LANGOUSTE présente là où la côte est rocheuse, du sud de l'Irlande et du sud-ouest de l'Angleterre jusqu'à la Méditerranée
LANGOSTA existente sobre fondos rocosos desde las costas sur de Irlanda y sudoeste de Inglaterra hasta el Mar Mediterráneo

LOBSTER and EDIBLE CRAB occur wherever there is a rocky coastline
HOMARD et TOURTEAU présents sur toutes les côtes rocheuses
BOGAVANTE y BUEY presentes en todas las costas rocosas

CRUSTACEANS
CRUSTACÉS
CRUSTACEOS

COMMON SHRIMP
CREVETTE GRISE (Crangon crangon)
QUISQUILLA

NORWAY LOBSTER
LANGOUSTINE
CIGALA

DEEPWATER SHRIMPS
CREVETTES PROFONDES
CARABINEROS

NORTHERN DEEPWATER PRAWN
CREVETTE NORDIQUE
GAMBA BOREAL

EDIBLE CRAB
TOURTEAU
BUEY

EUROPEAN LOBSTER
HOMARD EUROPÉEN
BOGAVANTE EUROPEO

FLAT OYSTER
HUÎTRE PLATE
OSTRA EUROPEA

PORTUGUESE CUPPED OYSTER
HUÎTRE PORTUGAISE
OSTION

Potential
Potentiel 500 000 t
Potencial

SEA SCALLOP
PECTEN D'AMÉRIQUE (Placopecten
VIEIRA AMERICANA   magellanicus)

WHELK
BUCCIN (Buccinum undatum)
BOCINA

MOLLUSCS
MOLLUSQUES
MOLUSCOS

TOTAL PRODUCTION
PRODUCTION TOTALE 370 000 t
PRODUCCION TOTAL

SEA SCALLOP-PECTEN D'AMÉRIQUE-VIEIRA AMERICANA
(Placopecten magellanicus)

COMMON SCALLOP-COQUILLE ST-JACQUES-VIEIRA
(Pecten maximus)

SHORT-FINNED SQUID
FAUX ENCORNET   (Illex illecebrosus) (May-Nov.)
CALAMAR (= volador)

Migrations - Migraciones

SCALLOP
PÉTONCLE (Chlamys islandicus)
VIEIRA

CRUSTACEANS
CRUSTACÉS
CRUSTACEOS

0 m
100
200
300

COMMON PRAWN AND SHRIMP
BOUQUET ET CREVETTE GRISE
CAMARON COMUN Y QUISQUILLA

EDIBLE CRAB
TOURTEAU (Cancer pagurus)
BUEY

NORTHERN DEEPWATER PRAWN
CREVETTE NORDIQUE (Pandalus borealis)
GAMBA BOREAL

EUROPEAN SPINY LOBSTER
LANGOUSTE EUROPÉENNE (Palinurus elephas)
LANGOSTA EUROPEA

NORWAY LOBSTER
LANGOUSTINE (Nephrops norvegicus)
CIGALA

NORTHERN LOBSTER
HOMARD AMERICAIN (Homarus americanus)
BOGAVANTE AMERICANO

EUROPEAN LOBSTER
HOMARD EUROPÉEN (Homarus gammarus)
BOGAVANTE EUROPEO

WHELK
BUCCIN
BOCINA

COMMON SCALLOP
COQUILLE ST-JACQUES
VIEIRA

BLUE MUSSEL
MOULE COMMUNE
MEJILLON COMUN

COCKLE
COQUE
BERBERECHO

0 m
50

SOFT CLAM-MYE-ALMEJA DE CAN (Mya arenaria)
WINKLE-BIGORNEAU-BIGARO (Litorina littorea)
COCKLE-COQUE-BERBERECHO (Cardium edule)
HARD CLAM-PRAIRE-ALMEJA (Mercenaria mercenaria)
MUSSEL-MOULE-MEJILLON (Mytilus edulis)
PORTUGUESE OYSTER-HUÎTRE PORTUGAISE-OSTION
(Crassostrea angulata)

MUSSEL-MOULE-MEJILLON (M. edulis)
WHELK-BUCCIN-BOCINA (Buccinum undatum)
SURF CLAM-MACTRE SOLIDE (Spisula solidissima)
OYSTERS-HUÎTRES-OSTRA Y OSTION (Ostrea edulis, C. virginica)

VERTICAL DISTRIBUTION - RÉPARTITION VERTICALE - DISTRIBUCION VERTICAL

VERTICAL DISTRIBUTION - RÉPARTITION VERTICALE - DISTRIBUCION VERTICAL

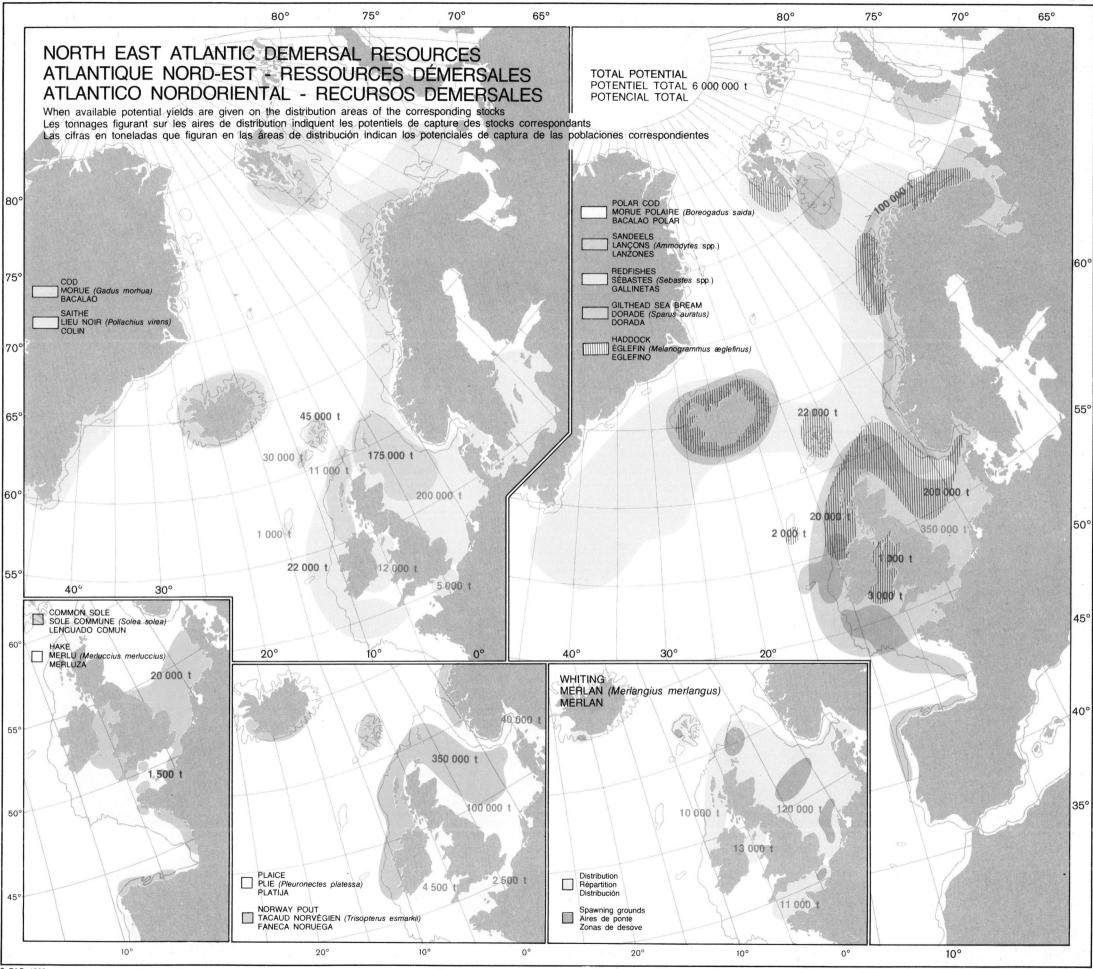

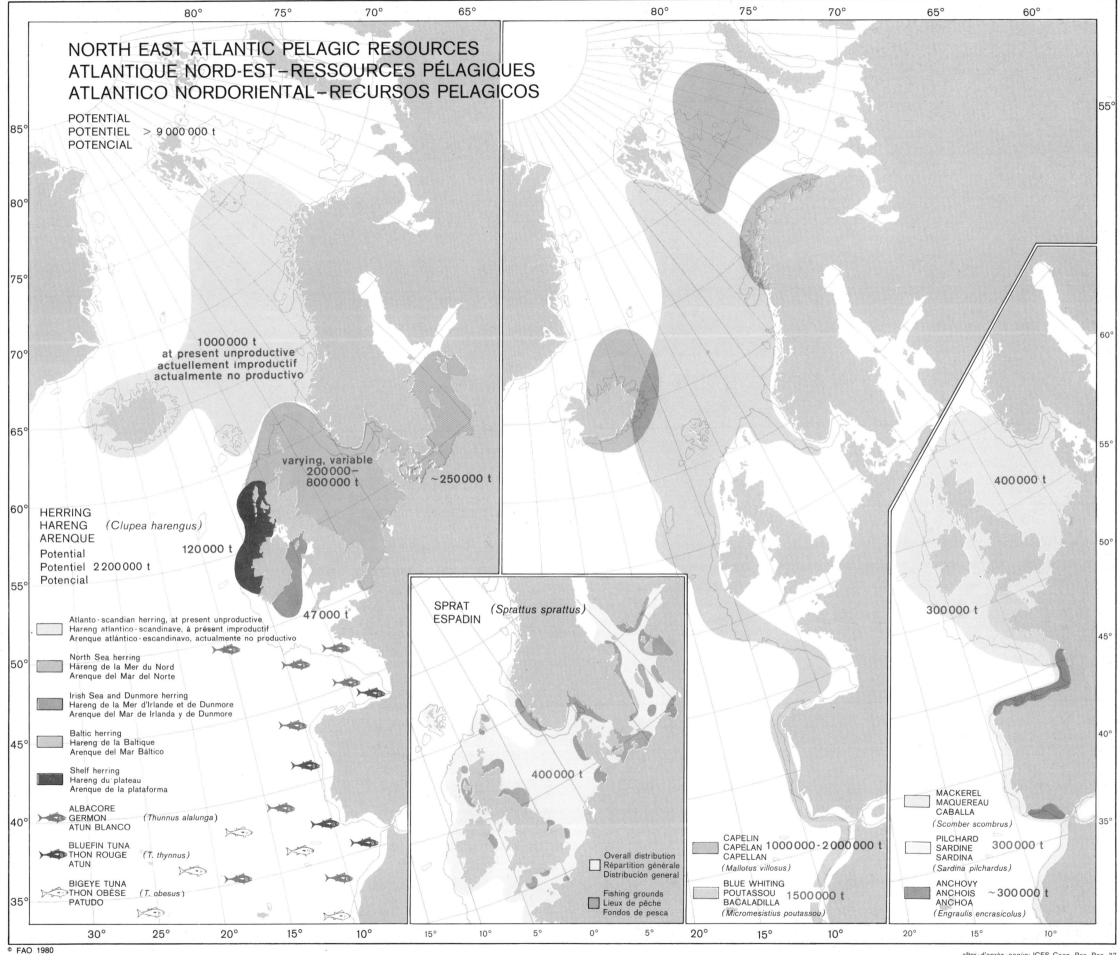

NORTH EAST ATLANTIC PELAGIC RESOURCES
ATLANTIQUE NORD-EST – RESSOURCES PÉLAGIQUES
ATLANTICO NORDORIENTAL – RECURSOS PELAGICOS

POTENTIAL
POTENTIEL > 9 000 000 t
POTENCIAL

1 000 000 t
at present unproductive
actuellement improductif
actualmente no productivo

varying, variable
200 000 –
800 000 t

~250 000 t

HERRING
HARENG   (Clupea harengus)
ARENQUE

Potential
Potentiel 2 200 000 t
Potencial

120 000 t

47 000 t

Atlanto-scandian herring, at present unproductive
Hareng atlantico-scandinave, à présent improductif
Arenque atlántico-escandinavo, actualmente no productivo

North Sea herring
Hareng de la Mer du Nord
Arenque del Mar del Norte

Irish Sea and Dunmore herring
Hareng de la Mer d'Irlande et de Dunmore
Arenque del Mar de Irlanda y de Dunmore

Baltic herring
Hareng de la Baltique
Arenque del Mar Báltico

Shelf herring
Hareng du plateau
Arenque de la plataforma

ALBACORE
GERMON   (Thunnus alalunga)
ATUN BLANCO

BLUEFIN TUNA
THON ROUGE   (T. thynnus)
ATUN

BIGEYE TUNA
THON OBÈSE   (T. obesus)
PATUDO

SPRAT
ESPADIN   (Sprattus sprattus)

400 000 t

Overall distribution
Répartition générale
Distribución general

Fishing grounds
Lieux de pêche
Fondos de pesca

400 000 t

300 000 t

CAPELIN
CAPELAN 1 000 000 - 2 000 000 t
CAPELLAN
(Mallotus villosus)

BLUE WHITING
POUTASSOU
BACALADILLA 1 500 000 t
(Micromesistius poutassou)

MACKEREL
MAQUEREAU
CABALLA
(Scomber scombrus)

PILCHARD
SARDINE   300 000 t
SARDINA
(Sardina pilchardus)

ANCHOVY
ANCHOIS   ~300 000 t
ANCHOA
(Engraulis encrasicolus)

© FAO 1980

after · d'après · según : ICES Coop. Res. Rep. 37

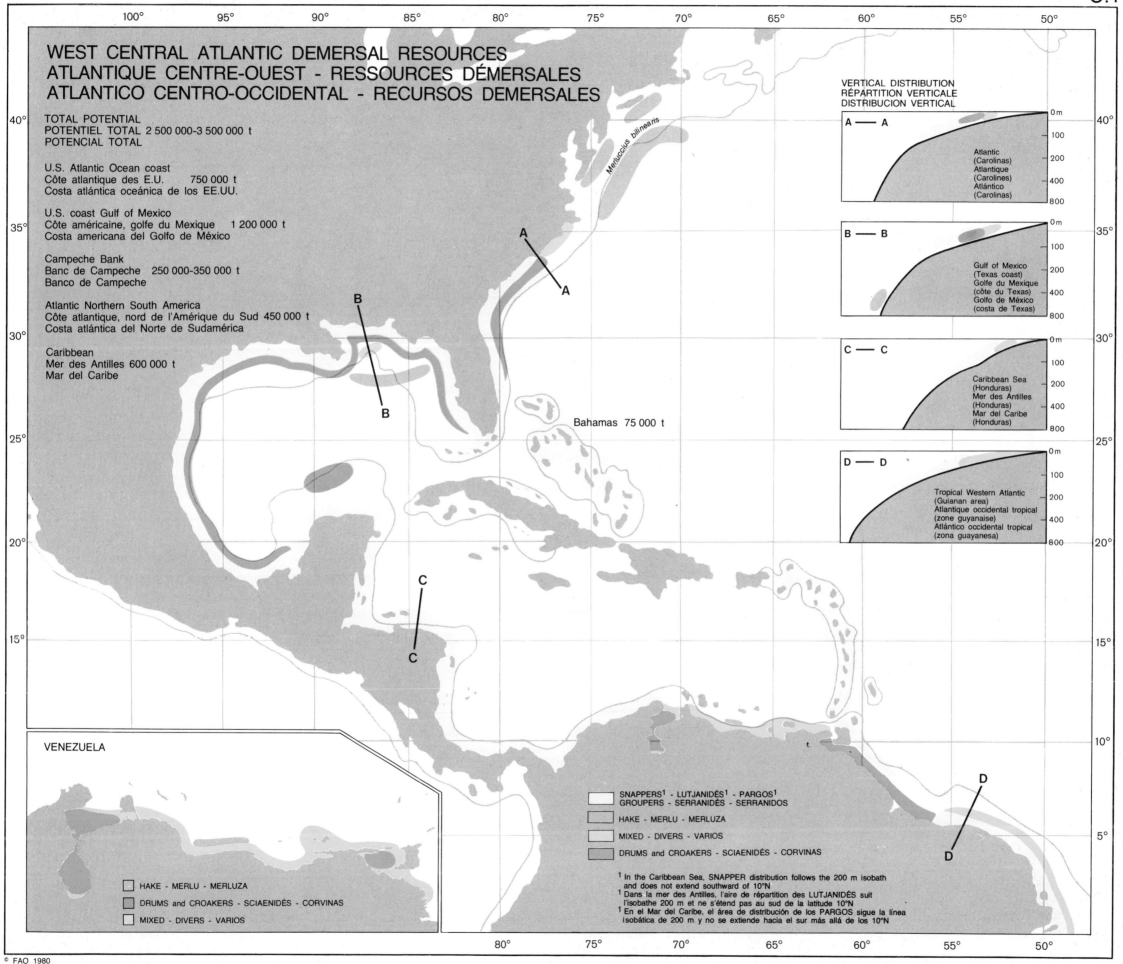

WEST CENTRAL ATLANTIC DEMERSAL RESOURCES
ATLANTIQUE CENTRE-OUEST - RESSOURCES DÉMERSALES
ATLANTICO CENTRO-OCCIDENTAL - RECURSOS DEMERSALES

TOTAL POTENTIAL
POTENTIEL TOTAL 2 500 000-3 500 000 t
POTENCIAL TOTAL

U.S. Atlantic Ocean coast
Côte atlantique des E.U.   750 000 t
Costa atlántica oceánica de los EE.UU.

U.S. coast Gulf of Mexico
Côte américaine, golfe du Mexique   1 200 000 t
Costa americana del Golfo de México

Campeche Bank
Banc de Campeche   250 000-350 000 t
Banco de Campeche

Atlantic Northern South America
Côte atlantique, nord de l'Amérique du Sud 450 000 t
Costa atlántica del Norte de Sudamérica

Caribbean
Mer des Antilles 600 000 t
Mar del Caribe

Bahamas 75 000 t

Merluccius bilinearis

VERTICAL DISTRIBUTION
RÉPARTITION VERTICALE
DISTRIBUCION VERTICAL

A — A
Atlantic
(Carolinas)
Atlantique
(Carolines)
Atlántico
(Carolinas)

B — B
Gulf of Mexico
(Texas coast)
Golfe du Mexique
(côte du Texas)
Golfo de México
(costa de Texas)

C — C
Caribbean Sea
(Honduras)
Mer des Antilles
(Honduras)
Mar del Caribe
(Honduras)

D — D
Tropical Western Atlantic
(Guianan area)
Atlantique occidental tropical
(zone guyanaise)
Atlántico occidental tropical
(zona guayanesa)

VENEZUELA

SNAPPERS[1] - LUTJANIDÉS[1] - PARGOS[1]
GROUPERS - SERRANIDÉS - SERRANIDOS

HAKE - MERLU - MERLUZA

MIXED - DIVERS - VARIOS

DRUMS and CROAKERS - SCIAENIDÉS - CORVINAS

HAKE - MERLU - MERLUZA

DRUMS and CROAKERS - SCIAENIDÉS - CORVINAS

MIXED - DIVERS - VARIOS

[1] In the Caribbean Sea, SNAPPER distribution follows the 200 m isobath
and does not extend southward of 10°N
[1] Dans la mer des Antilles, l'aire de répartition des LUTJANIDÉS suit
l'isobathe 200 m et ne s'étend pas au sud de la latitude 10°N
[1] En el Mar del Caribe, el área de distribución de los PARGOS sigue la línea
isobática de 200 m y no se extiende hacia el sur más allá de los 10°N

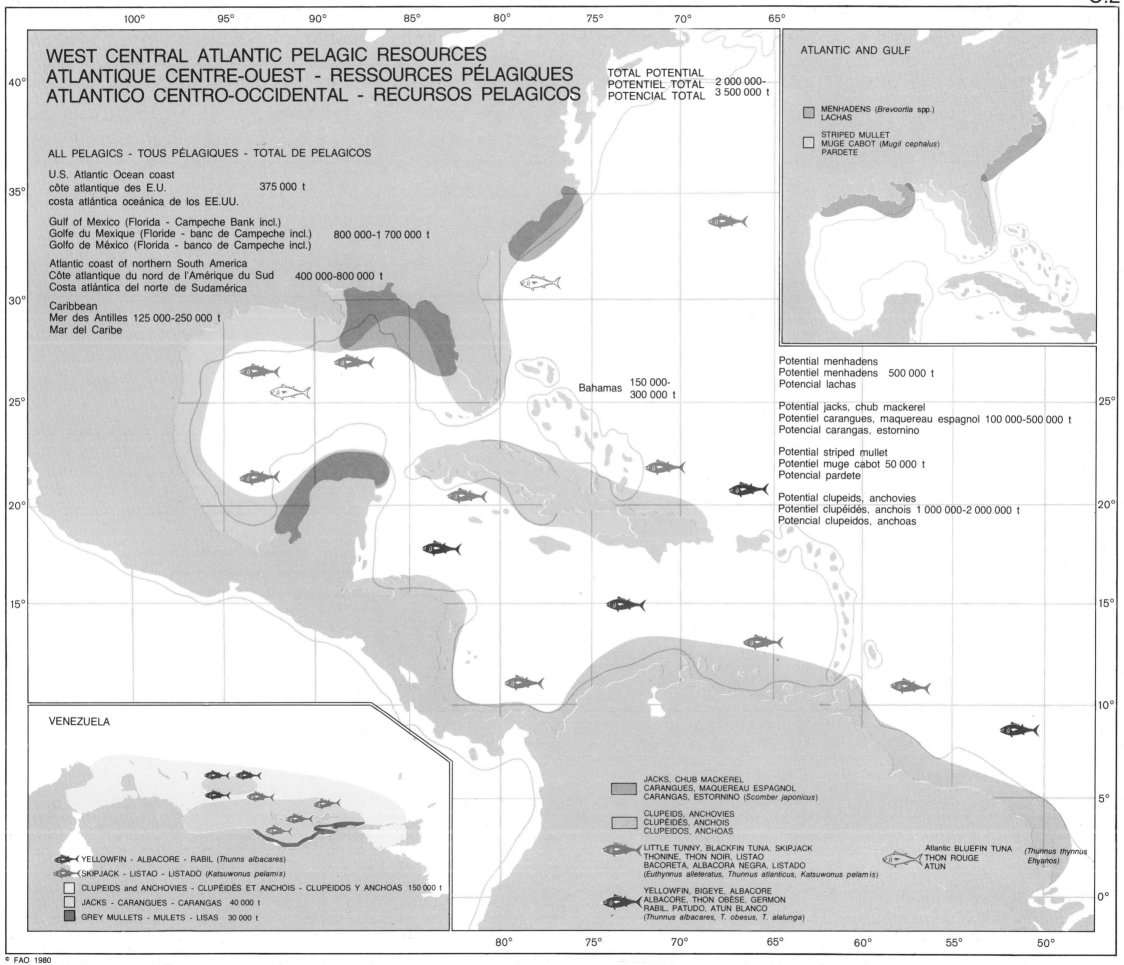

WEST CENTRAL ATLANTIC PELAGIC RESOURCES
ATLANTIQUE CENTRE-OUEST - RESSOURCES PÉLAGIQUES
ATLANTICO CENTRO-OCCIDENTAL - RECURSOS PELAGICOS

TOTAL POTENTIAL
POTENTIEL TOTAL   2 000 000-
POTENCIAL TOTAL   3 500 000 t

ALL PELAGICS - TOUS PÉLAGIQUES - TOTAL DE PELAGICOS

U.S. Atlantic Ocean coast
côte atlantique des E.U.   375 000 t
costa atlántica oceánica de los EE.UU.

Gulf of Mexico (Florida - Campeche Bank incl.)
Golfe du Mexique (Floride - banc de Campeche incl.)   800 000-1 700 000 t
Golfo de México (Florida - banco de Campeche incl.)

Atlantic coast of northern South America
Côte atlantique du nord de l'Amérique du Sud   400 000-800 000 t
Costa atlántica del norte de Sudamérica

Caribbean
Mer des Antilles 125 000-250 000 t
Mar del Caribe

Bahamas   150 000-
           300 000 t

ATLANTIC AND GULF

☐ MENHADENS (*Brevoortia* spp.)
  LACHAS

☐ STRIPED MULLET
  MUGE CABOT (*Mugil cephalus*)
  PARDETE

Potential menhadens
Potentiel menhadens   500 000 t
Potencial lachas

Potential jacks, chub mackerel
Potentiel carangues, maquereau espagnol 100 000-500 000 t
Potencial carangas, estornino

Potential striped mullet
Potentiel muge cabot 50 000 t
Potencial pardete

Potential clupeids, anchovies
Potentiel clupéidés, anchois 1 000 000-2 000 000 t
Potencial clupeidos, anchoas

VENEZUELA

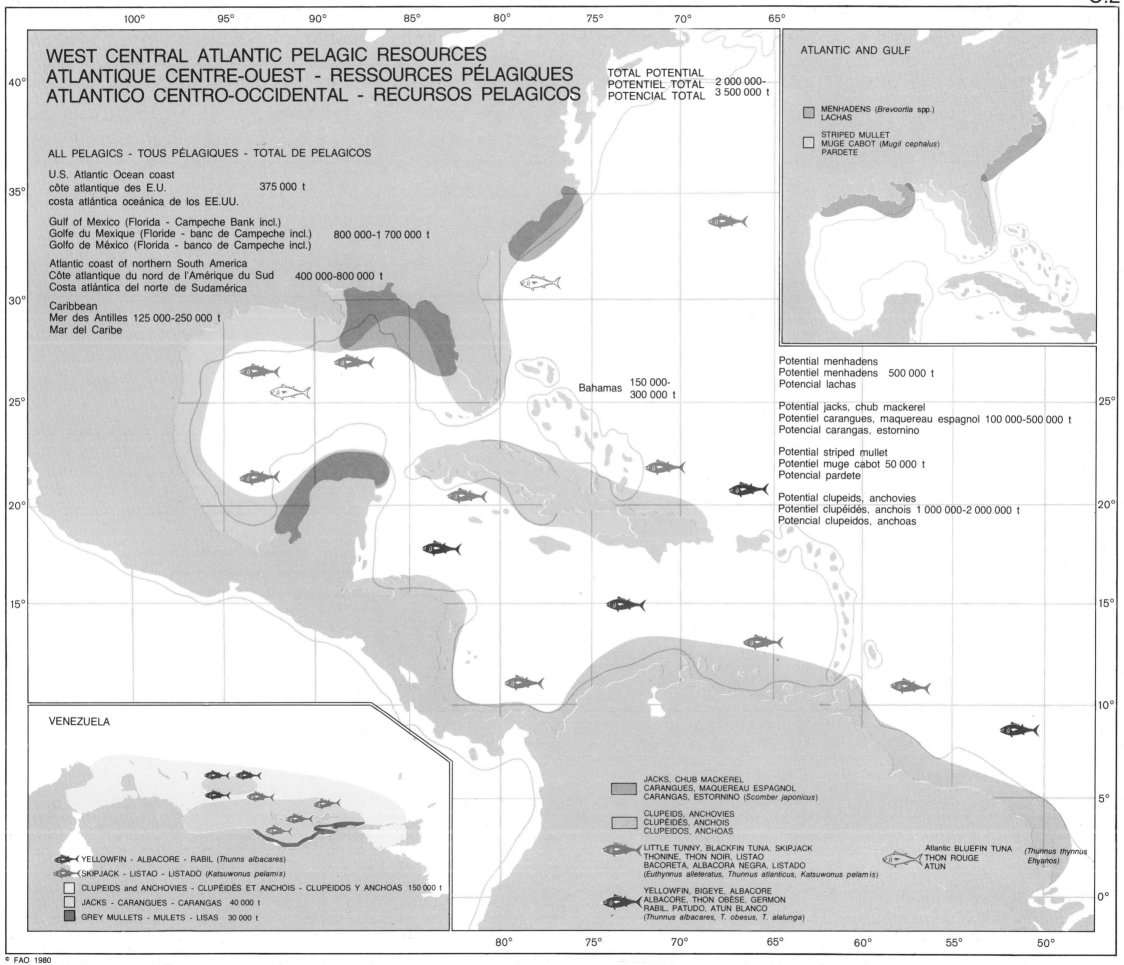 YELLOWFIN - ALBACORE - RABIL (*Thunns albacares*)

SKIPJACK - LISTAO - LISTADO (*Katsuwonus pelamis*)

☐ CLUPEIDS and ANCHOVIES - CLUPÉIDÉS ET ANCHOIS - CLUPEIDOS Y ANCHOAS 150 000 t
☐ JACKS - CARANGUES - CARANGAS 40 000 t
■ GREY MULLETS - MULETS - LISAS 30 000 t

☐ JACKS, CHUB MACKEREL
  CARANGUES, MAQUEREAU ESPAGNOL
  CARANGAS, ESTORNINO (*Scomber japonicus*)

☐ CLUPEIDS, ANCHOVIES
  CLUPÉIDÉS, ANCHOIS
  CLUPEIDOS, ANCHOAS

LITTLE TUNNY, BLACKFIN TUNA, SKIPJACK
THONINE, THON NOIR, LISTAO
BACORETA, ALBACORA NEGRA, LISTADO
(*Euthynnus alleteratus, Thunnus atlanticus, Katsuwonus pelamis*)

Atlantic BLUEFIN TUNA   (*Thunnus thynnus*
THON ROUGE   *Ehyanos*)
ATUN

YELLOWFIN, BIGEYE, ALBACORE
ALBACORE, THON OBÈSE, GERMON
RABIL, PATUDO, ATUN BLANCO
(*Thunnus albacares, T. obesus, T. alalunga*)

© FAO 1980

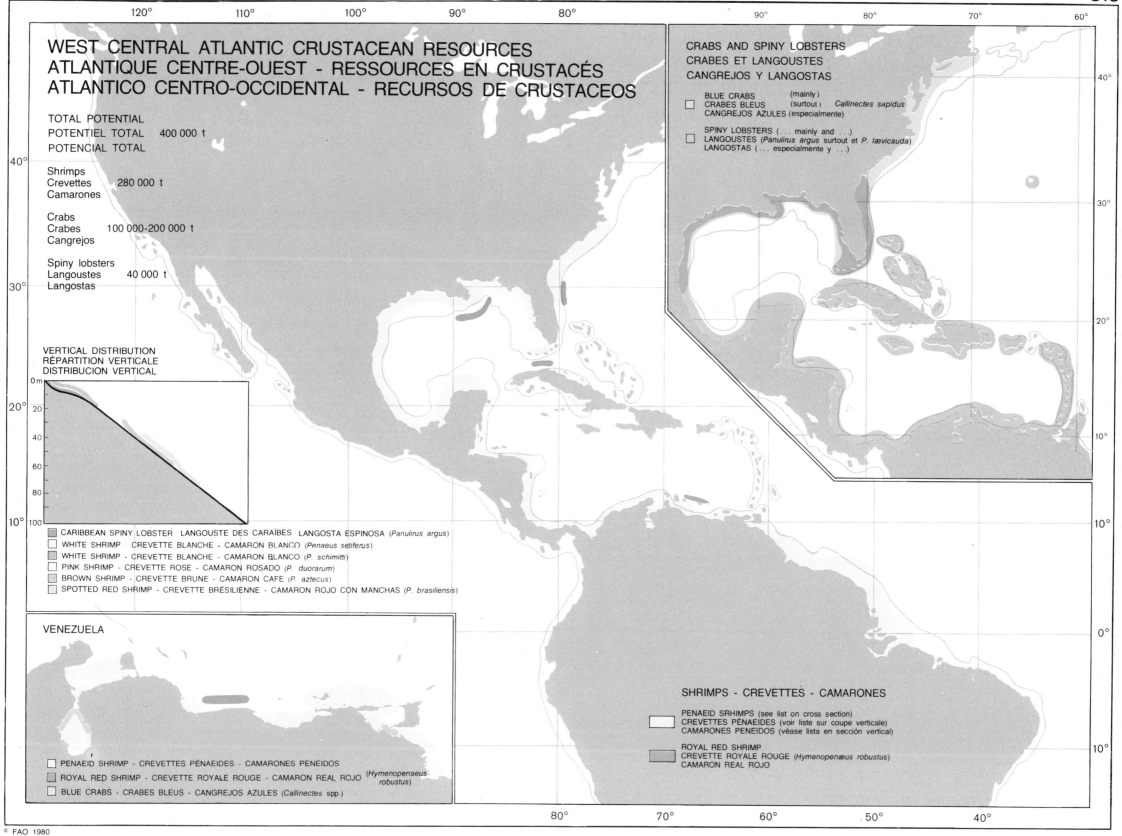

WEST CENTRAL ATLANTIC CRUSTACEAN RESOURCES
ATLANTIQUE CENTRE-OUEST - RESSOURCES EN CRUSTACÉS
ATLANTICO CENTRO-OCCIDENTAL - RECURSOS DE CRUSTACEOS

TOTAL POTENTIAL
POTENTIEL TOTAL   400 000 t
POTENCIAL TOTAL

Shrimps
Crevettes   280 000 t
Camarones

Crabs
Crabes   100 000-200 000 t
Cangrejos

Spiny lobsters
Langoustes   40 000 t
Langostas

VERTICAL DISTRIBUTION
RÉPARTITION VERTICALE
DISTRIBUCION VERTICAL

CARIBBEAN SPINY LOBSTER LANGOUSTE DES CARAÏBES LANGOSTA ESPINOSA (Panulirus argus)
WHITE SHRIMP   CREVETTE BLANCHE - CAMARON BLANCO (Penaeus setiferus)
WHITE SHRIMP - CREVETTE BLANCHE - CAMARON BLANCO (P. schimitti)
PINK SHRIMP - CREVETTE ROSE - CAMARON ROSADO (P. duorarum)
BROWN SHRIMP - CREVETTE BRUNE - CAMARON CAFE (P. aztecus)
SPOTTED RED SHRIMP - CREVETTE BRÉSILIENNE - CAMARON ROJO CON MANCHAS (P. brasiliensis)

CRABS AND SPINY LOBSTERS
CRABES ET LANGOUSTES
CANGREJOS Y LANGOSTAS

BLUE CRABS   (mainly)
CRABES BLEUS   (surtout)   Callinectes sapidus
CANGREJOS AZULES (especialmente)

SPINY LOBSTERS (... mainly and ...)
LANGOUSTES (Panulirus argus surtout et P. lævicauda)
LANGOSTAS (... especialmente y ...)

VENEZUELA

PENAEID SHRIMP - CREVETTES PÉNAEIDES - CAMARONES PENEIDOS
ROYAL RED SHRIMP - CREVETTE ROYALE ROUGE - CAMARON REAL ROJO (Hymenopenaeus robustus)
BLUE CRABS - CRABES BLEUS - CANGREJOS AZULES (Callinectes spp.)

SHRIMPS - CREVETTES - CAMARONES

PENAEID SRHIMPS (see list on cross section)
CREVETTES PÉNAEIDES (voir liste sur coupe verticale)
CAMARONES PENEIDOS (véase lista en sección vertical)

ROYAL RED SHRIMP
CREVETTE ROYALE ROUGE (Hymenopenæus robustus)
CAMARON REAL ROJO

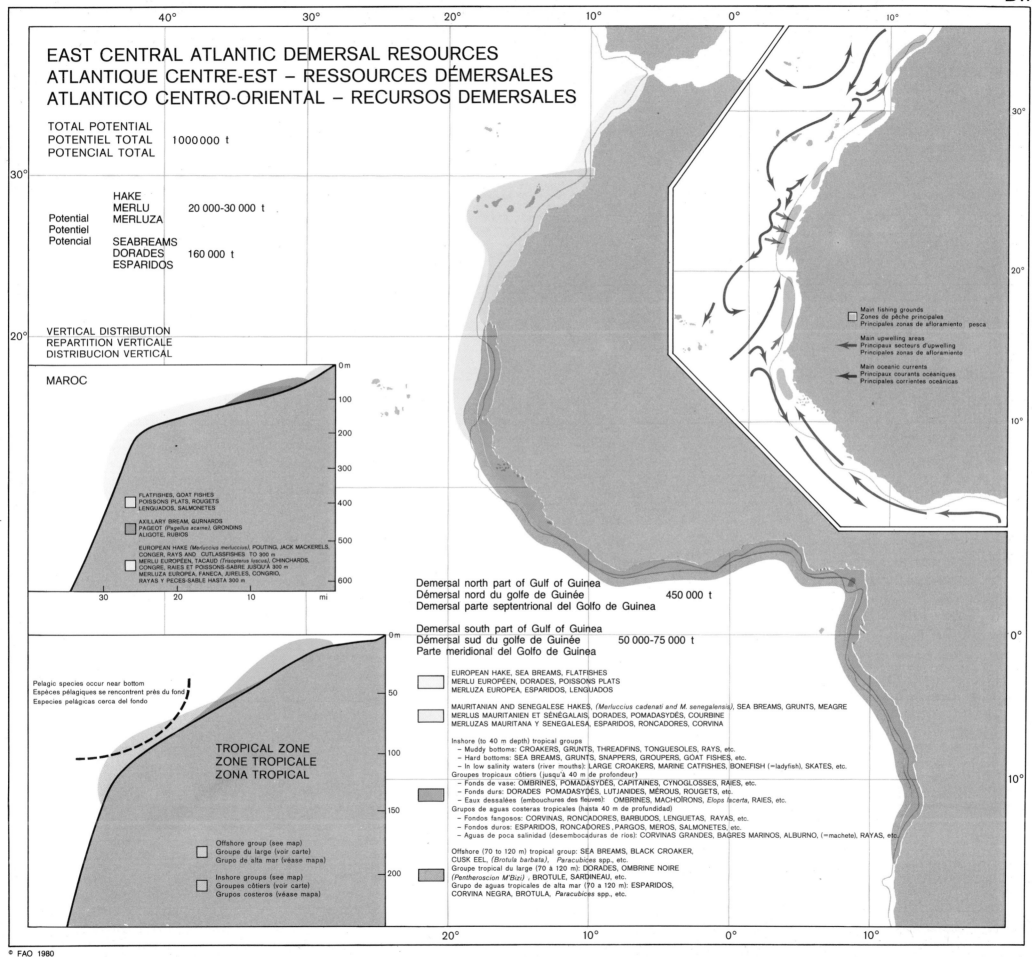

EAST CENTRAL ATLANTIC DEMERSAL RESOURCES
ATLANTIQUE CENTRE-EST – RESSOURCES DÉMERSALES
ATLANTICO CENTRO-ORIENTAL – RECURSOS DEMERSALES

TOTAL POTENTIAL
POTENTIEL TOTAL   1 000 000 t
POTENCIAL TOTAL

Potential
Potentiel
Potencial

HAKE
MERLU   20 000-30 000 t
MERLUZA

SEABREAMS
DORADES   160 000 t
ESPARIDOS

VERTICAL DISTRIBUTION
REPARTITION VERTICALE
DISTRIBUCION VERTICAL

MAROC

0m
100
200
300
400
500
600

FLATFISHES, GOAT FISHES
POISSONS PLATS, ROUGETS
LENGUADOS, SALMONETES

AXILLARY BREAM, GURNARDS
PAGEOT (*Pagellus acarne*), GRONDINS
ALIGOTE, RUBIOS

EUROPEAN HAKE (*Merluccius merluccius*), POUTING, JACK MACKERELS,
CONGER, RAYS AND CUTLASSFISHES TO 300 m
MERLU EUROPÉEN, TACAUD (*Trisopterus luscus*), CHINCHARDS,
CONGRE, RAIES ET POISSONS-SABRE JUSQU'À 300 m
MERLUZA EUROPEA, FANECA, JURELES, CONGRIO,
RAYAS Y PECES-SABLE HASTA 300 m

30   20   10   mi

Pelagic species occur near bottom
Espèces pélagiques se rencontrent près du fond
Especies pelágicas cerca del fondo

TROPICAL ZONE
ZONE TROPICALE
ZONA TROPICAL

0m
50
100
150
200

Offshore group (see map)
Groupe du large (voir carte)
Grupo de alta mar (véase mapa)

Inshore groups (see map)
Groupes côtiers (voir carte)
Grupos costeros (véase mapa)

Demersal north part of Gulf of Guinea
Démersal nord du golfe de Guinée   450 000 t
Demersal parte septentrional del Golfo de Guinea

Demersal south part of Gulf of Guinea
Démersal sud du golfe de Guinée   50 000-75 000 t
Parte meridional del Golfo de Guinea

EUROPEAN HAKE, SEA BREAMS, FLATFISHES
MERLU EUROPÉEN, DORADES, POISSONS PLATS
MERLUZA EUROPEA, ESPARIDOS, LENGUADOS

MAURITANIAN AND SENEGALESE HAKES, (*Merluccius cadenati and M. senegalensis*), SEA BREAMS, GRUNTS, MEAGRE
MERLUS MAURITANIEN ET SÉNÉGALAIS, DORADES, POMADASYDÉS, COURBINE
MERLUZAS MAURITANA Y SENEGALESA, ESPARIDOS, RONCADORES, CORVINA

Inshore (to 40 m depth) tropical groups
 – Muddy bottoms: CROAKERS, GRUNTS, THREADFINS, TONGUESOLES, RAYS, etc.
 – Hard bottoms: SEA BREAMS, GRUNTS, SNAPPERS, GROUPERS, GOAT FISHES, etc.
 – In low salinity waters (river mouths): LARGE CROAKERS, MARINE CATFISHES, BONEFISH (=ladyfish), SKATES, etc.
Groupes tropicaux côtiers (jusqu'à 40 m de profondeur)
 – Fonds de vase: OMBRINES, POMADASYDÉS, CAPITAINES, CYNOGLOSSES, RAIES, etc.
 – Fonds durs: DORADES POMADASYDÉS, LUTJANIDES, MÉROUS, ROUGETS, etc.
 – Eaux dessalées (embouchures des fleuves): OMBRINES, MACHOÏRONS, *Elops lacerta*, RAIES, etc.
Grupos de aguas costeras tropicales (hasta 40 m de profundidad)
 – Fondos fangosos: CORVINAS, RONCADORES, BARBUDOS, LENGUETAS, RAYAS, etc.
 – Fondos duros: ESPARIDOS, RONCADORES, PARGOS, MEROS, SALMONETES, etc.
 – Aguas de poca salinidad (desembocaduras de rios): CORVINAS GRANDES, BAGRES MARINOS, ALBURNO, (=machete), RAYAS, etc.

Offshore (70 to 120 m) tropical group: SEA BREAMS, BLACK CROAKER,
CUSK EEL, (*Brotula barbata*), *Paracubices* spp., etc.
Groupe tropical du large (70 à 120 m): DORADES, OMBRINE NOIRE
(*Pentheroscion M'Bizi*), BROTULE, SARDINEAU, etc.
Grupo de aguas tropicales de alta mar (70 a 120 m): ESPARIDOS,
CORVINA NEGRA, BROTULA, *Paracubices* spp., etc.

Main fishing grounds
Zones de pêche principales
Principales zonas de afloramiento   pesca

Main upwelling areas
Principaux secteurs d'upwelling
Principales zonas de afloramiento

Main oceanic currents
Principaux courants océaniques
Principales corrientes oceánicas

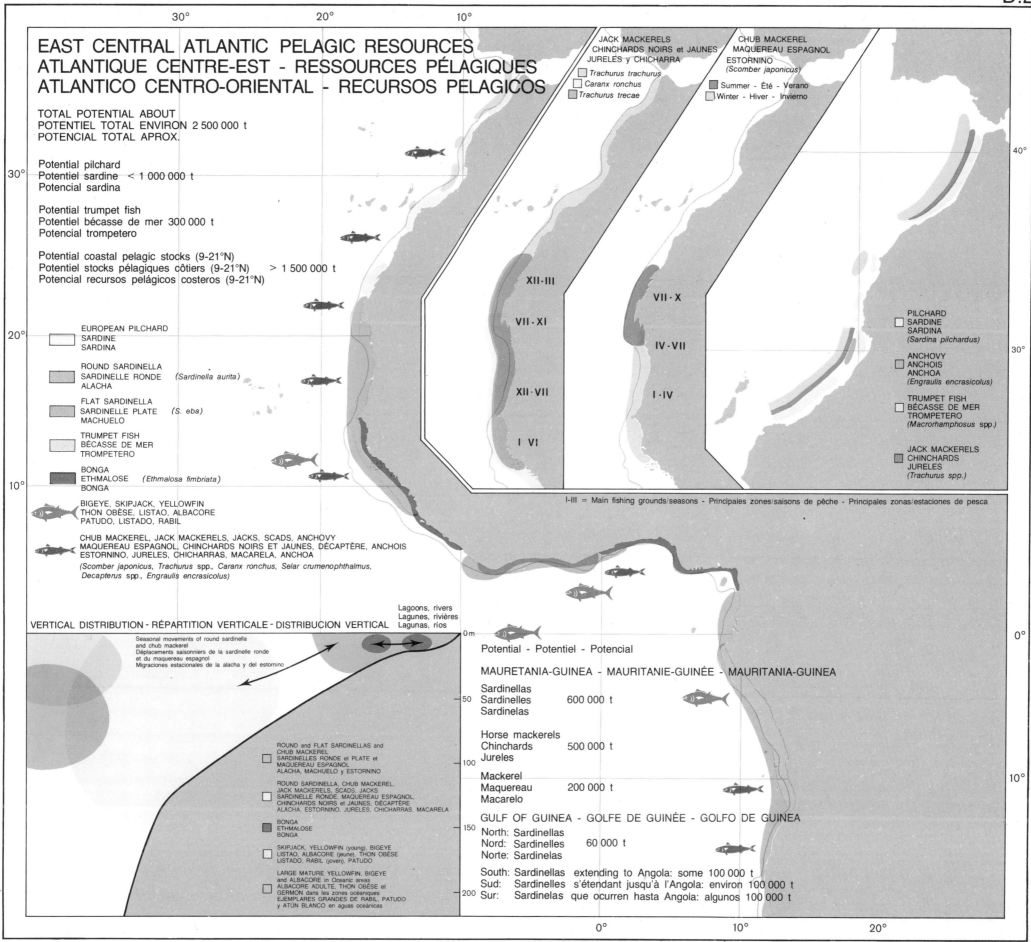

EAST CENTRAL ATLANTIC PELAGIC RESOURCES

D.2

EAST CENTRAL ATLANTIC PELAGIC RESOURCES
ATLANTIQUE CENTRE-EST - RESSOURCES PÉLAGIQUES
ATLANTICO CENTRO-ORIENTAL - RECURSOS PELAGICOS

TOTAL POTENTIAL ABOUT
POTENTIEL TOTAL ENVIRON 2 500 000 t
POTENCIAL TOTAL APROX.

Potential pilchard
Potentiel sardine   < 1 000 000 t
Potencial sardina

Potential trumpet fish
Potentiel bécasse de mer 300 000 t
Potencial trompetero

Potential coastal pelagic stocks (9-21°N)
Potentiel stocks pélagiques côtiers (9-21°N)   > 1 500 000 t
Potencial recursos pelágicos costeros (9-21°N)

EUROPEAN PILCHARD
SARDINE
SARDINA

ROUND SARDINELLA
SARDINELLE RONDE   (Sardinella aurita)
ALACHA

FLAT SARDINELLA
SARDINELLE PLATE   (S. eba)
MACHUELO

TRUMPET FISH
BÉCASSE DE MER
TROMPETERO

BONGA
ETHMALOSE   (Ethmalosa fimbriata)
BONGA

BIGEYE, SKIPJACK, YELLOWFIN
THON OBÈSE, LISTAO, ALBACORE
PATUDO, LISTADO, RABIL

CHUB MACKEREL, JACK MACKERELS, JACKS, SCADS, ANCHOVY
MAQUEREAU ESPAGNOL, CHINCHARDS NOIRS ET JAUNES, DÉCAPTÈRE, ANCHOIS
ESTORNINO, JURELES, CHICHARRAS, MACARELA, ANCHOA
(Scomber japonicus, Trachurus spp., Caranx ronchus, Selar crumenophthalmus,
Decapterus spp., Engraulis encrasicolus)

JACK MACKERELS
CHINCHARDS NOIRS et JAUNES
JURELES y CHICHARRA

☐ Trachurus trachurus
☐ Caranx ronchus
☐ Trachurus trecae

CHUB MACKEREL
MAQUEREAU ESPAGNOL
ESTORNINO
(Scomber japonicus)

☐ Summer - Été - Verano
☐ Winter - Hiver - Invierno

XII-III
VII-XI
XII-VII
I-VI

VII-X
IV-VII
I-IV

PILCHARD
SARDINE
SARDINA
(Sardina pilchardus)

ANCHOVY
ANCHOIS
ANCHOA
(Engraulis encrasicolus)

TRUMPET FISH
BÉCASSE DE MER
TROMPETERO
(Macrorhamphosus spp.)

JACK MACKERELS
CHINCHARDS
JURELES
(Trachurus spp.)

I-III = Main fishing grounds/seasons - Principales zones/saisons de pêche - Principales zonas/estaciones de pesca

VERTICAL DISTRIBUTION - RÉPARTITION VERTICALE - DISTRIBUCION VERTICAL

Lagoons, rivers
Lagunes, rivières
Lagunas, ríos

Seasonal movements of round sardinella
and chub mackerel
Déplacements saisonniers de la sardinelle ronde
et du maquereau espagnol
Migraciones estacionales de la alacha y del estornino

0 m

50

100

150

200

ROUND and FLAT SARDINELLAS and
CHUB MACKEREL
SARDINELLES RONDE et PLATE et
MAQUEREAU ESPAGNOL
ALACHA, MACHUELO y ESTORNINO

ROUND SARDINELLA, CHUB MACKEREL,
JACK MACKERELS, SCADS, JACKS
SARDINELLE RONDE, MAQUEREAU ESPAGNOL,
CHINCHARDS NOIRS et JAUNES, DÉCAPTÈRE
ALACHA, ESTORNINO, JURELES, CHICHARRAS, MACARELA

BONGA
ETHMALOSE
BONGA

SKIPJACK, YELLOWFIN (young), BIGEYE
LISTAO, ALBACORE (jeune), THON OBÈSE
LISTADO, RABIL (joven), PATUDO

LARGE MATURE YELLOWFIN, BIGEYE
and ALBACORE in Oceanic areas
ALBACORE ADULTE, THON OBÈSE et
GERMON dans les zones océaniques
EJEMPLARES GRANDES DE RABIL, PATUDO
y ATÚN BLANCO en aguas oceánicas

Potential - Potentiel - Potencial

MAURETANIA-GUINEA - MAURITANIE-GUINÉE - MAURITANIA-GUINEA

Sardinellas
Sardinelles   600 000 t
Sardinelas

Horse mackerels
Chinchards   500 000 t
Jureles

Mackerel
Maquereau   200 000 t
Macarelo

GULF OF GUINEA - GOLFE DE GUINÉE - GOLFO DE GUINEA

North: Sardinellas
Nord: Sardinelles   60 000 t
Norte: Sardinelas

South: Sardinellas extending to Angola: some 100 000 t
Sud: Sardinelles s'étendant jusqu'à l'Angola: environ 100 000 t
Sur: Sardinelas que ocurren hasta Angola: algunos 100 000 t

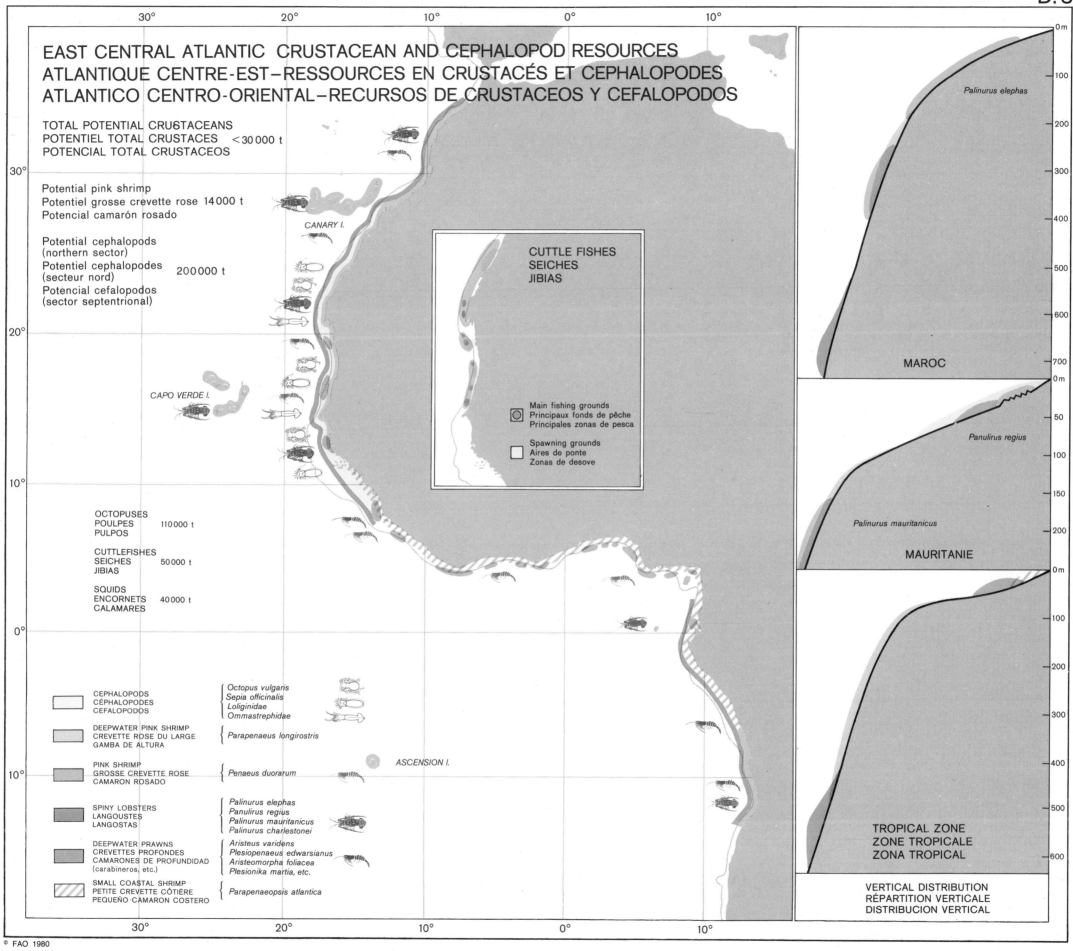

EAST CENTRAL ATLANTIC CRUSTACEAN AND CEPHALOPOD RESOURCES
ATLANTIQUE CENTRE-EST–RESSOURCES EN CRUSTACÉS ET CEPHALOPODES
ATLANTICO CENTRO-ORIENTAL–RECURSOS DE CRUSTACEOS Y CEFALOPODOS

TOTAL POTENTIAL CRUSTACEANS
POTENTIEL TOTAL CRUSTACES   <30 000 t
POTENCIAL TOTAL CRUSTACEOS

Potential pink shrimp
Potentiel grosse crevette rose 14 000 t
Potencial camarón rosado

Potential cephalopods
(northern sector)
Potentiel cephalopodes   200 000 t
(secteur nord)
Potencial cefalopodos
(sector septentrional)

CANARY I.

CAPO VERDE I.

OCTOPUSES
POULPES   110 000 t
PULPOS

CUTTLEFISHES
SEICHES   50 000 t
JIBIAS

SQUIDS
ENCORNETS   40 000 t
CALAMARES

CUTTLE FISHES
SEICHES
JIBIAS

Main fishing grounds
Principaux fonds de pêche
Principales zonas de pesca

Spawning grounds
Aires de ponte
Zonas de desove

ASCENSION I.

	CEPHALOPODS CÉPHALOPODES CEFALOPODOS	Octopus vulgaris Sepia officinalis Loliginidae Ommastrephidae
	DEEPWATER PINK SHRIMP CREVETTE ROSE DU LARGE GAMBA DE ALTURA	Parapenaeus longirostris
	PINK SHRIMP GROSSE CREVETTE ROSE CAMARON ROSADO	Penaeus duorarum
	SPINY LOBSTERS LANGOUSTES LANGOSTAS	Palinurus elephas Panulirus regius Palinurus mauritanicus Palinurus charlestonei
	DEEPWATER PRAWNS CREVETTES PROFONDES CAMARONES DE PROFUNDIDAD (carabineros, etc.)	Aristeus varidens Plesiopenaeus edwarsianus Aristeomorpha foliacea Plesionika martia, etc.
	SMALL COASTAL SHRIMP PETITE CREVETTE CÔTIÉRE PEQUEÑO·CAMARON COSTERO	Parapenaeopsis atlantica

Palinurus elephas

MAROC

Panulirus regius

Palinurus mauritanicus

MAURITANIE

TROPICAL ZONE
ZONE TROPICALE
ZONA TROPICAL

VERTICAL DISTRIBUTION
RÉPARTITION VERTICALE
DISTRIBUCION VERTICAL

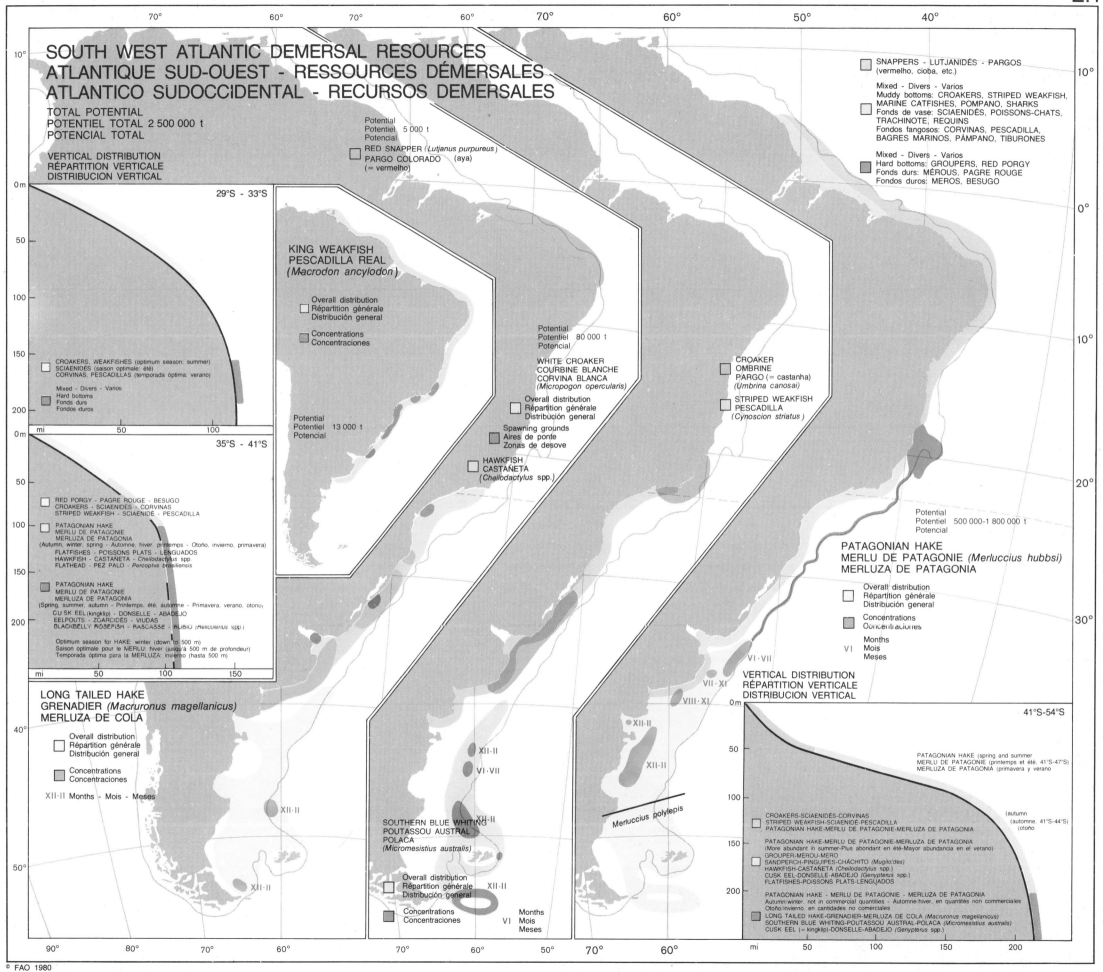

SOUTH WEST ATLANTIC DEMERSAL RESOURCES
ATLANTIQUE SUD-OUEST - RESSOURCES DÉMERSALES -
ATLANTICO SUDOCCIDENTAL - RECURSOS DEMERSALES

TOTAL POTENTIAL
POTENTIEL TOTAL 2 500 000 t
POTENCIAL TOTAL

VERTICAL DISTRIBUTION
RÉPARTITION VERTICALE
DISTRIBUCION VERTICAL

29°S - 33°S

CROAKERS, WEAKFISHES (optimum season: summer)
SCIAENIDÉS (saison optimale: été)
CORVINAS, PESCADILLAS (temporada óptima: verano)

Mixed - Divers - Varios
Hard bottoms
Fonds durs
Fondos duros

35°S - 41°S

RED PORGY - PAGRE ROUGE - BESUGO
CROAKERS - SCIAENIDÉS - CORVINAS
STRIPED WEAKFISH - SCIAENIDÉ - PESCADILLA

PATAGONIAN HAKE
MERLU DE PATAGONIE
MERLUZA DE PATAGONIA
(Autumn, winter, spring - Automne, hiver, printemps - Otoño, invierno, primavera)
FLATFISHES - POISSONS PLATS - LENGUADOS
HAWKFISH - CASTAÑETA - Cheilodactylus spp.
FLATHEAD - PEZ PALO - Percophis brasiliensis

PATAGONIAN HAKE
MERLU DE PATAGONIE
MERLUZA DE PATAGONIA
(Spring, summer, autumn - Printemps, été, automne - Primavera, verano, otoño)
CUSK EEL (kingklip) - DONSELLE - ABADEJO
EELPOUTS - ZOARCIDÉS - VIUDAS
BLACKBELLY ROSEFISH - RASCASSE - RUBIO (Helicolenus spp.)

Optimum season for HAKE: winter (down to 500 m)
Saison optimale pour le MERLU: hiver (jusqu'à 500 m de profondeur)
Temporada óptima para la MERLUZA: invierno (hasta 500 m)

LONG TAILED HAKE
GRENADIER (Macruronus magellanicus)
MERLUZA DE COLA

Overall distribution
Répartition générale
Distribución general

Concentrations
Concentraciones

XII-II Months - Mois - Meses

RED SNAPPER (Lutjanus purpureus)
PARGO COLORADO (aya)
(= vermelho)

Potential
Potentiel 5 000 t
Potencial

KING WEAKFISH
PESCADILLA REAL
(Macrodon ancylodon)

Overall distribution
Répartition générale
Distribución general

Concentrations
Concentraciones

Potential
Potentiel 13 000 t
Potencial

WHITE CROAKER
COURBINE BLANCHE
CORVINA BLANCA
(Micropogon opercularis)

Overall distribution
Répartition générale
Distribución general

Spawning grounds
Aires de ponte
Zonas de desove

HAWKFISH
CASTAÑETA
(Cheilodactylus spp.)

Potential
Potentiel 80 000 t
Potencial

CROAKER
OMBRINE
PARGO (= castanha)
(Umbrina canosai)

STRIPED WEAKFISH
PESCADILLA
(Cynoscion striatus)

SNAPPERS - LUTJANIDÉS - PARGOS
(vermelho, cioba, etc.)

Mixed - Divers - Varios
Muddy bottoms: CROAKERS, STRIPED WEAKFISH,
MARINE CATFISHES, POMPANO, SHARKS
Fonds de vase: SCIAENIDÉS, POISSONS-CHATS,
TRACHINOTE, REQUINS
Fondos fangosos: CORVINAS, PESCADILLA,
BAGRES MARINOS, PÁMPANO, TIBURONES

Mixed - Divers - Varios
Hard bottoms: GROUPERS, RED PORGY
Fonds durs: MÉROUS, PAGRE ROUGE
Fondos duros: MEROS, BESUGO

Potential
Potentiel 500 000-1 800 000 t
Potencial

PATAGONIAN HAKE
MERLU DE PATAGONIE (Merluccius hubbsi)
MERLUZA DE PATAGONIA

Overall distribution
Répartition générale
Distribución general

Concentrations
Concentraciones

VI Months
Mois
Meses

VERTICAL DISTRIBUTION
RÉPARTITION VERTICALE
DISTRIBUCION VERTICAL

41°S-54°S

PATAGONIAN HAKE (spring and summer)
MERLU DE PATAGONIE (printemps et été, 41°S-47°S)
MERLUZA DE PATAGONIA (primavera y verano)

(autumn)
(automne, 41°S-44°S)
(otoño)

CROAKERS-SCIAENIDÉS-CORVINAS
STRIPED WEAKFISH-SCIAENIDÉ-PESCADILLA
PATAGONIAN HAKE-MERLU DE PATAGONIE-MERLUZA DE PATAGONIA

PATAGONIAN HAKE-MERLU DE PATAGONIE-MERLUZA DE PATAGONIA
(More abundant in summer-Plus abondant en été-Mayor abundancia en el verano)
SANDPERCH-PINGUIPES-CHÁCHITO (Mugiloides)
HAWKFISH-CASTAÑETA (Cheilodactylus spp.)
CUSK EEL-DONSELLE-ABADEJO (Genypterus spp.)
FLATFISHES-POISSONS PLATS-LENGUADOS

PATAGONIAN HAKE - MERLU DE PATAGONIE - MERLUZA DE PATAGONIA
Autumn/winter, not in commercial quantities - Automne/hiver, en quantités non commerciales
Otoño/invierno, en cantidades no comerciales
LONG TAILED HAKE-GRENADIER-MERLUZA DE COLA (Macruronus magellanicus)
SOUTHERN BLUE WHITING-POUTASSOU AUSTRAL-POLACA (Micromesistius australis)
CUSK EEL (= kingklip)-DONSELLE-ABADEJO (Genypterus spp.)

Merluccius polylepis

SOUTHERN BLUE WHITING
POUTASSOU AUSTRAL
POLACA
(Micromesistius australis)

Overall distribution
Répartition générale
Distribución general

Concentrations
Concentraciones

VI Months
Mois
Meses

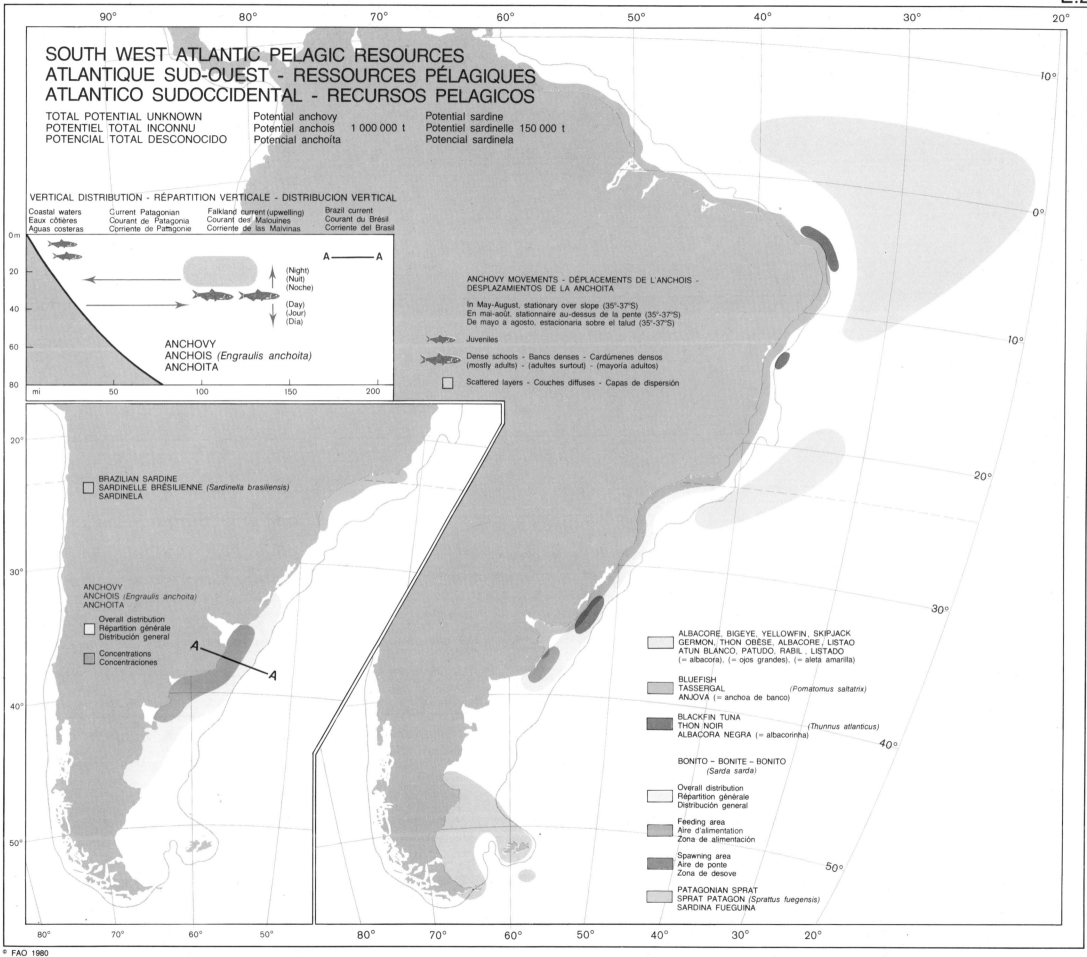

SOUTH WEST ATLANTIC PELAGIC RESOURCES
ATLANTIQUE SUD-OUEST - RESSOURCES PÉLAGIQUES
ATLANTICO SUDOCCIDENTAL - RECURSOS PELAGICOS

TOTAL POTENTIAL UNKNOWN
POTENTIEL TOTAL INCONNU
POTENCIAL TOTAL DESCONOCIDO

Potential anchovy
Potentiel anchois   1 000 000 t
Potencial anchoíta

Potential sardine
Potentiel sardinelle 150 000 t
Potencial sardinela

VERTICAL DISTRIBUTION - RÉPARTITION VERTICALE - DISTRIBUCION VERTICAL

Coastal waters
Eaux côtières
Aguas costeras

Current Patagonian
Courant de Patagonia
Corriente de Patagonie

Falkland current (upwelling)
Courant des Malouines
Corriente de las Malvinas

Brazil current
Courant du Brésil
Corriente del Brasil

(Night)
(Nuit)
(Noche)

(Day)
(Jour)
(Día)

A ———— A

ANCHOVY
ANCHOIS (Engraulis anchoita)
ANCHOITA

mi   50   100   150   200

ANCHOVY MOVEMENTS - DÉPLACEMENTS DE L'ANCHOIS -
DESPLAZAMIENTOS DE LA ANCHOITA

In May-August, stationary over slope (35°-37°S)
En mai-août, stationnaire au-dessus de la pente (35°-37°S)
De mayo a agosto, estacionaria sobre el talud (35°-37°S)

Juveniles

Dense schools - Bancs denses - Cardúmenes densos
(mostly adults) - (adultes surtout) - (mayoría adultos)

Scattered layers - Couches diffuses - Capas de dispersión

BRAZILIAN SARDINE
SARDINELLE BRÉSILIENNE (Sardinella brasiliensis)
SARDINELA

ANCHOVY
ANCHOIS (Engraulis anchoita)
ANCHOITA

Overall distribution
Répartition générale
Distribución general

Concentrations
Concentraciones

ALBACORE, BIGEYE, YELLOWFIN, SKIPJACK
GERMON, THON OBÈSE, ALBACORE, LISTAO
ATUN BLANCO, PATUDO, RABIL , LISTADO
(= albacora), (= ojos grandes), (= aleta amarilla)

BLUEFISH
TASSERGAL   (Pomatomus saltatrix)
ANJOVA (= anchoa de banco)

BLACKFIN TUNA
THON NOIR   (Thunnus atlanticus)
ALBACORA NEGRA (= albacorinha)

BONITO – BONITE – BONITO
(Sarda sarda)

Overall distribution
Répartition générale
Distribución general

Feeding area
Aire d'alimentation
Zona de alimentación

Spawning area
Aire de ponte
Zona de desove

PATAGONIAN SPRAT
SPRAT PATAGON (Sprattus fuegensis)
SARDINA FUEGUINA

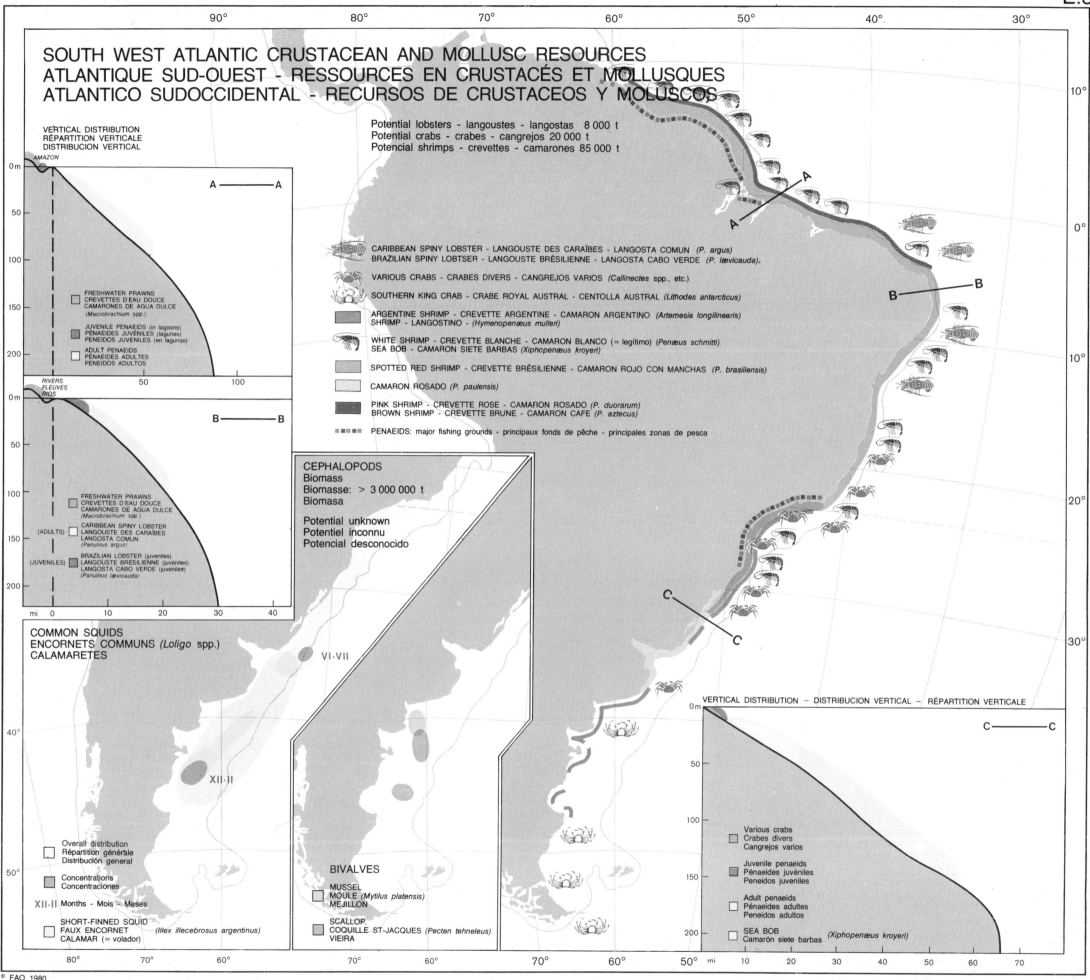

SOUTH WEST ATLANTIC CRUSTACEAN AND MOLLUSC RESOURCES
ATLANTIQUE SUD-OUEST - RESSOURCES EN CRUSTACÉS ET MOLLUSQUES
ATLANTICO SUDOCCIDENTAL - RECURSOS DE CRUSTACEOS Y MOLUSCOS

VERTICAL DISTRIBUTION
RÉPARTITION VERTICALE
DISTRIBUCION VERTICAL

AMAZON

A ——— A

FRESHWATER PRAWNS
CREVETTES D'EAU DOUCE
CAMARONES DE AGUA DULCE
(*Macrobrachium* spp.)

JUVENILE PENAEIDS (in lagoons)
PÉNAEIDES JUVÉNILES (lagunes)
PENEIDOS JUVENILES (en lagunas)

ADULT PENAEIDS
PÉNAEIDES ADULTES
PENEIDOS ADULTOS

RIVERS
FLEUVES
RIOS

B ——— B

FRESHWATER PRAWNS
CREVETTES D'EAU DOUCE
CAMARONES DE AGUA DULCE
(*Macrobrachium* spp.)

(ADULTS) CARIBBEAN SPINY LOBSTER
LANGOUSTE DES CARAÏBES
LANGOSTA COMUN
(*Panulirus argus*)

(JUVENILES) BRAZILIAN LOBSTER (juveniles)
LANGOUSTE BRÉSILIENNE (juveniles)
LANGOSTA CABO VERDE (juveniles)
(*Panulirus lævicauda*)

mi 0   10   20   30   40

Potential lobsters - langoustes - langostas 8 000 t
Potential crabs - crabes - cangrejos 20 000 t
Potencial shrimps - crevettes - camarones 85 000 t

CARIBBEAN SPINY LOBSTER - LANGOUSTE DES CARAÏBES - LANGOSTA COMUN (*P. argus*)
BRAZILIAN SPINY LOBTSER - LANGOUSTE BRÉSILIENNE - LANGOSTA CABO VERDE (*P. lævicauda*).

VARIOUS CRABS - CRABES DIVERS - CANGREJOS VARIOS (*Callinectes* spp., etc.)

SOUTHERN KING CRAB - CRABE ROYAL AUSTRAL - CENTOLLA AUSTRAL (*Lithodes antarcticus*)

ARGENTINE SHRIMP - CREVETTE ARGENTINE - CAMARON ARGENTINO (*Artemesia longilinearis*)
SHRIMP - LANGOSTINO - (*Hymenopenæus mulleri*)

WHITE SHRIMP - CREVETTE BLANCHE - CAMARON BLANCO (= legítimo) (*Penæus schmitti*)
SEA BOB - CAMARON SIETE BARBAS (*Xiphopenæus kroyeri*)

SPOTTED RED SHRIMP - CREVETTE BRÉSILIENNE - CAMARON ROJO CON MANCHAS (*P. brasiliensis*)

CAMARON ROSADO (*P. paulensis*)

PINK SHRIMP - CREVETTE ROSE - CAMARON ROSADO (*P. duorarum*)
BROWN SHRIMP - CREVETTE BRUNE - CAMARON CAFE (*P. aztecus*)

PENAEIDS: major fishing grounds - principaux fonds de pêche - principales zonas de pesca

CEPHALOPODS
Biomass
Biomasse: > 3 000 000 t
Biomasa

Potential unknown
Potentiel inconnu
Potencial desconocido

COMMON SQUIDS
ENCORNETS COMMUNS (*Loligo* spp.)
CALAMARETES

VI·VII

XII·II

Overall distribution
Répartition générale
Distribución general

Concentrations
Concentraciones

XII·II Months - Mois - Meses

SHORT-FINNED SQUID
FAUX ENCORNET   (*Illex illecebrosus argentinus*)
CALAMAR (= volador)

BIVALVES

MUSSEL
MOULE (*Mytilus platensis*)
MEJILLON

SCALLOP
COQUILLE ST-JACQUES (*Pecten tehneleus*)
VIEIRA

VERTICAL DISTRIBUTION - DISTRIBUCION VERTICAL - RÉPARTITION VERTICALE

C ——— C

Various crabs
Crabes divers
Cangrejos varios

Juvenile penaeids
Pénaeides juvéniles
Peneidos juveniles

Adult penaeids
Pénaeides adultes
Peneidos adultos

SEA BOB   (*Xiphopenæus kroyeri*)
Camarón siete barbas

mi 10   20   30   40   50   60   70

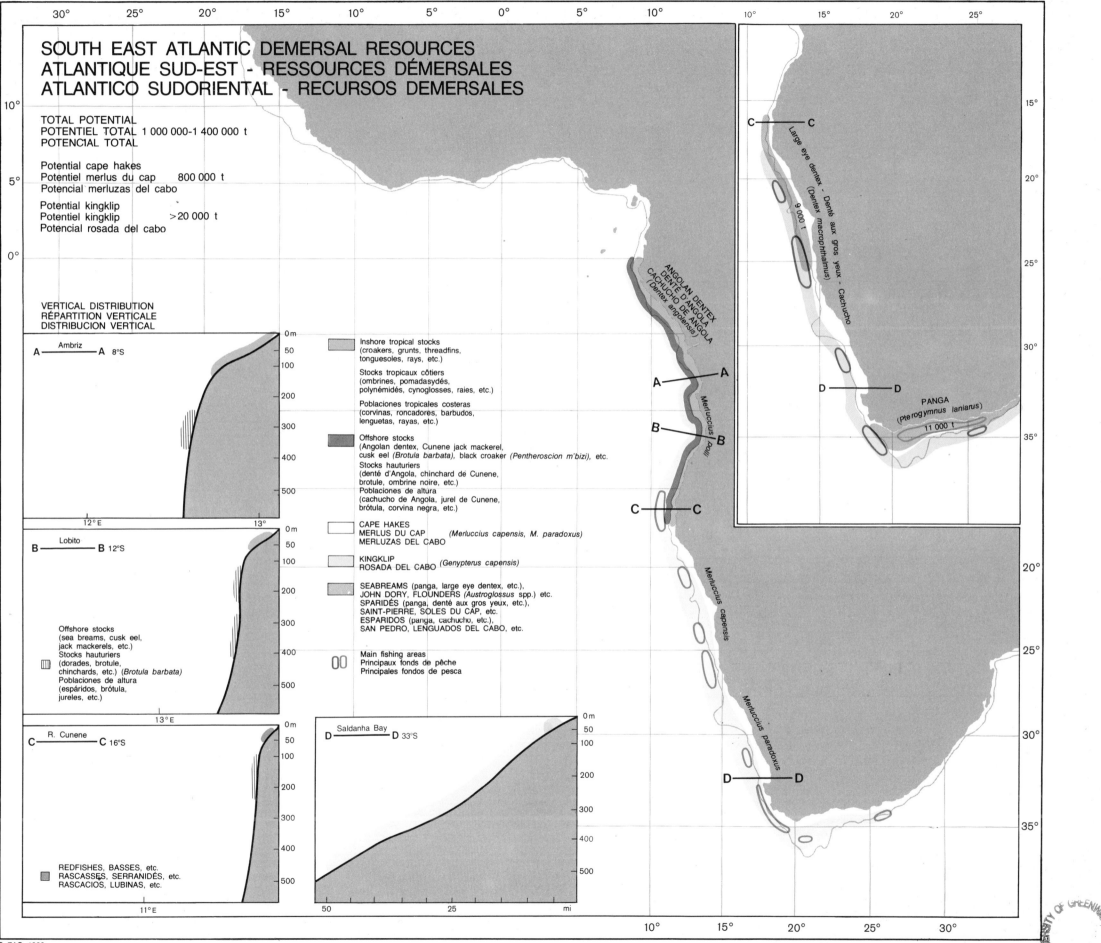

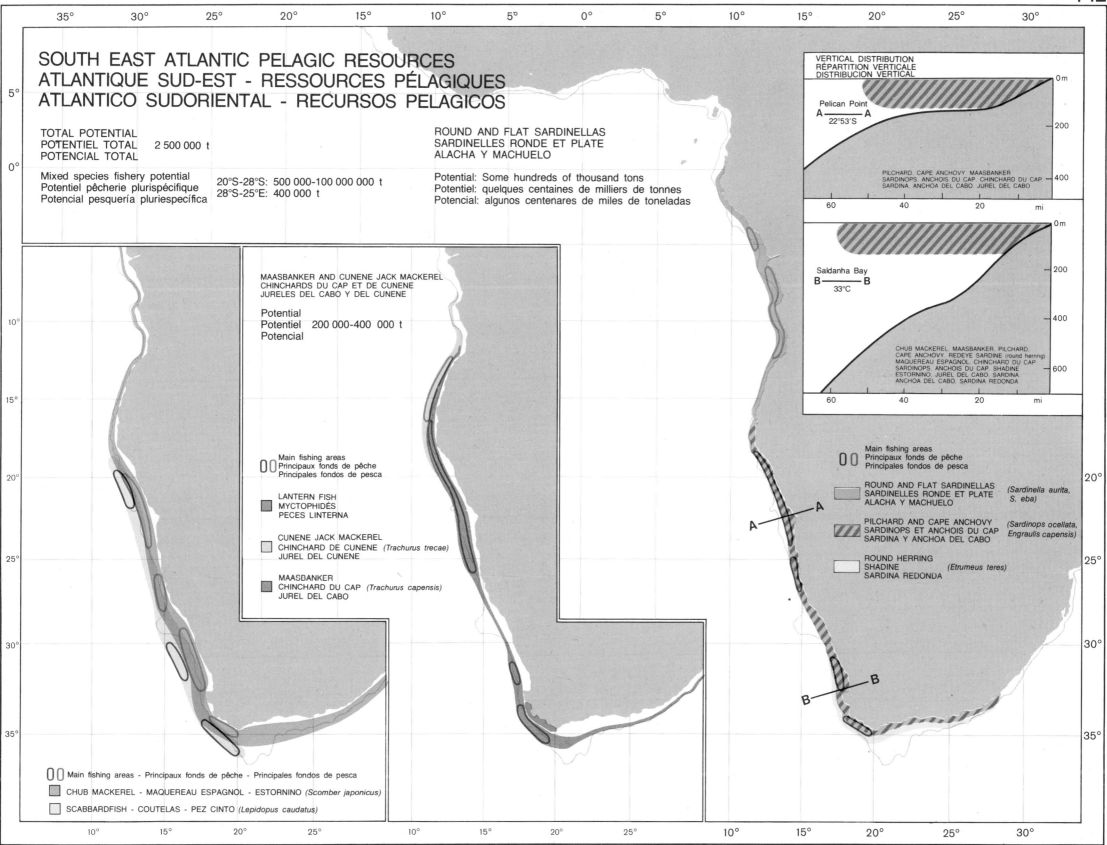

SOUTH EAST ATLANTIC PELAGIC RESOURCES
ATLANTIQUE SUD-EST - RESSOURCES PÉLAGIQUES
ATLANTICO SUDORIENTAL - RECURSOS PELAGICOS

TOTAL POTENTIAL
POTENTIEL TOTAL   2 500 000 t
POTENCIAL TOTAL

Mixed species fishery potential
Potentiel pêcherie plurispécifique   20°S-28°S: 500 000-100 000 000 t
Potencial pesquería pluriespecífica   28°S-25°E: 400 000 t

ROUND AND FLAT SARDINELLAS
SARDINELLES RONDE ET PLATE
ALACHA Y MACHUELO

Potential: Some hundreds of thousand tons
Potentiel: quelques centaines de milliers de tonnes
Potencial: algunos centenares de miles de toneladas

VERTICAL DISTRIBUTION
RÉPARTITION VERTICALE
DISTRIBUCION VERTICAL

Pelican Point
A —————— A
22°53'S

PILCHARD, CAPE ANCHOVY, MAASBANKER
SARDINOPS, ANCHOIS DU CAP, CHINCHARD DU CAP
SARDINA, ANCHOA DEL CABO, JUREL DEL CABO

Saldanha Bay
B —————— B
33°C

CHUB MACKEREL, MAASBANKER, PILCHARD,
CAPE ANCHOVY, REDEYE SARDINE (round herring)
MAQUEREAU ESPAGNOL, CHINCHARD DU CAP,
SARDINOPS, ANCHOIS DU CAP, SHADINE
ESTORNINO, JUREL DEL CABO, SARDINA,
ANCHOA DEL CABO, SARDINA REDONDA

MAASBANKER AND CUNENE JACK MACKEREL
CHINCHARDS DU CAP ET DE CUNENE
JURELES DEL CABO Y DEL CUNENE

Potential
Potentiel   200 000-400 000 t
Potencial

○○ Main fishing areas
Principaux fonds de pêche
Principales fondos de pesca

■ LANTERN FISH
MYCTOPHIDÉS
PECES LINTERNA

□ CUNENE JACK MACKEREL
CHINCHARD DE CUNENE *(Trachurus trecae)*
JUREL DEL CUNENE

■ MAASBANKER
CHINCHARD DU CAP *(Trachurus capensis)*
JUREL DEL CABO

○○ Main fishing areas
Principaux fonds de pêche
Principales fondos de pesca

■ ROUND AND FLAT SARDINELLAS   *(Sardinella aurita,*
SARDINELLES RONDE ET PLATE   *S. eba)*
ALACHA Y MACHUELO

▨ PILCHARD AND CAPE ANCHOVY   *(Sardinops ocellata,*
SARDINOPS ET ANCHOIS DU CAP   *Engraulis capensis)*
SARDINA Y ANCHOA DEL CABO

□ ROUND HERRING
SHADINE   *(Etrumeus teres)*
SARDINA REDONDA

○○ Main fishing areas - Principaux fonds de pêche - Principales fondos de pesca

■ CHUB MACKEREL - MAQUEREAU ESPAGNOL - ESTORNINO *(Scomber japonicus)*

□ SCABBARDFISH - COUTELAS - PEZ CINTO *(Lepidopus caudatus)*

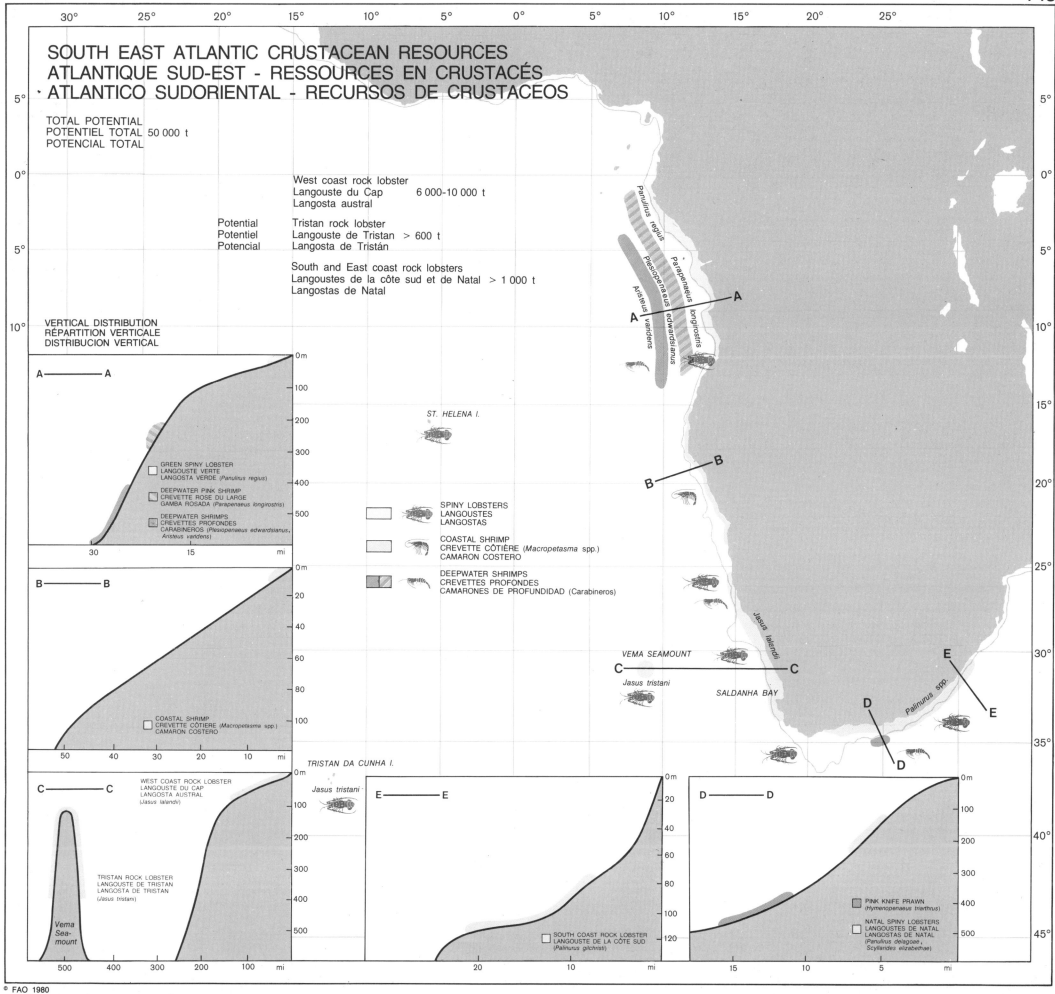

SOUTH EAST ATLANTIC CRUSTACEAN RESOURCES
ATLANTIQUE SUD-EST - RESSOURCES EN CRUSTACÉS
ATLANTICO SUDORIENTAL - RECURSOS DE CRUSTACEOS

TOTAL POTENTIAL
POTENTIEL TOTAL 50 000 t
POTENCIAL TOTAL

West coast rock lobster
Langouste du Cap   6 000-10 000 t
Langosta austral

Potential   Tristan rock lobster
Potentiel   Langouste de Tristan > 600 t
Potencial   Langosta de Tristán

South and East coast rock lobsters
Langoustes de la côte sud et de Natal > 1 000 t
Langostas de Natal

VERTICAL DISTRIBUTION
RÉPARTITION VERTICALE
DISTRIBUCION VERTICAL

A ———— A

GREEN SPINY LOBSTER
LANGOUSTE VERTE
LANGOSTA VERDE (Panulirus regius)

DEEPWATER PINK SHRIMP
CREVETTE ROSE DU LARGE
GAMBA ROSADA (Parapenaeus longirostris)

DEEPWATER SHRIMPS
CREVETTES PROFONDES
CARABINEROS (Plesiopenaeus edwardsianus,
Aristeus varidens)

B ———— B

COASTAL SHRIMP
CREVETTE CÔTIERE (Macropetasma spp.)
CAMARON COSTERO

C ———— C
WEST COAST ROCK LOBSTER
LANGOUSTE DU CAP
LANGOSTA AUSTRAL
(Jasus lalandii)

TRISTAN ROCK LOBSTER
LANGOUSTE DE TRISTAN
LANGOSTA DE TRISTAN
(Jasus tristani)

Vema Sea-mount

SPINY LOBSTERS
LANGOUSTES
LANGOSTAS

COASTAL SHRIMP
CREVETTE CÔTIERE (Macropetasma spp.)
CAMARON COSTERO

DEEPWATER SHRIMPS
CREVETTES PROFONDES
CAMARONES DE PROFUNDIDAD (Carabineros)

ST. HELENA I.

VEMA SEAMOUNT

Jasus tristani

SALDANHA BAY

Jasus lalandii

Palinurus spp.

TRISTAN DA CUNHA I.

Jasus tristani

E ———— E

SOUTH COAST ROCK LOBSTER
LANGOUSTE DE LA CÔTE SUD
(Palinurus gilchristi)

D ———— D

PINK KNIFE PRAWN
(Hymenopenaeus triarthrus)

NATAL SPINY LOBSTERS
LANGOUSTES DE NATAL
LANGOSTAS DE NATAL
(Panulirus delagoae,
Scyllarides elizabethae)

Panulirus regius
Parapenaeus longirostris
Plesiopenaeus edwardsianus
Aristeus varidens

© FAO 1980

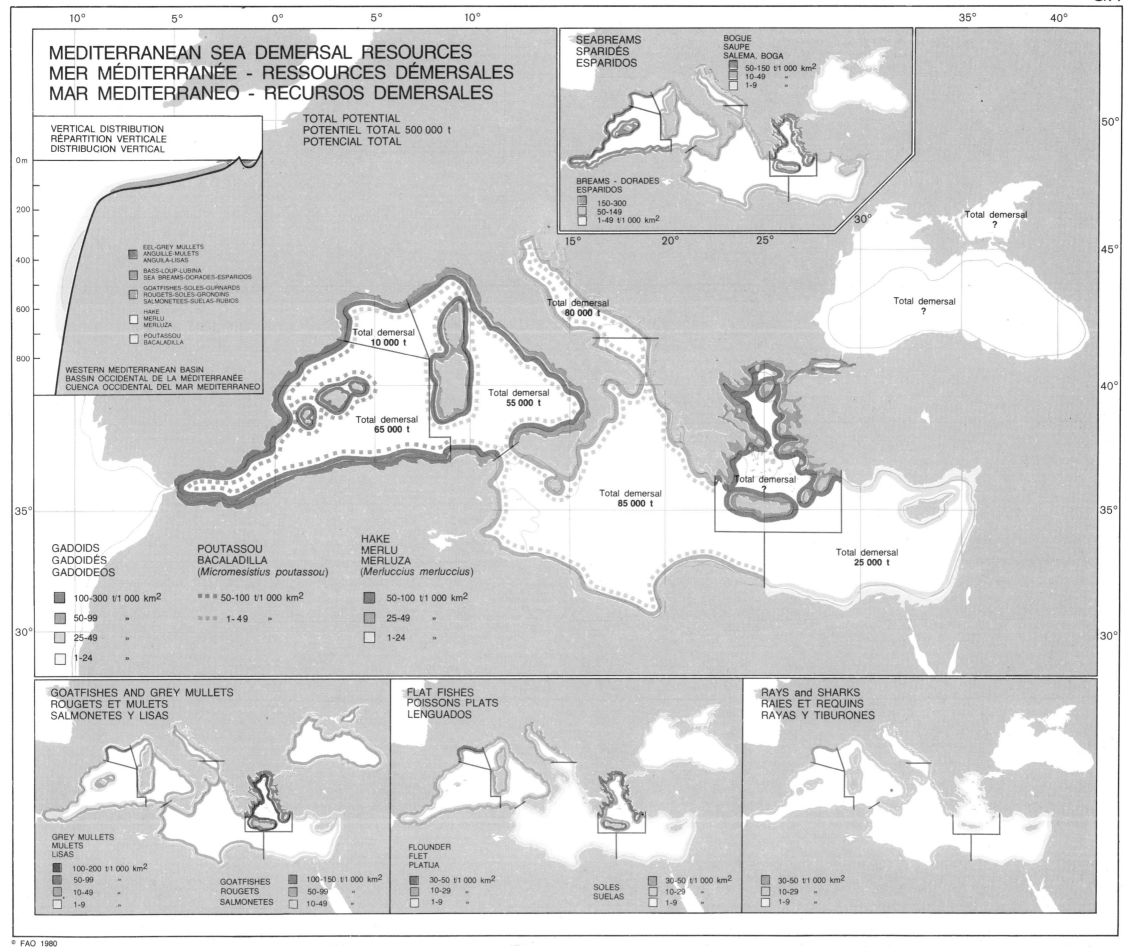

MEDITERRANEAN SEA DEMERSAL RESOURCES
MER MÉDITERRANÉE - RESSOURCES DÉMERSALES
MAR MEDITERRANEO - RECURSOS DEMERSALES

VERTICAL DISTRIBUTION
RÉPARTITION VERTICALE
DISTRIBUCION VERTICAL

TOTAL POTENTIAL
POTENTIEL TOTAL 500 000 t
POTENCIAL TOTAL

EEL-GREY MULLETS
ANGUILLE-MULETS
ANGUILA-LISAS

BASS-LOUP-LUBINA
SEA BREAMS-DORADES-ESPARIDOS

GOATFISHES-SOLES-GURNARDS
ROUGETS-SOLES-GRONDINS
SALMONETES-SUELAS-RUBIOS

HAKE
MERLU
MERLUZA

POUTASSOU
BACALADILLA

WESTERN MEDITERRANEAN BASIN
BASSIN OCCIDENTAL DE LA MÉDITERRANÉE
CUENCA OCCIDENTAL DEL MAR MEDITERRANEO

SEABREAMS
SPARIDÉS
ESPARIDOS

BOGUE
SAUPE
SALEMA, BOGA
50-150 t/1 000 km²
10-49 »
1-9 »

BREAMS - DORADES
ESPARIDOS
150-300
50-149
1-49 t/1 000 km²

Total demersal
?

Total demersal
?

Total demersal
80 000 t

Total demersal
10 000 t

Total demersal
55 000 t

Total demersal
65 000 t

Total demersal
?

Total demersal
85 000 t

Total demersal
25 000 t

GADOIDS
GADOIDÉS
GADOIDEOS

100-300 t/1 000 km²
50-99 »
25-49 »
1-24 »

POUTASSOU
BACALADILLA
(Micromesistius poutassou)

50-100 t/1 000 km²
1-49 »

HAKE
MERLU
MERLUZA
(Merluccius merluccius)

50-100 t/1 000 km²
25-49 »
1-24 »

GOATFISHES AND GREY MULLETS
ROUGETS ET MULETS
SALMONETES Y LISAS

GREY MULLETS
MULETS
LISAS
100-200 t/1 000 km²
50-99 »
10-49 »
1-9 »

GOATFISHES
ROUGETS
SALMONETES
100-150 t/1 000 km²
50-99 »
10-49 »

FLAT FISHES
POISSONS PLATS
LENGUADOS

FLOUNDER
FLET
PLATIJA
30-50 t/1 000 km²
10-29 »
1-9 »

SOLES
SUELAS
30-50 t/1 000 km²
10-29 »
1-9 »

RAYS and SHARKS
RAIES ET REQUINS
RAYAS Y TIBURONES

30-50 t/1 000 km²
10-29 »
1-9 »

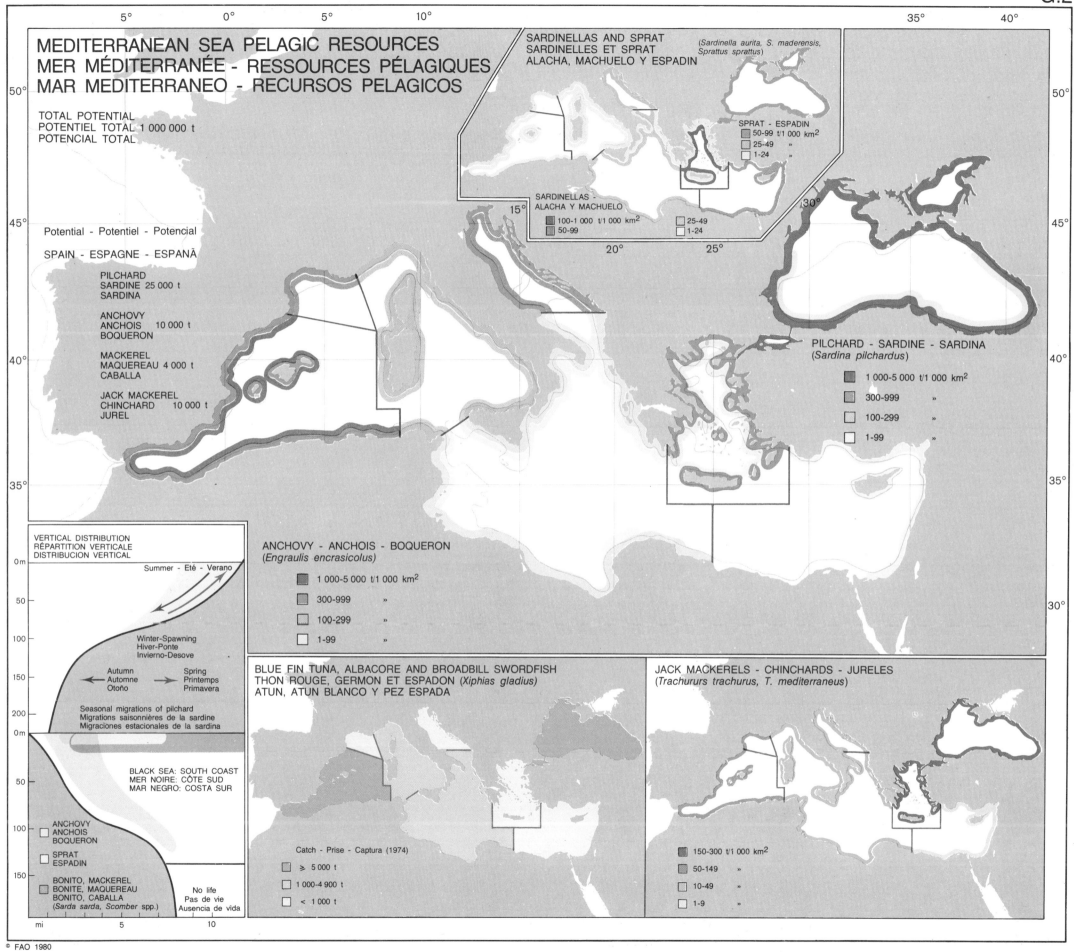

MEDITERRANEAN SEA PELAGIC RESOURCES
MER MÉDITERRANÉE - RESSOURCES PÉLAGIQUES
MAR MEDITERRANEO - RECURSOS PELAGICOS

TOTAL POTENTIAL
POTENTIEL TOTAL 1 000 000 t
POTENCIAL TOTAL

Potential - Potentiel - Potencial

SPAIN - ESPAGNE - ESPAÑA

PILCHARD
SARDINE 25 000 t
SARDINA

ANCHOVY
ANCHOIS 10 000 t
BOQUERON

MACKEREL
MAQUEREAU 4 000 t
CABALLA

JACK MACKEREL
CHINCHARD 10 000 t
JUREL

SARDINELLAS AND SPRAT
SARDINELLES ET SPRAT
ALACHA, MACHUELO Y ESPADIN

(Sardinella aurita, S. maderensis, Sprattus sprattus)

SPRAT - ESPADIN
- 50-99 t/1 000 km²
- 25-49 »
- 1-24 »

SARDINELLAS -
ALACHA Y MACHUELO
- 100-1 000 t/1 000 km²
- 50-99
- 25-49
- 1-24

PILCHARD - SARDINE - SARDINA
(Sardina pilchardus)
- 1 000-5 000 t/1 000 km²
- 300-999 »
- 100-299 »
- 1-99 »

VERTICAL DISTRIBUTION
RÉPARTITION VERTICALE
DISTRIBUCION VERTICAL

0 m
50
100
150
200

Summer - Eté - Verano

Winter-Spawning
Hiver-Ponte
Invierno-Desove

Autumn   Spring
Automne   Printemps
Otoño   Primavera

Seasonal migrations of pilchard
Migrations saisonnières de la sardine
Migraciones estacionales de la sardina

0 m
50
100
150

BLACK SEA: SOUTH COAST
MER NOIRE: CÔTE SUD
MAR NEGRO: COSTA SUR

ANCHOVY
ANCHOIS
BOQUERON

SPRAT
ESPADIN

BONITO, MACKEREL
BONITE, MAQUEREAU
BONITO, CABALLA
(Sarda sarda, Scomber spp.)

No life
Pas de vie
Ausencia de vida

mi   5   10

ANCHOVY - ANCHOIS - BOQUERON
(Engraulis encrasicolus)
- 1 000-5 000 t/1 000 km²
- 300-999 »
- 100-299 »
- 1-99 »

BLUE FIN TUNA, ALBACORE AND BROADBILL SWORDFISH
THON ROUGE, GERMON ET ESPADON *(Xiphias gladius)*
ATUN, ATUN BLANCO Y PEZ ESPADA

Catch - Prise - Captura (1974)
- ≥ 5 000 t
- 1 000-4 900 t
- < 1 000 t

JACK MACKERELS - CHINCHARDS - JURELES
(Trachurus trachurus, T. mediterraneus)
- 150-300 t/1 000 km²
- 50-149 »
- 10-49 »
- 1-9 »

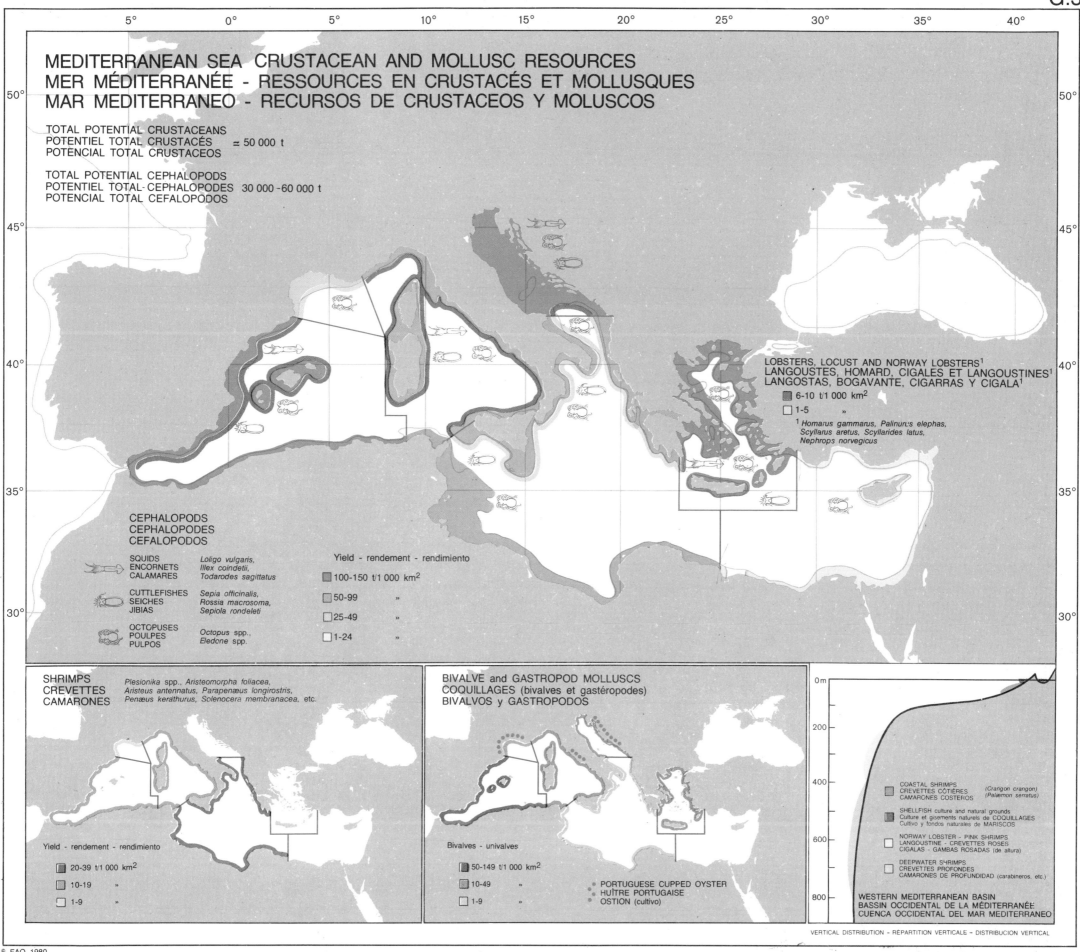

MEDITERRANEAN SEA CRUSTACEAN AND MOLLUSC RESOURCES
MER MÉDITERRANÉE - RESSOURCES EN CRUSTACÉS ET MOLLUSQUES
MAR MEDITERRANEO - RECURSOS DE CRUSTACEOS Y MOLUSCOS

TOTAL POTENTIAL CRUSTACEANS
POTENTIEL TOTAL CRUSTACÉS   ≃ 50 000 t
POTENCIAL TOTAL CRUSTACEOS

TOTAL POTENTIAL CEPHALOPODS
POTENTIEL TOTAL CEPHALOPODES   30 000 - 60 000 t
POTENCIAL TOTAL CEFALOPODOS

LOBSTERS, LOCUST AND NORWAY LOBSTERS[1]
LANGOUSTES, HOMARD, CIGALES ET LANGOUSTINES[1]
LANGOSTAS, BOGAVANTE, CIGARRAS Y CIGALA[1]

- 6-10 t/1 000 km²
- 1-5 »

[1] Homarus gammarus, Palinurus elephas,
Scyllarus arctus, Scyllarides latus,
Nephrops norvegicus

CEPHALOPODS
CEPHALOPODES
CEFALOPODOS

SQUIDS ENCORNETS CALAMARES	Loligo vulgaris, Illex coindetii, Todarodes sagittatus	
CUTTLEFISHES SEICHES JIBIAS	Sepia officinalis, Rossia macrosoma, Sepiola rondeleti	
OCTOPUSES POULPES PULPOS	Octopus spp., Eledone spp.	

Yield - rendement - rendimiento

- 100-150 t/1 000 km²
- 50-99 »
- 25-49 »
- 1-24 »

SHRIMPS
CREVETTES
CAMARONES

Plesionika spp., Aristeomorpha foliacea,
Aristeus antennatus, Parapenæus longirostris,
Penæus kerathurus, Solenocera membranacea, etc.

Yield - rendement - rendimiento

- 20-39 t/1 000 km²
- 10-19 »
- 1-9 »

BIVALVE and GASTROPOD MOLLUSCS
COQUILLAGES (bivalves et gastéropodes)
BIVALVOS y GASTROPODOS

Bivalves - univalves

- 50-149 t/1 000 km²
- 10-49 »
- 1-9 »

- • PORTUGUESE CUPPED OYSTER
- HUÎTRE PORTUGAISE
- OSTION (cultivo)

COASTAL SHRIMPS CREVETTES CÔTIÈRES CAMARONES COSTEROS	(Crangon crangon) (Palæmon serratus)
SHELLFISH culture and natural grounds Culture et gisements naturels de COQUILLAGES Cultivo y fondos naturales de MARISCOS	
NORWAY LOBSTER - PINK SHRIMPS LANGOUSTINE - CREVETTES ROSES CIGALAS - GAMBAS ROSADAS (de altura)	
DEEPWATER SHRIMPS CREVETTES PROFONDES CAMARONES DE PROFUNDIDAD (carabineros. etc.)	

WESTERN MEDITERRANEAN BASIN
BASSIN OCCIDENTAL DE LA MÉDITERRANÉE
CUENCA OCCIDENTAL DEL MAR MEDITERRANEO

VERTICAL DISTRIBUTION - RÉPARTITION VERTICALE - DISTRIBUCION VERTICAL

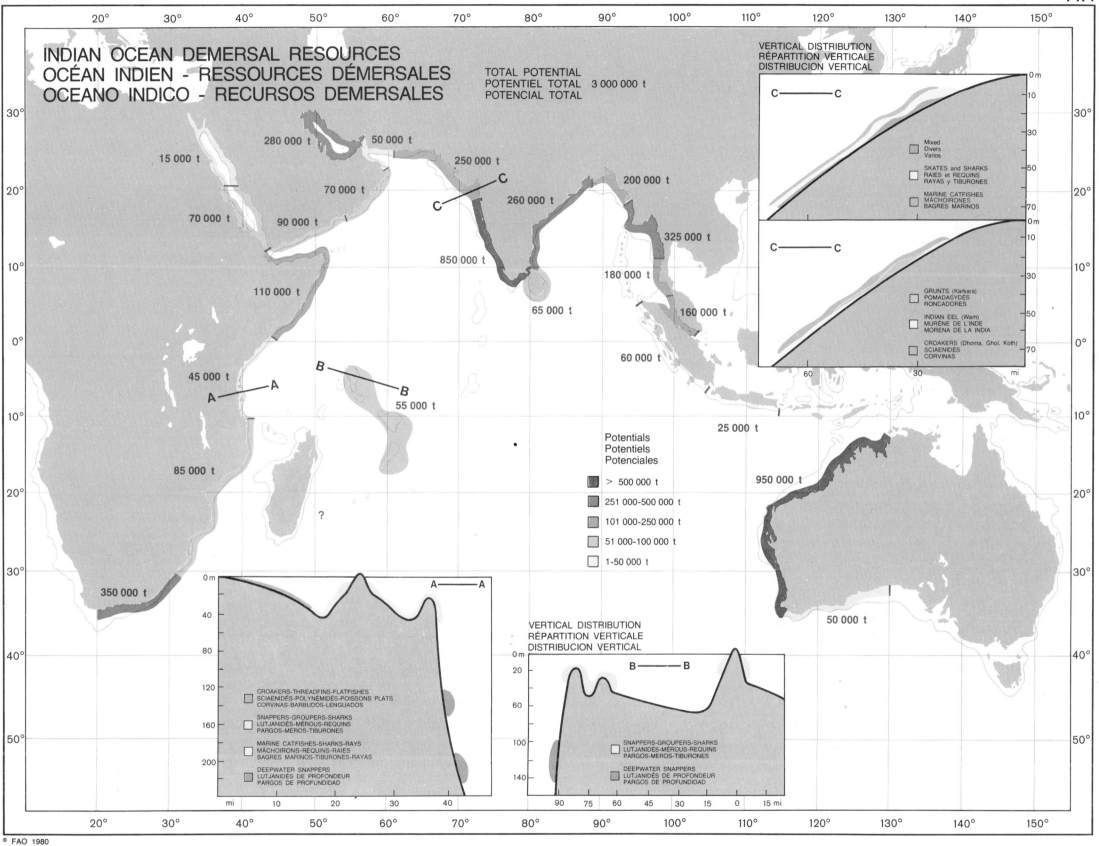

INDIAN OCEAN DEMERSAL RESOURCES
OCÉAN INDIEN - RESSOURCES DÉMERSALES
OCEANO INDICO - RECURSOS DEMERSALES

TOTAL POTENTIAL
POTENTIEL TOTAL   3 000 000 t
POTENCIAL TOTAL

15 000 t

280 000 t

50 000 t

70 000 t

250 000 t

70 000 t

90 000 t

260 000 t

200 000 t

C
C

325 000 t

110 000 t

850 000 t

180 000 t

65 000 t

160 000 t

45 000 t

B

A   A

B

55 000 t

60 000 t

85 000 t

950 000 t

25 000 t

?

350 000 t

50 000 t

VERTICAL DISTRIBUTION
RÉPARTITION VERTICALE
DISTRIBUCION VERTICAL

C ——— C

Mixed
Divers
Varios

SKATES and SHARKS
RAIES et REQUINS
RAYAS y TIBURONES

MARINE CATFISHES
MÂCHOIRONES
BAGRES MARINOS

C ——— C

GRUNTS (Karkara)
POMADASYDÉS
RONCADORES

INDIAN EEL (Wam)
MURÈNE DE L'INDE
MORENA DE LA INDIA

CROAKERS (Dhoma, Ghol, Koth)
SCIAENIDÉS
CORVINAS

Potentials
Potentiels
Potenciales

> 500 000 t

251 000-500 000 t

101 000-250 000 t

51 000-100 000 t

1-50 000 t

VERTICAL DISTRIBUTION
RÉPARTITION VERTICALE
DISTRIBUCION VERTICAL

A ——— A

CROAKERS-THREADFINS-FLATFISHES
SCIAENIDÉS-POLYNÉMIDÉS-POISSONS PLATS
CORVINAS-BARBUDOS-LENGUADOS

SNAPPERS-GROUPERS-SHARKS
LUTJANIDÉS-MÉROUS-REQUINS
PARGOS-MEROS-TIBURONES

MARINE CATFISHES-SHARKS-RAYS
MÂCHOIRONS-REQUINS-RAIES
BAGRES MARINOS-TIBURONES-RAYAS

DEEPWATER SNAPPERS
LUTJANIDÉS DE PROFONDEUR
PARGOS DE PROFUNDIDAD

B ——— B

SNAPPERS-GROUPERS-SHARKS
LUTJANIDÉS-MÉROUS-REQUINS
PARGOS-MEROS-TIBURONES

DEEPWATER SNAPPERS
LUTJANIDÉS DE PROFONDEUR
PARGOS DE PROFUNDIDAD

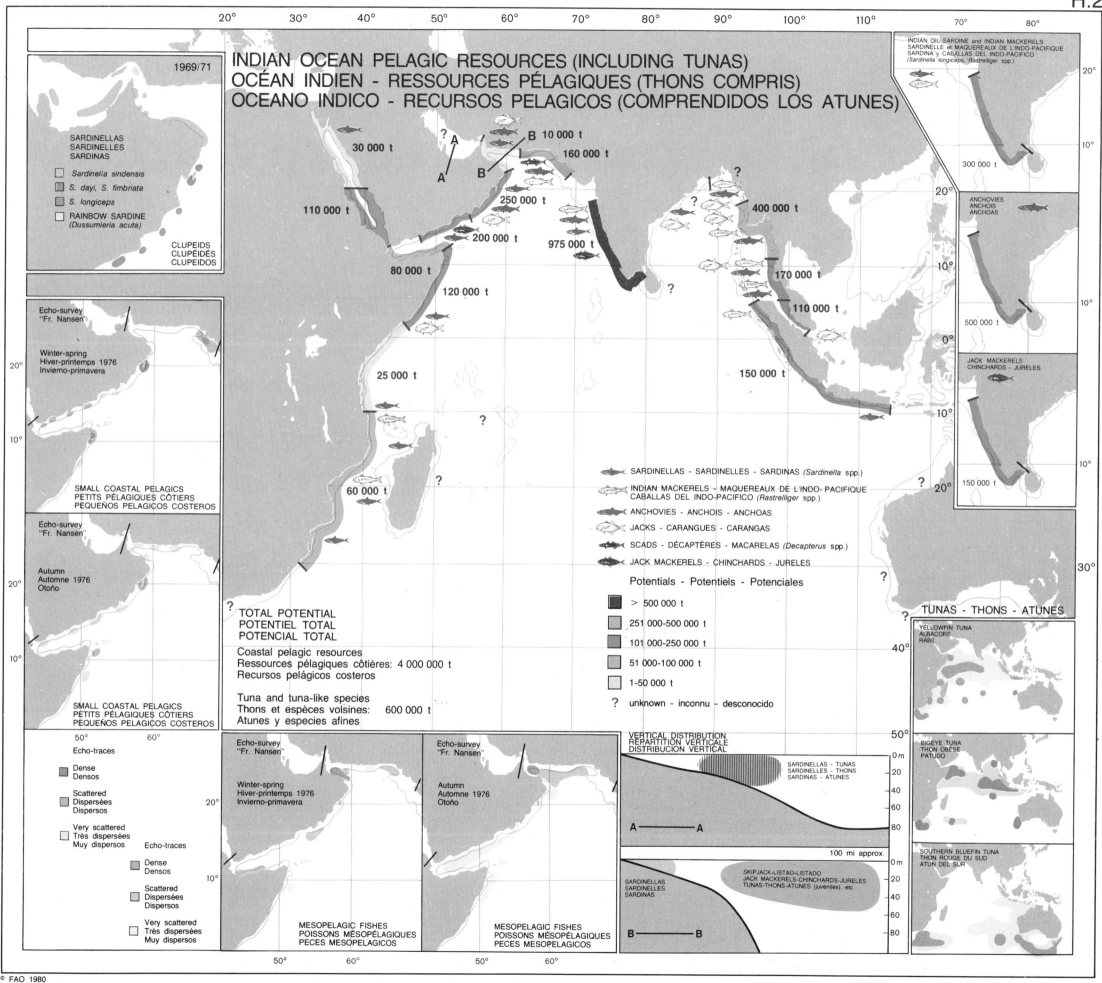

INDIAN OCEAN PELAGIC RESOURCES (INCLUDING TUNAS)
OCÉAN INDIEN - RESSOURCES PÉLAGIQUES (THONS COMPRIS)
OCEANO INDICO - RECURSOS PELAGICOS (COMPRENDIDOS LOS ATUNES)

1969/71

SARDINELLAS
SARDINELLES
SARDINAS

☐ *Sardinella sindensis*
■ *S. dayi, S. fimbriata*
■ *S. longiceps*
☐ RAINBOW SARDINE
(*Dussumieria acuta*)

CLUPEIDS
CLUPÉIDÉS
CLUPEIDOS

30 000 t
? A
B 10 000 t
160 000 t
110 000 t
250 000 t
200 000 t
80 000 t
975 000 t
120 000 t
400 000 t
170 000 t
110 000 t
25 000 t
150 000 t
60 000 t

INDIAN OIL SARDINE and INDIAN MACKERELS
SARDINELLE et MAQUEREAUX DE L'INDO-PACIFIQUE
SARDINA y CABALLAS DEL INDO-PACIFICO
(*Sardinella longiceps, Rastrelliger* spp.)

300 000 t

ANCHOVIES
ANCHOIS
ANCHOAS

500 000 t

JACK MACKERELS
CHINCHARDS - JURELES

150 000 t

Echo-survey
"Fr. Nansen"

Winter-spring
Hiver-printemps 1976
Invierno-primavera

SMALL COASTAL PELAGICS
PETITS PÉLAGIQUES CÔTIERS
PEQUEÑOS PELAGICOS COSTEROS

Echo-survey
"Fr. Nansen"

Autumn
Automne 1976
Otoño

SMALL COASTAL PELAGICS
PETITS PÉLAGIQUES CÔTIERS
PEQUEÑOS PELAGICOS COSTEROS

Echo-traces

■ Dense
Densos

■ Scattered
Dispersées
Dispersos

☐ Very scattered
Très dispersées
Muy dispersos

Echo-traces

■ Dense
Densos

■ Scattered
Dispersées
Dispersos

☐ Very scattered
Très dispersées
Muy dispersos

⤙ SARDINELLAS - SARDINELLES - SARDINAS (*Sardinella* spp.)

⤙ INDIAN MACKERELS - MAQUEREAUX DE L'INDO-PACIFIQUE
CABALLAS DEL INDO-PACIFICO (*Rastrelliger* spp.)

⤙ ANCHOVIES - ANCHOIS - ANCHOAS

⤙ JACKS - CARANGUES - CARANGAS

⤙ SCADS - DÉCAPTÈRES - MACARELAS (*Decapterus* spp.)

⤙ JACK MACKERELS - CHINCHARDS - JURELES

Potentials - Potentiels - Potenciales

■ > 500 000 t
▨ 251 000-500 000 t
■ 101 000-250 000 t
■ 51 000-100 000 t
☐ 1-50 000 t

? unknown - inconnu - desconocido

TOTAL POTENTIAL
POTENTIEL TOTAL
POTENCIAL TOTAL

Coastal pelagic resources
Ressources pélagiques côtières: 4 000 000 t
Recursos pelágicos costeros

Tuna and tuna-like species
Thons et espèces voisines: 600 000 t
Atunes y especies afines

VERTICAL DISTRIBUTION
RÉPARTITION VERTICALE
DISTRIBUCIÓN VERTICAL

SARDINELLAS - TUNAS
SARDINELLES - THONS
SARDINAS - ATUNES

A —————— A

0 m
20
40
60
80

100 mi approx.

SARDINELLAS
SARDINELLES
SARDINAS

SKIPJACK-LISTAO-LISTADO
JACK MACKERELS-CHINCHARDS-JURELES
TUNAS-THONS-ATUNES (juveniles), etc.

B —————— B

0 m
20
40
60
80

TUNAS - THONS - ATUNES

YELLOWFIN TUNA
ALBACORE
RABIL

BIGEYE TUNA
THON OBÈSE
PATUDO

SOUTHERN BLUEFIN TUNA
THON ROUGE DU SUD
ATUN DEL SUR

Echo-survey
"Fr. Nansen"

Winter-spring
Hiver-printemps 1976
Invierno-primavera

MESOPELAGIC FISHES
POISSONS MÉSOPÉLAGIQUES
PECES MESOPELAGICOS

Echo-survey
"Fr. Nansen"

Autumn
Automne 1976
Otoño

MESOPELAGIC FISHES
POISSONS MÉSOPÉLAGIQUES
PECES MESOPELAGICOS

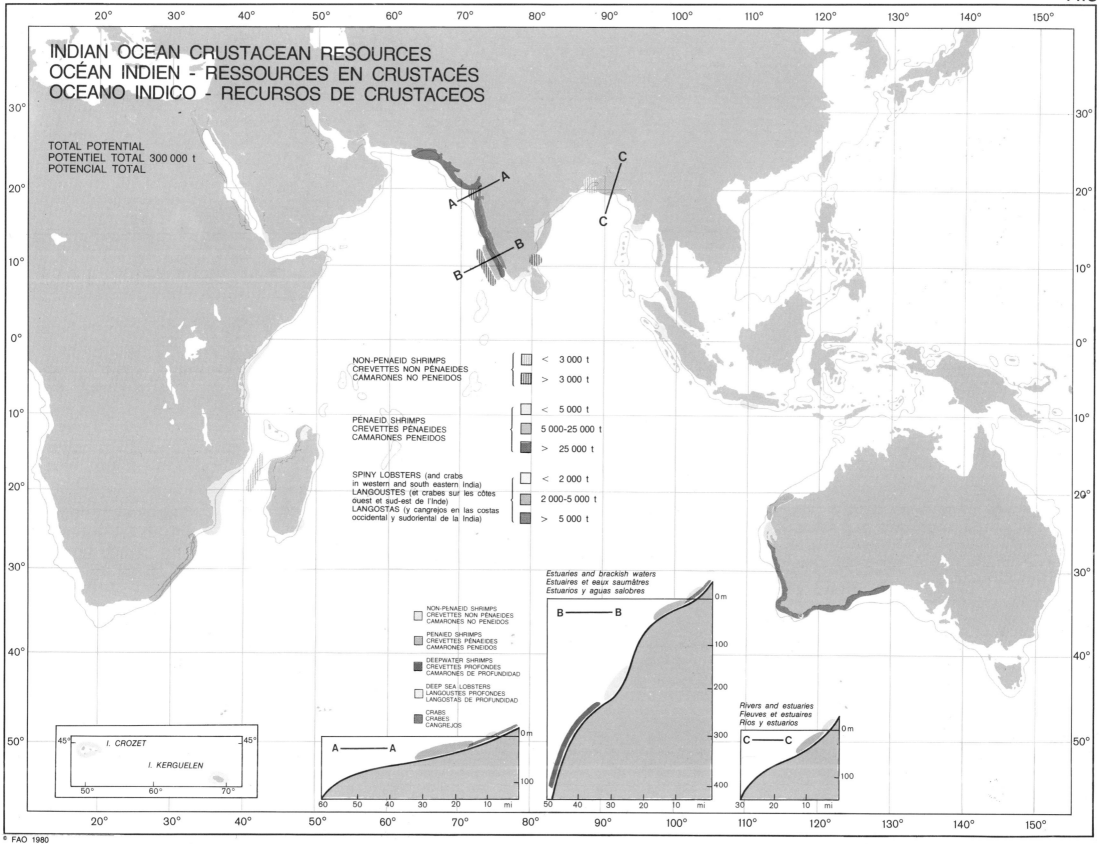

INDIAN OCEAN CRUSTACEAN RESOURCES
OCÉAN INDIEN - RESSOURCES EN CRUSTACÉS
OCEANO INDICO - RECURSOS DE CRUSTACEOS

TOTAL POTENTIAL
POTENTIEL TOTAL 300 000 t
POTENCIAL TOTAL

NON-PENAEID SHRIMPS
CREVETTES NON PÉNAEIDES
CAMARONES NO PENEIDOS
- < 3 000 t
- > 3 000 t

PÉNAEID SHRIMPS
CREVETTES PÉNAEIDES
CAMARONES PENEIDOS
- < 5 000 t
- 5 000-25 000 t
- > 25 000 t

SPINY LOBSTERS (and crabs
in western and south eastern India)
LANGOUSTES (et crabes sur les côtes
ouest et sud-est de l'Inde)
LANGOSTAS (y cangrejos en las costas
occidental y sudoriental de la India)
- < 2 000 t
- 2 000-5 000 t
- > 5 000 t

NON-PENAEID SHRIMPS
CREVETTES NON PÉNAEIDES
CAMARONES NO PENEIDOS

PENAEID SHRIMPS
CREVETTES PÉNAEIDES
CAMARONES PENEIDOS

DEEPWATER SHRIMPS
CREVETTES PROFONDES
CAMARONES DE PROFUNDIDAD

DEEP SEA LOBSTERS
LANGOUSTES PROFONDES
LANGOSTAS DE PROFUNDIDAD

CRABS
CRABES
CANGREJOS

Estuaries and brackish waters
Estuaires et eaux saumâtres
Estuarios y aguas salobres

B —— B

Rivers and estuaries
Fleuves et estuaires
Ríos y estuarios

C —— C

A —— A

I. CROZET
I. KERGUELEN

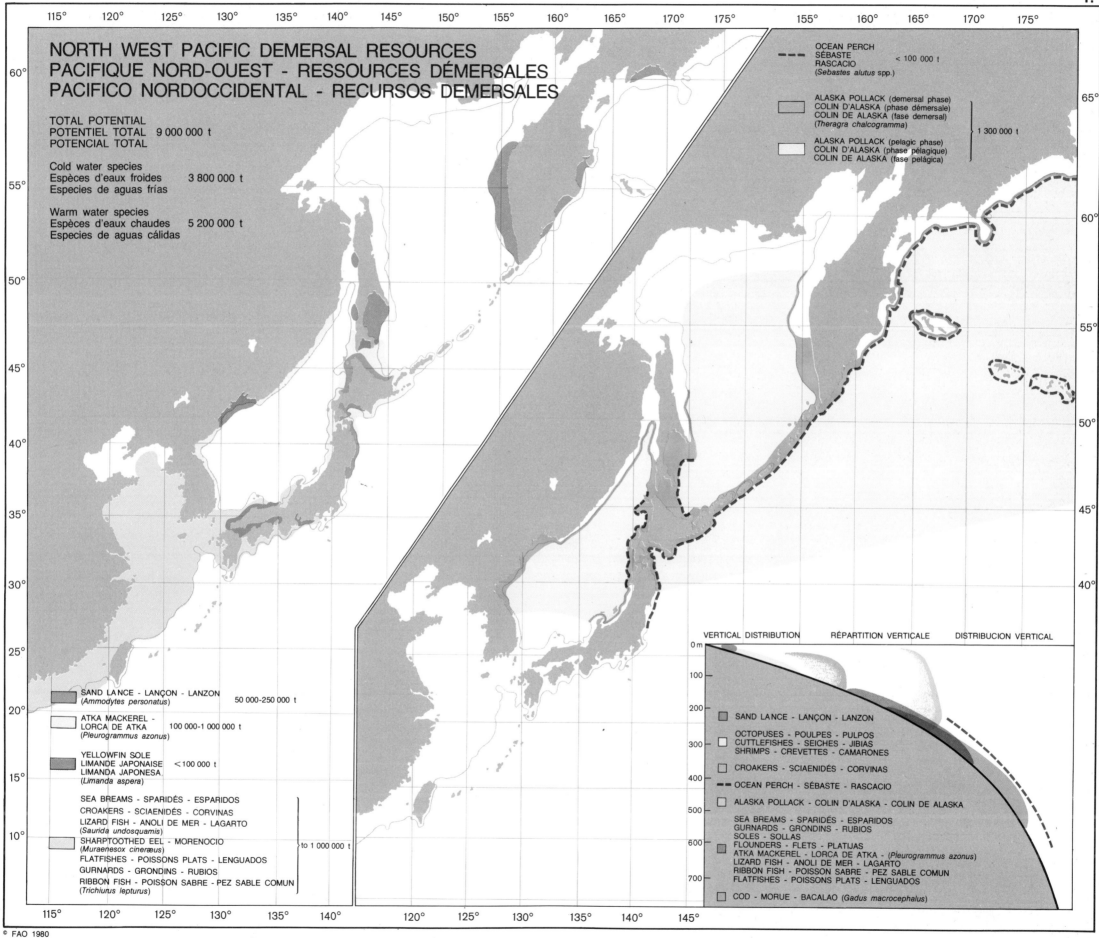

NORTH WEST PACIFIC DEMERSAL RESOURCES
PACIFIQUE NORD-OUEST - RESSOURCES DÉMERSALES
PACIFICO NORDOCCIDENTAL - RECURSOS DEMERSALES

TOTAL POTENTIAL
POTENTIEL TOTAL   9 000 000 t
POTENCIAL TOTAL

Cold water species
Espèces d'eaux froides   3 800 000 t
Especies de aguas frías

Warm water species
Espèces d'eaux chaudes   5 200 000 t
Especies de aguas cálidas

OCEAN PERCH
SÉBASTE   < 100 000 t
RASCACIO
(Sebastes alutus spp.)

ALASKA POLLACK (demersal phase)
COLIN D'ALASKA (phase démersale)
COLIN DE ALASKA (fase demersal)
(Theragra chalcogramma)   1 300 000 t

ALASKA POLLACK (pelagic phase)
COLIN D'ALASKA (phase pélagique)
COLIN DE ALASKA (fase pelágica)

SAND LANCE - LANÇON - LANZON   50 000-250 000 t
(Ammodytes personatus)

ATKA MACKEREL -
LORCA DE ATKA   100 000-1 000 000 t
(Pleurogrammus azonus)

YELLOWFIN SOLE
LIMANDE JAPONAISE   < 100 000 t
LIMANDA JAPONESA
(Limanda aspera)

SEA BREAMS - SPARIDÉS - ESPARIDOS
CROAKERS - SCIAENIDÉS - CORVINAS
LIZARD FISH - ANOLI DE MER - LAGARTO
(Saurida undosquamis)
SHARPTOOTHED EEL - MORENOCIO   to 1 000 000 t
(Muraenesox cinereæus)
FLATFISHES - POISSONS PLATS - LENGUADOS
GURNARDS - GRONDINS - RUBIOS
RIBBON FISH - POISSON SABRE - PEZ SABLE COMUN
(Trichiurus lepturus)

VERTICAL DISTRIBUTION   RÉPARTITION VERTICALE   DISTRIBUCION VERTICAL

SAND LANCE - LANÇON - LANZON

OCTOPUSES - POULPES - PULPOS
CUTTLEFISHES - SEICHES - JIBIAS
SHRIMPS - CREVETTES - CAMARONES

CROAKERS - SCIAENIDÉS - CORVINAS

OCEAN PERCH - SÉBASTE - RASCACIO

ALASKA POLLACK - COLIN D'ALASKA - COLIN DE ALASKA

SEA BREAMS - SPARIDÉS - ESPARIDOS
GURNARDS - GRONDINS - RUBIOS
SOLES - SOLLAS
FLOUNDERS - FLETS - PLATIJAS
ATKA MACKEREL - LORCA DE ATKA - (Pleurogrammus azonus)
LIZARD FISH - ANOLI DE MER - LAGARTO
RIBBON FISH - POISSON SABRE - PEZ SABLE COMUN
FLATFISHES - POISSONS PLATS - LENGUADOS

COD - MORUE - BACALAO (Gadus macrocephalus)

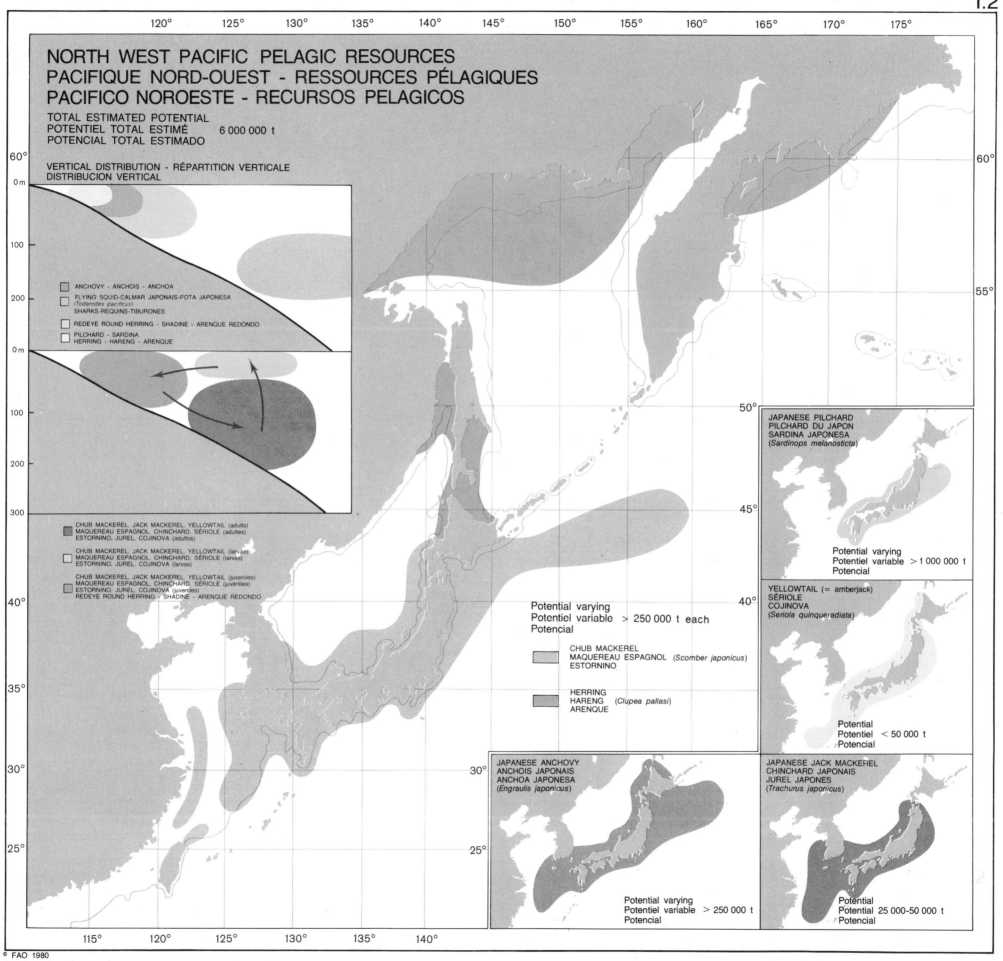

I.2

NORTH WEST PACIFIC PELAGIC RESOURCES
PACIFIQUE NORD-OUEST - RESSOURCES PÉLAGIQUES
PACIFICO NOROESTE - RECURSOS PELAGICOS

TOTAL ESTIMATED POTENTIAL
POTENTIEL TOTAL ESTIMÉ   6 000 000 t
POTENCIAL TOTAL ESTIMADO

VERTICAL DISTRIBUTION - RÉPARTITION VERTICALE
DISTRIBUCION VERTICAL

ANCHOVY - ANCHOIS - ANCHOA

FLYING SQUID-CALMAR JAPONAIS-POTA JAPONESA
(Todarodes pacificus)
SHARKS-REQUINS-TIBURONES

REDEYE ROUND HERRING - SHADINE - ARENQUE REDONDO

PILCHARD - SARDINA
HERRING - HARENG - ARENQUE

CHUB MACKEREL, JACK MACKEREL, YELLOWTAIL (adults)
MAQUEREAU ESPAGNOL, CHINCHARD, SÉRIOLE (adultes)
ESTORNINO, JUREL, COJINOVA (adultos)

CHUB MACKEREL, JACK MACKEREL, YELLOWTAIL (larvae)
MAQUEREAU ESPAGNOL, CHINCHARD, SÉRIOLE (larves)
ESTORNINO, JUREL, COJINOVA (larvas)

CHUB MACKEREL, JACK MACKEREL, YELLOWTAIL (juveniles)
MAQUEREAU ESPAGNOL, CHINCHARD, SÉRIOLE (juvéniles)
ESTORNINO, JUREL, COJINOVA (juveniles)
REDEYE ROUND HERRING - SHADINE - ARENQUE REDONDO

Potential varying
Potentiel variable > 250 000 t each
Potencial

CHUB MACKEREL
MAQUEREAU ESPAGNOL (Scomber japonicus)
ESTORNINO

HERRING
HARENG (Clupea pallasi)
ARENQUE

JAPANESE PILCHARD
PILCHARD DU JAPON
SARDINA JAPONESA
(Sardinops melanosticta)

Potential varying
Potentiel variable > 1 000 000 t
Potencial

YELLOWTAIL (= amberjack)
SÉRIOLE
COJINOVA
(Seriola quinqueradiata)

Potential
Potentiel < 50 000 t
Potencial

JAPANESE ANCHOVY
ANCHOIS JAPONAIS
ANCHOA JAPONESA
(Engraulis japonicus)

Potential varying
Potentiel variable > 250 000 t
Potencial

JAPANESE JACK MACKEREL
CHINCHARD JAPONAIS
JUREL JAPONES
(Trachurus japonicus)

Potential
Potential 25 000-50 000 t
Potencial

© FAO 1980

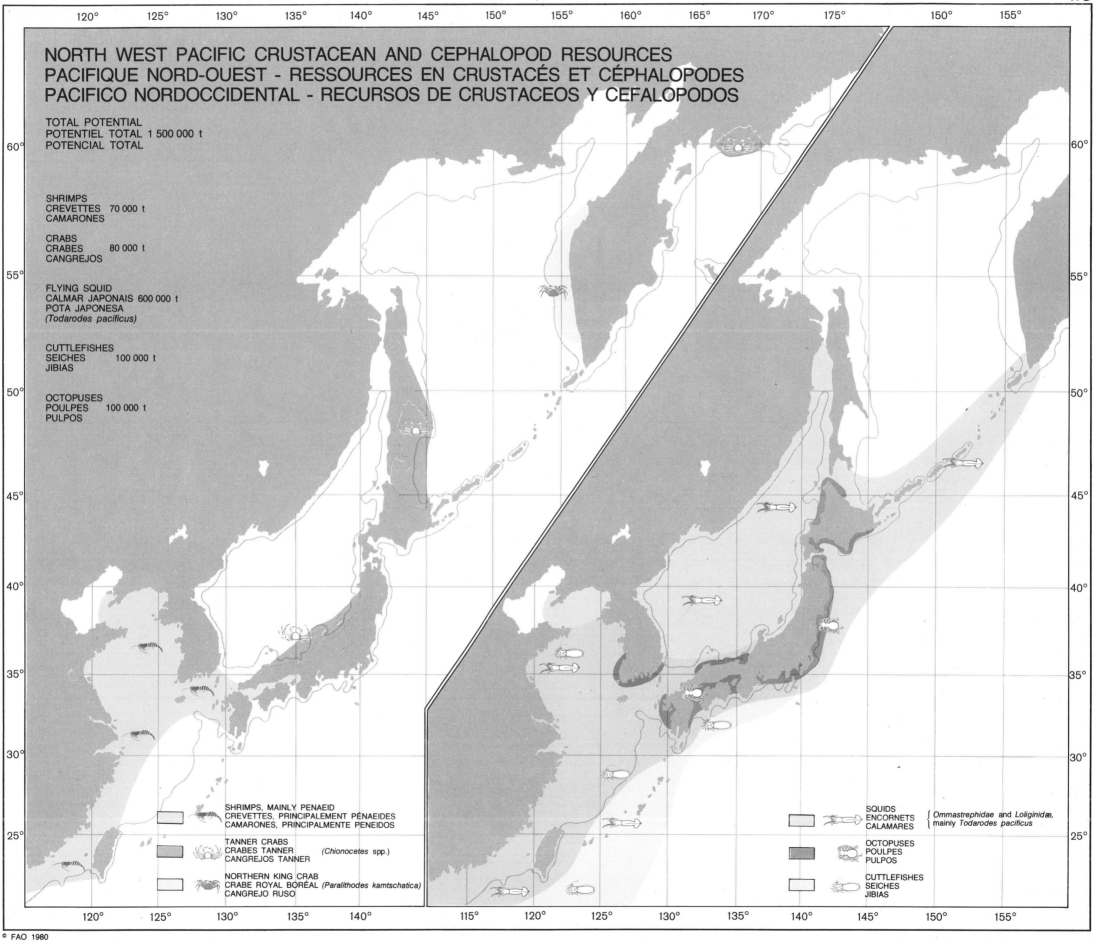

NORTH WEST PACIFIC CRUSTACEAN AND CEPHALOPOD RESOURCES
PACIFIQUE NORD-OUEST - RESSOURCES EN CRUSTACÉS ET CÉPHALOPODES
PACIFICO NORDOCCIDENTAL - RECURSOS DE CRUSTACEOS Y CEFALOPODOS

TOTAL POTENTIAL
POTENTIEL TOTAL 1 500 000 t
POTENCIAL TOTAL

SHRIMPS
CREVETTES 70 000 t
CAMARONES

CRABS
CRABES 80 000 t
CANGREJOS

FLYING SQUID
CALMAR JAPONAIS 600 000 t
POTA JAPONESA
(Todarodes pacificus)

CUTTLEFISHES
SEICHES 100 000 t
JIBIAS

OCTOPUSES
POULPES 100 000 t
PULPOS

SHRIMPS, MAINLY PENAEID
CREVETTES, PRINCIPALEMENT PÉNAEIDES
CAMARONES, PRINCIPALMENTE PENEIDOS

TANNER CRABS
CRABES TANNER (Chionocetes spp.)
CANGREJOS TANNER

NORTHERN KING CRAB
CRABE ROYAL BORÉAL (Paralithodes kamtschatica)
CANGREJO RUSO

SQUIDS
ENCORNETS { Ommastrephidae and Loliginidæ,
CALAMARES { mainly Todarodes pacificus

OCTOPUSES
POULPES
PULPOS

CUTTLEFISHES
SEICHES
JIBIAS

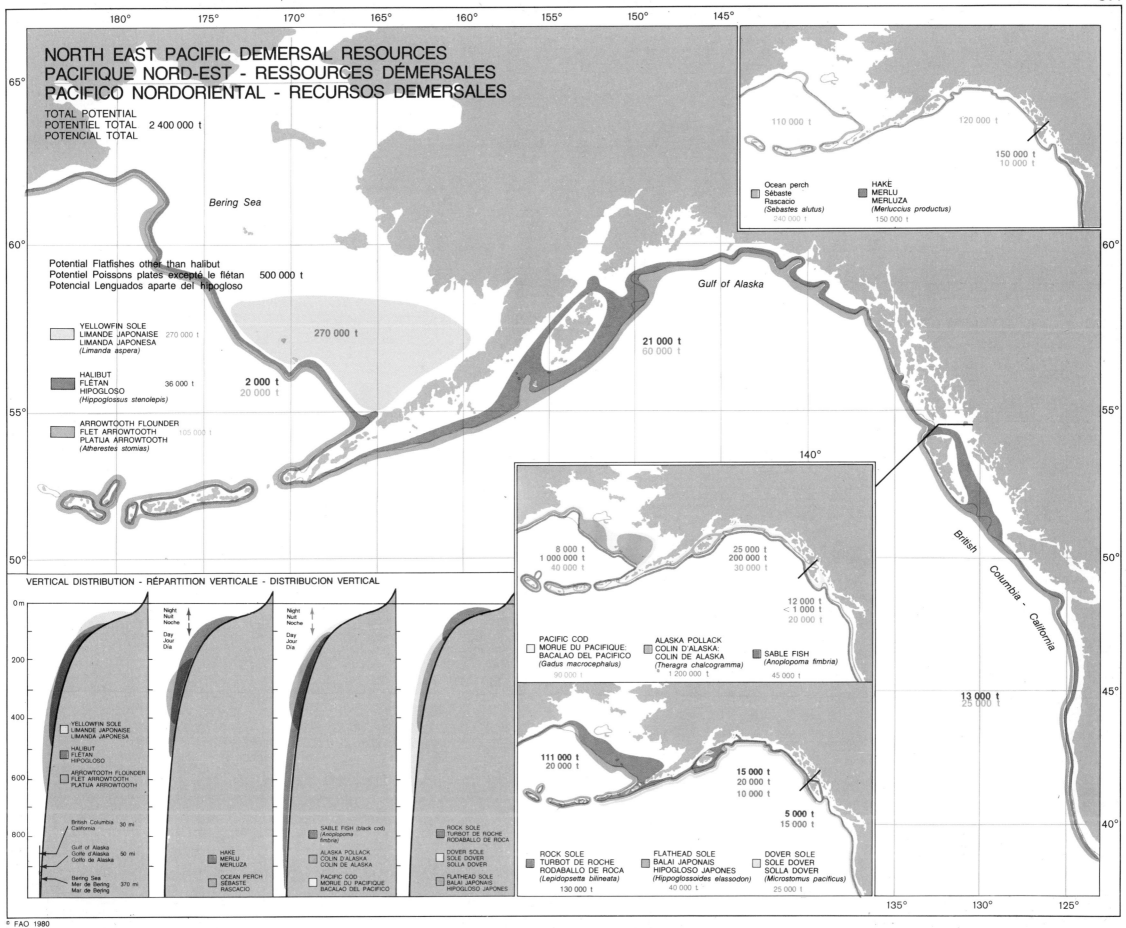

NORTH EAST PACIFIC DEMERSAL RESOURCES
PACIFIQUE NORD-EST - RESSOURCES DÉMERSALES
PACIFICO NORDORIENTAL - RECURSOS DEMERSALES

TOTAL POTENTIAL
POTENTIEL TOTAL   2 400 000 t
POTENCIAL TOTAL

Potential Flatfishes other than halibut
Potentiel Poissons plates excepté le flétan   500 000 t
Potencial Lenguados aparte del hipogloso

YELLOWFIN SOLE
LIMANDE JAPONAISE   270 000 t
LIMANDA JAPONESA
(Limanda aspera)

HALIBUT
FLÉTAN   36 000 t
HIPOGLOSO
(Hippoglossus stenolepis)

ARROWTOOTH FLOUNDER
FLET ARROWTOOTH   105 000 t
PLATIJA ARROWTOOTH
(Atherestes stomias)

Bering Sea

Gulf of Alaska

British Columbia - California

270 000 t

2 000 t
20 000 t

21 000 t
60 000 t

Ocean perch inset
110 000 t   120 000 t
150 000 t
10 000 t

Ocean perch
Sébaste
Rascacio
(Sebastes alutus)
240 000 t

HAKE
MERLU
MERLUZA
(Merluccius productus)
150 000 t

Pacific cod / Alaska pollack / Sable fish inset
8 000 t   25 000 t
1 000 000 t   200 000 t
40 000 t   30 000 t

12 000 t
< 1 000 t
20 000 t

PACIFIC COD
MORUE DU PACIFIQUE:
BACALAO DEL PACIFICO
(Gadus macrocephalus)
90 000 t

ALASKA POLLACK
COLIN D'ALASKA:
COLIN DE ALASKA
(Theragra chalcogramma)
1 200 000 t

SABLE FISH
(Anoplopoma fimbria)
45 000 t

13 000 t
25 000 t

Rock sole / Flathead sole / Dover sole inset
111 000 t
20 000 t

15 000 t
20 000 t
10 000 t

5 000 t
15 000 t

ROCK SOLE
TURBOT DE ROCHE
RODABALLO DE ROCA
(Lepidopsetta bilineata)
130 000 t

FLATHEAD SOLE
BALAI JAPONAIS
HIPOGLOSO JAPONES
(Hippoglossoides elassodon)
40 000 t

DOVER SOLE
SOLE DOVER
SOLLA DOVER
(Microstomus pacificus)
25 000 t

VERTICAL DISTRIBUTION - RÉPARTITION VERTICALE - DISTRIBUCION VERTICAL

0 m
200
400
600
800

Night
Nuit
Noche

Day
Jour
Dia

YELLOWFIN SOLE
LIMANDE JAPONAISE
LIMANDA JAPONESA

HALIBUT
FLÉTAN
HIPOGLOSO

ARROWTOOTH FLOUNDER
FLET ARROWTOOTH
PLATIJA ARROWTOOTH

British Columbia
California   30 mi

Gulf of Alaska
Golfe d'Alaska   50 mi
Golfo de Alaska

Bering Sea
Mer de Bering   370 mi
Mar de Bering

HAKE
MERLU
MERLUZA

OCEAN PERCH
SÉBASTE
RASCACIO

SABLE FISH (black cod)
(Anoplopoma
fimbria)

ALASKA POLLACK
COLIN D'ALASKA
COLIN DE ALASKA

PACIFIC COD
MORUE DU PACIFIQUE
BACALAO DEL PACIFICO

ROCK SOLE
TURBOT DE ROCHE
RODABALLO DE ROCA

DOVER SOLE
SOLE DOVER
SOLLA DOVER

FLATHEAD SOLE
BALAI JAPONAIS
HIPOGLOSO JAPONES

© FAO 1980

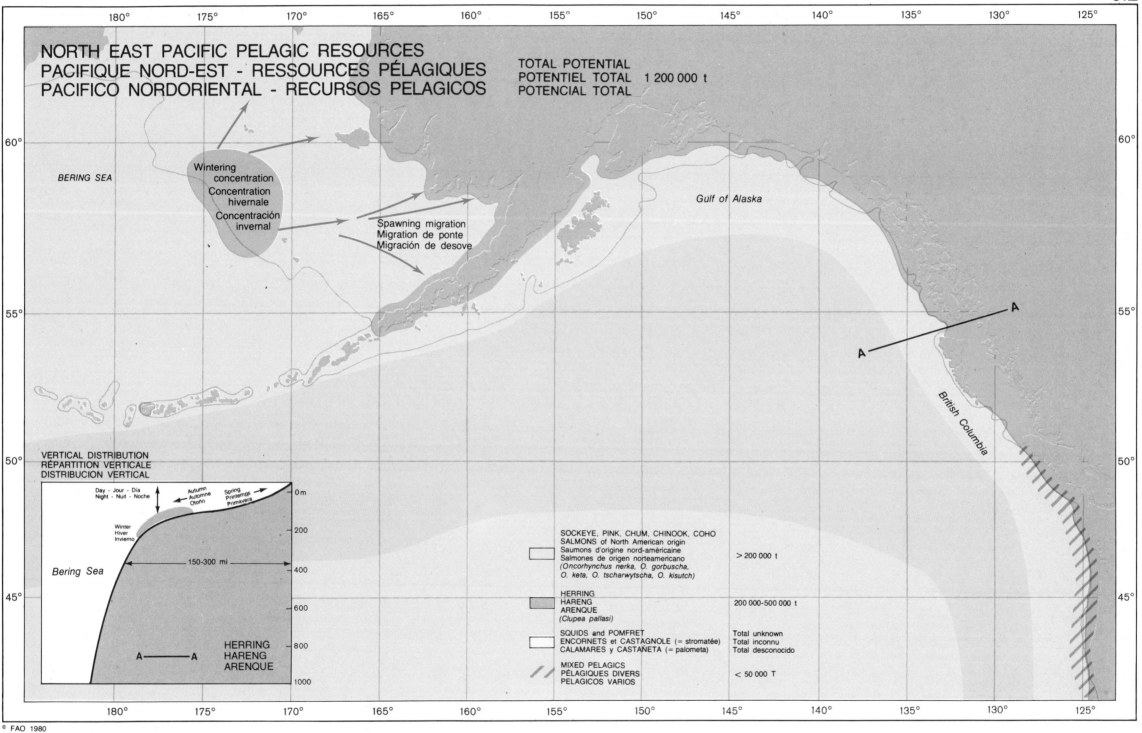

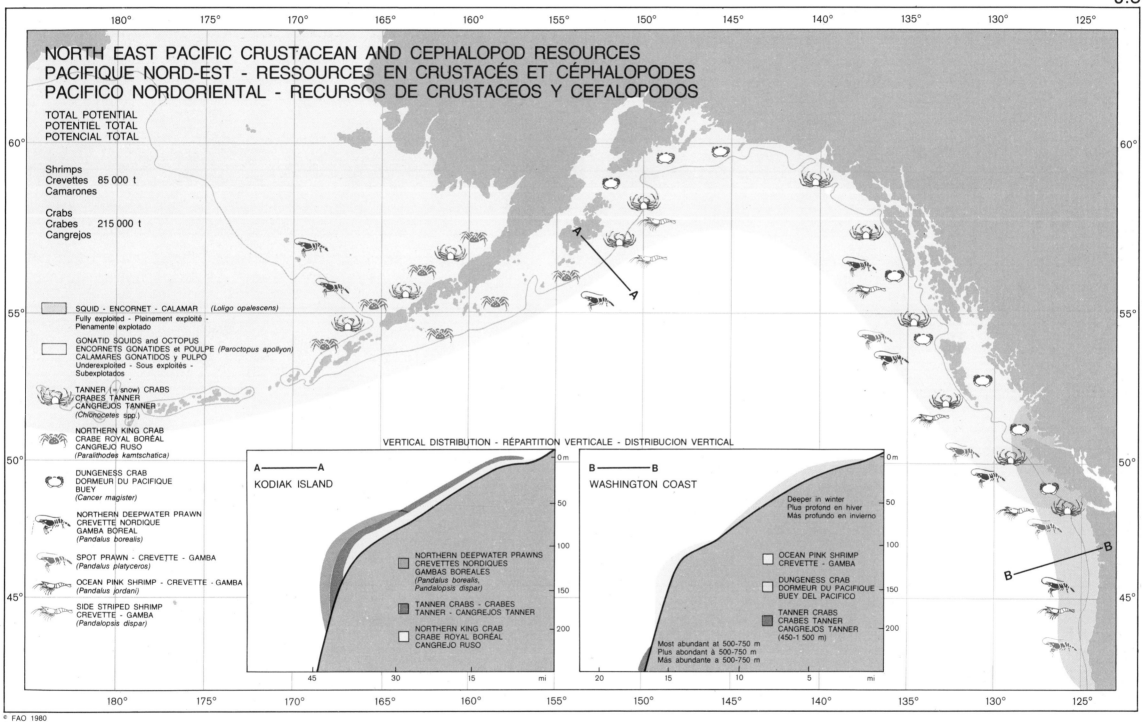

NORTH EAST PACIFIC CRUSTACEAN AND CEPHALOPOD RESOURCES
PACIFIQUE NORD-EST - RESSOURCES EN CRUSTACÉS ET CÉPHALOPODES
PACIFICO NORDORIENTAL - RECURSOS DE CRUSTACEOS Y CEFALOPODOS

TOTAL POTENTIAL
POTENTIEL TOTAL
POTENCIAL TOTAL

Shrimps
Crevettes 85 000 t
Camarones

Crabs
Crabes 215 000 t
Cangrejos

SQUID - ENCORNET - CALAMAR (Loligo opalescens)
Fully exploited - Pleinement exploité -
Plenamente explotado

GONATID SQUIDS and OCTOPUS
ENCORNETS GONATIDES et POULPE (Paroctopus apollyon)
CALAMARES GONATIDOS y PULPO
Underexploited - Sous exploités -
Subexplotados

TANNER (= snow) CRABS
CRABES TANNER
CANGREJOS TANNER
(Chionocetes spp.)

NORTHERN KING CRAB
CRABE ROYAL BORÉAL
CANGREJO RUSO
(Paralithodes kamtschatica)

DUNGENESS CRAB
DORMEUR DU PACIFIQUE
BUEY
(Cancer magister)

NORTHERN DEEPWATER PRAWN
CREVETTE NORDIQUE
GAMBA BOREAL
(Pandalus borealis)

SPOT PRAWN - CREVETTE - GAMBA
(Pandalus platyceros)

OCEAN PINK SHRIMP - CREVETTE - GAMBA
(Pandalus jordani)

SIDE STRIPED SHRIMP
CREVETTE - GAMBA
(Pandalopsis dispar)

VERTICAL DISTRIBUTION - RÉPARTITION VERTICALE - DISTRIBUCION VERTICAL

A ——— A
KODIAK ISLAND

NORTHERN DEEPWATER PRAWNS
CREVETTES NORDIQUES
GAMBAS BOREALES
(Pandalus borealis,
Pandalopsis dispar)

TANNER CRABS - CRABES
TANNER - CANGREJOS TANNER

NORTHERN KING CRAB
CRABE ROYAL BORÉAL
CANGREJO RUSO

45   30   15   mi

B ——— B
WASHINGTON COAST

Deeper in winter
Plus profond en hiver
Más profundo en invierno

OCEAN PINK SHRIMP
CREVETTE - GAMBA

DUNGENESS CRAB
DORMEUR DU PACIFICO
BUEY DEL PACIFICO

TANNER CRABS
CRABES TANNER
CANGREJOS TANNER
(450-1 500 m)

Most abundant at 500-750 m
Plus abondant à 500-750 m
Más abundante a 500-750 m

20   15   10   5   mi

© FAO 1980

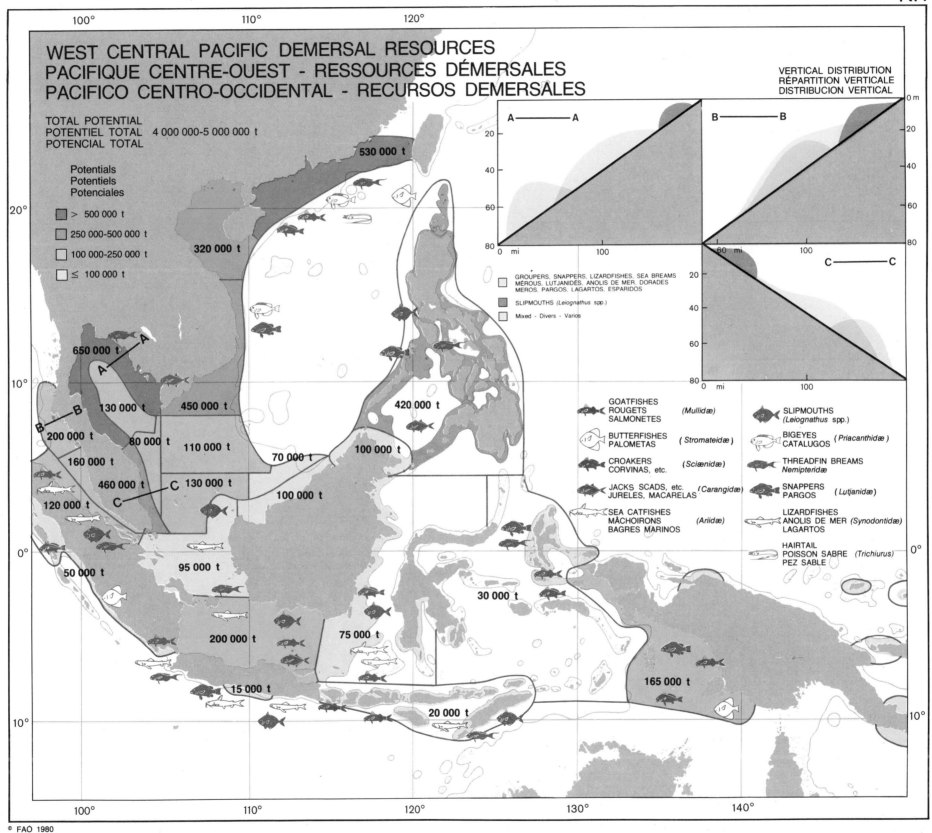

WEST CENTRAL PACIFIC DEMERSAL RESOURCES
PACIFIQUE CENTRE-OUEST - RESSOURCES DÉMERSALES
PACIFICO CENTRO-OCCIDENTAL - RECURSOS DEMERSALES

TOTAL POTENTIAL
POTENTIEL TOTAL   4 000 000-5 000 000 t
POTENCIAL TOTAL

Potentials
Potentiels
Potenciales

> 500 000 t
250 000-500 000 t
100 000-250 000 t
≤ 100 000 t

VERTICAL DISTRIBUTION
RÉPARTITION VERTICALE
DISTRIBUCION VERTICAL

GROUPERS, SNAPPERS, LIZARDFISHES, SEA BREAMS
MÉROUS, LUTJANIDÉS, ANOLIS DE MER, DORADES
MEROS, PARGOS, LAGARTOS, ESPARIDOS

SLIPMOUTHS (Leiognathus spp.)

Mixed - Divers - Varios

530 000 t
320 000 t
650 000 t
130 000 t   450 000 t
200 000 t
80 000 t   110 000 t
160 000 t
460 000 t   130 000 t
120 000 t
70 000 t   100 000 t
420 000 t
100 000 t
50 000 t
95 000 t
30 000 t
200 000 t   75 000 t
165 000 t
15 000 t
20 000 t

GOATFISHES
ROUGETS   (Mullidæ)
SALMONETES

BUTTERFISHES
PALOMETAS   (Stromateidæ)

CROAKERS
CORVINAS, etc.   (Sciænidæ)

JACKS SCADS, etc.
JURELES, MACARELAS   (Carangidæ)

SEA CATFISHES
MÂCHOIRONS   (Ariidæ)
BAGRES MARINOS

SLIPMOUTHS
(Leiognathus spp.)

BIGEYES
CATALUGOS   (Priacanthidæ)

THREADFIN BREAMS
Nemipteridæ

SNAPPERS
PARGOS   (Lutjanidæ)

LIZARDFISHES
ANOLIS DE MER (Synodontidæ)
LAGARTOS

HAIRTAIL
POISSON SABRE   (Trichiurus)
PEZ SABLE

© FAO 1980

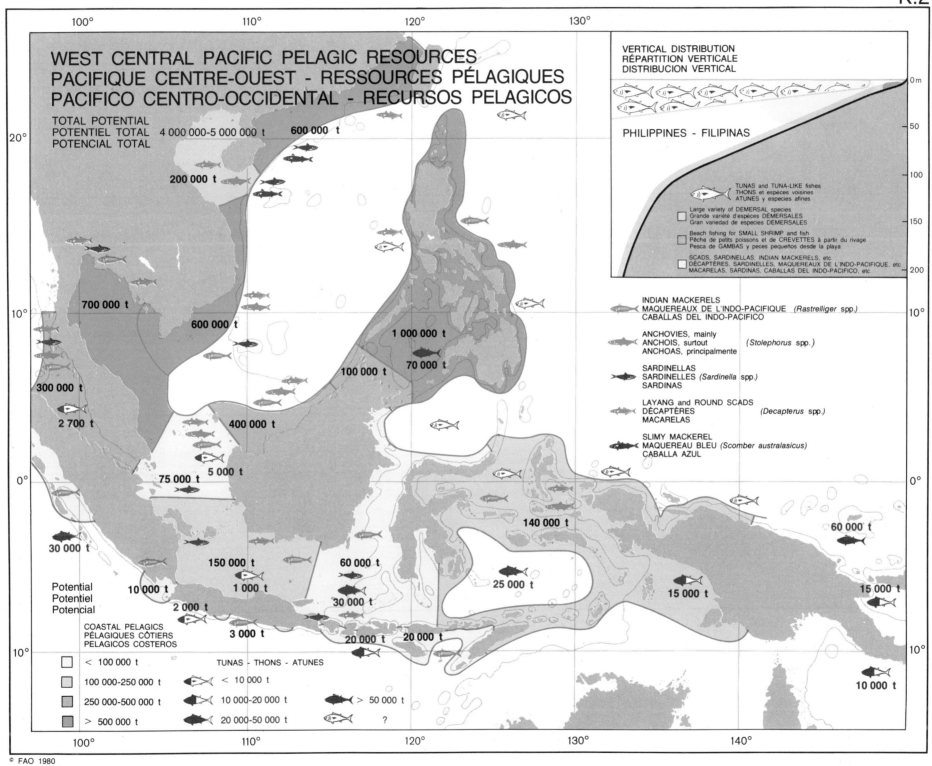

WEST CENTRAL PACIFIC PELAGIC RESOURCES
PACIFIQUE CENTRE-OUEST - RESSOURCES PÉLAGIQUES
PACIFICO CENTRO-OCCIDENTAL - RECURSOS PELAGICOS

TOTAL POTENTIAL
POTENTIEL TOTAL   4 000 000-5 000 000 t
POTENCIAL TOTAL

600 000 t

200 000 t

700 000 t

600 000 t

1 000 000 t

70 000 t

300 000 t

100 000 t

2 700 t

400 000 t

75 000 t   5 000 t

140 000 t

60 000 t

30 000 t

150 000 t

60 000 t

25 000 t

15 000 t

15 000 t

10 000 t   1 000 t

30 000 t

Potential
Potentiel
Potencial

2 000 t

3 000 t

20 000 t   20 000 t

10 000 t

COASTAL PELAGICS
PÉLAGIQUES CÔTIERS
PELAGICOS COSTEROS

TUNAS - THONS - ATUNES

☐	< 100 000 t	
☐	100 000-250 000 t	< 10 000 t
☐	250 000-500 000 t	10 000-20 000 t
☐	> 500 000 t	20 000-50 000 t

> 50 000 t

?

VERTICAL DISTRIBUTION
RÉPARTITION VERTICALE
DISTRIBUCION VERTICAL

0 m

50

PHILIPPINES - FILIPINAS

100

150

TUNAS and TUNA-LIKE fishes
THONS et espèces voisines
ATUNES y especies afines

Large variety of DEMERSAL species
Grande variété d'espèces DÉMERSALES
Gran variedad de especies DEMERSALES

Beach fishing for SMALL SHRIMP and fish
Pêche de petits poissons et de CREVETTES à partir du rivage
Pesca de GAMBAS y peces pequeños desde la playa

SCADS, SARDINELLAS, INDIAN MACKERELS, etc
DÉCAPTÈRES, SARDINELLES, MAQUEREAUX DE L'INDO-PACIFIQUE, etc.
MACARELAS, SARDINAS, CABALLAS DEL INDO-PACIFICO, etc.

200

INDIAN MACKERELS
MAQUEREAUX DE L'INDO-PACIFIQUE   (Rastrelliger spp.)
CABALLAS DEL INDO-PACIFICO

ANCHOVIES, mainly
ANCHOIS, surtout   (Stolephorus spp.)
ANCHOAS, principalmente

SARDINELLAS
SARDINELLES (Sardinella spp.)
SARDINAS

LAYANG and ROUND SCADS
DÉCAPTÈRES   (Decapterus spp.)
MACARELAS

SLIMY MACKEREL
MAQUEREAU BLEU (Scomber australasicus)
CABALLA AZUL

© FAO 1980

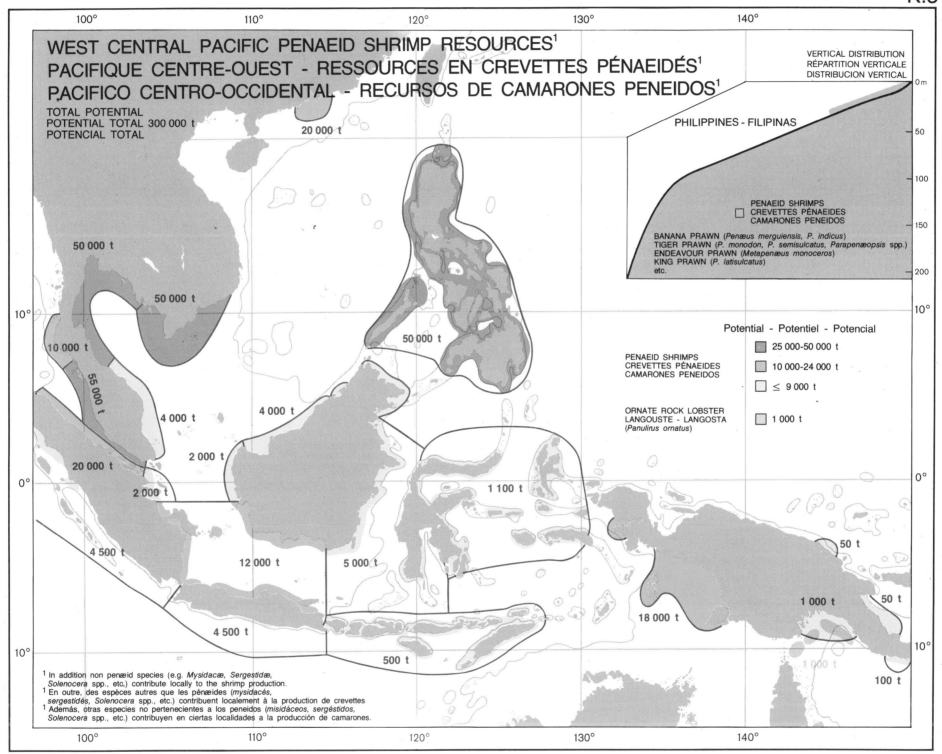

WEST CENTRAL PACIFIC PENAEID SHRIMP RESOURCES[1]
PACIFIQUE CENTRE-OUEST - RESSOURCES EN CREVETTES PÉNAEIDÉS[1]
PACIFICO CENTRO-OCCIDENTAL - RECURSOS DE CAMARONES PENEIDOS[1]

TOTAL POTENTIAL
POTENTIAL TOTAL 300 000 t
POTENCIAL TOTAL

VERTICAL DISTRIBUTION
RÉPARTITION VERTICALE
DISTRIBUCION VERTICAL

PHILIPPINES - FILIPINAS

PENAEID SHRIMPS
CREVETTES PÉNAEIDES
CAMARONES PENEIDOS

BANANA PRAWN (*Penæus merguiensis, P. indicus*)
TIGER PRAWN (*P. monodon, P. semisulcatus, Parapenæopsis* spp.)
ENDEAVOUR PRAWN (*Metapenæus monoceros*)
KING PRAWN (*P. latisulcatus*)
etc.

Potential - Potentiel - Potencial

PENAEID SHRIMPS
CREVETTES PÉNAEIDES
CAMARONES PENEIDOS

25 000-50 000 t
10 000-24 000 t
≤ 9 000 t

ORNATE ROCK LOBSTER
LANGOUSTE - LANGOSTA
(*Panulirus ornatus*)

1 000 t

[1] In addition non penæid species (e.g. *Mysidacæ, Sergestidæ, Solenocera* spp., etc.) contribute locally to the shrimp production.
[1] En outre, des espèces autres que les pénæides (*mysidacés, sergestidés, Solenocera* spp., etc.) contribuent localement à la production de crevettes
[1] Además, otras especies no pertenecientes a los peneidos (*misidáceos, sergéstidos, Solenocera* spp., etc.) contribuyen en ciertas localidades a la producción de camarones.

© FAO 1980

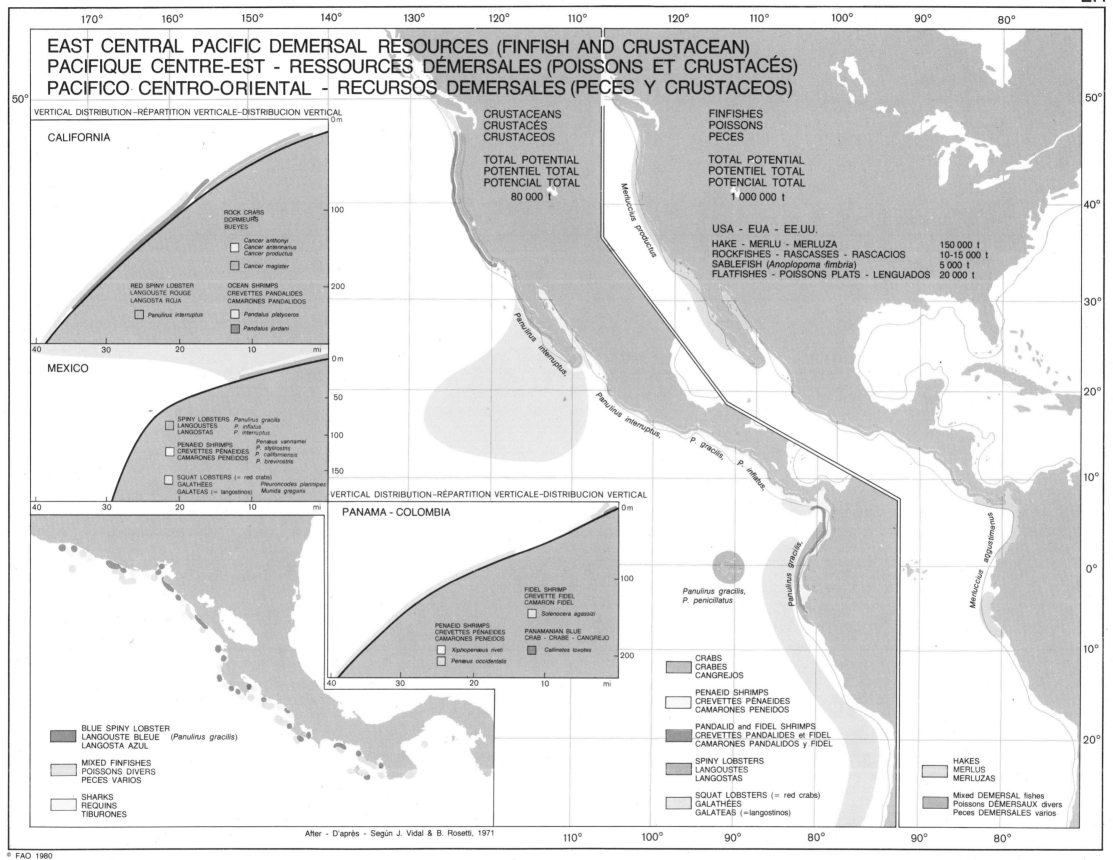

EAST CENTRAL PACIFIC DEMERSAL RESOURCES (FINFISH AND CRUSTACEAN)
PACIFIQUE CENTRE-EST - RESSOURCES DÉMERSALES (POISSONS ET CRUSTACÉS)
PACIFICO CENTRO-ORIENTAL - RECURSOS DEMERSALES (PECES Y CRUSTACEOS)

After - D'après - Según J. Vidal & B. Rosetti, 1971

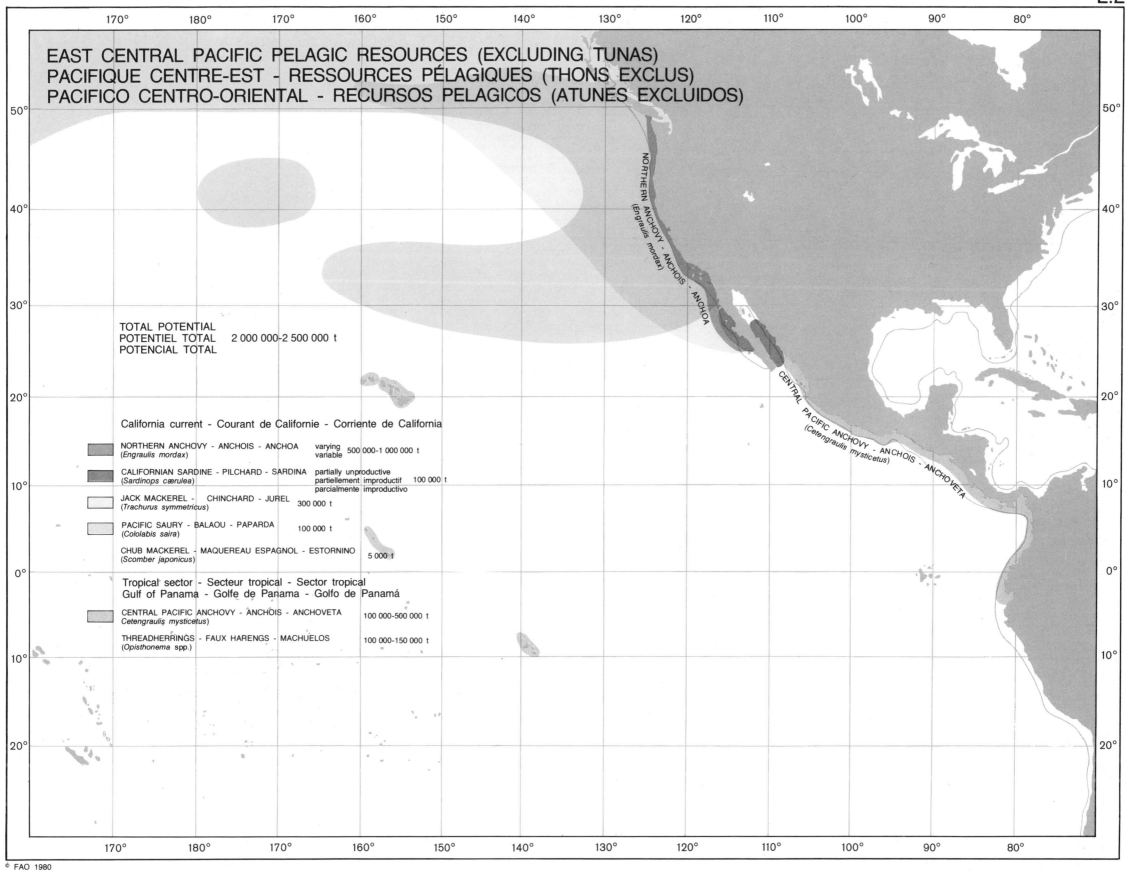

EAST CENTRAL PACIFIC PELAGIC RESOURCES (EXCLUDING TUNAS)
PACIFIQUE CENTRE-EST - RESSOURCES PÉLAGIQUES (THONS EXCLUS)
PACIFICO CENTRO-ORIENTAL - RECURSOS PELAGICOS (ATUNES EXCLUIDOS)

TOTAL POTENTIAL
POTENTIEL TOTAL   2 000 000-2 500 000 t
POTENCIAL TOTAL

California current - Courant de Californie - Corriente de California

NORTHERN ANCHOVY - ANCHOIS - ANCHOA   varying   500 000-1 000 000 t
(Engraulis mordax)   variable

CALIFORNIAN SARDINE - PILCHARD - SARDINA   partially unproductive
(Sardinops cærulea)   partiellement improductif   100 000 t
                                             parcialmente improductivo

JACK MACKEREL -   CHINCHARD - JUREL
(Trachurus symmetricus)   300 000 t

PACIFIC SAURY - BALAOU - PAPARDA
(Cololabis saira)   100 000 t

CHUB MACKEREL - MAQUEREAU ESPAGNOL - ESTORNINO
(Scomber japonicus)   5 000 t

Tropical sector - Secteur tropical - Sector tropical
Gulf of Panama - Golfe de Panama - Golfo de Panamá

CENTRAL PACIFIC ANCHOVY - ANCHOIS - ANCHOVETA
Cetengraulis mysticetus)   100 000-500 000 t

THREADHERRINGS - FAUX HARENGS - MACHUELOS
(Opisthonema spp.)   100 000-150 000 t

NORTHERN ANCHOVY - ANCHOIS - ANCHOA
(Engraulis mordax)

CENTRAL PACIFIC ANCHOVY - ANCHOIS - ANCHOVETA
(Cetengraulis mysticetus)

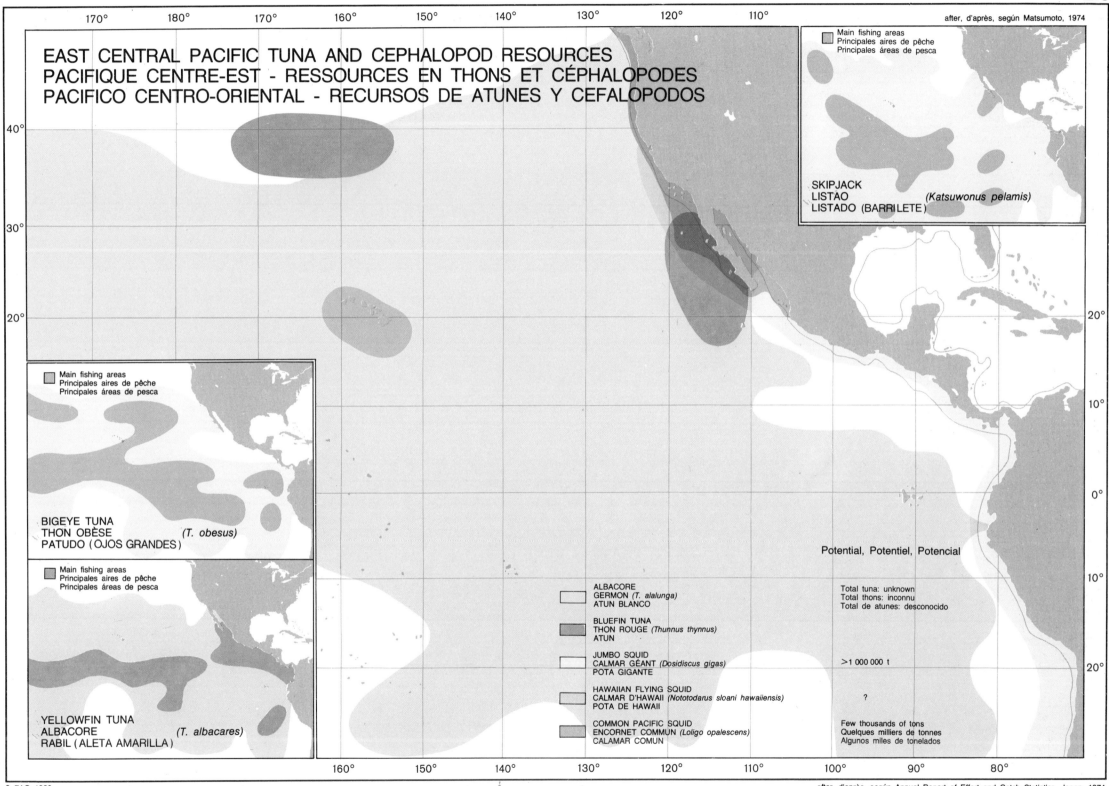

L.3

after, d'après, según Matsumoto, 1974

EAST CENTRAL PACIFIC TUNA AND CEPHALOPOD RESOURCES
PACIFIQUE CENTRE-EST - RESSOURCES EN THONS ET CÉPHALOPODES
PACIFICO CENTRO-ORIENTAL - RECURSOS DE ATUNES Y CEFALOPODOS

Main fishing areas
Principales aires de pêche
Principales áreas de pesca

SKIPJACK
LISTAO   (Katsuwonus pelamis)
LISTADO (BARRILETE)

Main fishing areas
Principales aires de pêche
Principales áreas de pesca

BIGEYE TUNA
THON OBÈSE   (T. obesus)
PATUDO (OJOS GRANDES)

Main fishing areas
Principales aires de pêche
Principales áreas de pesca

YELLOWFIN TUNA
ALBACORE   (T. albacares)
RABIL (ALETA AMARILLA)

Potential, Potentiel, Potencial

ALBACORE
GERMON (T. alalunga)
ATUN BLANCO

Total tuna: unknown
Total thons: inconnu
Total de atunes: desconocido

BLUEFIN TUNA
THON ROUGE (Thunnus thynnus)
ATUN

JUMBO SQUID
CALMAR GÉANT (Dosidiscus gigas)
POTA GIGANTE

>1 000 000 t

HAWAIIAN FLYING SQUID
CALMAR D'HAWAII (Nototodarus sloani hawaiiensis)
POTA DE HAWAII

?

COMMON PACIFIC SQUID
ENCORNET COMMUN (Loligo opalescens)
CALAMAR COMUN

Few thousands of tons
Quelques milliers de tonnes
Algunos miles de toneladas

© FAO 1980

after, d'après, según Annual Report of Effort and Catch Statistics, Japan, 1974

EAST CENTRAL PACIFIC - VERTICAL DISTRIBUTION OF PELAGIC RESOURCES
PACIFIQUE CENTRE-EST - RÉPARTITION VERTICALE DES RESSOURCES PÉLAGIQUES
PACIFICO CENTRO-ORIENTAL - DISTRIBUCION VERTICAL DE RECURSOS PELAGICOS

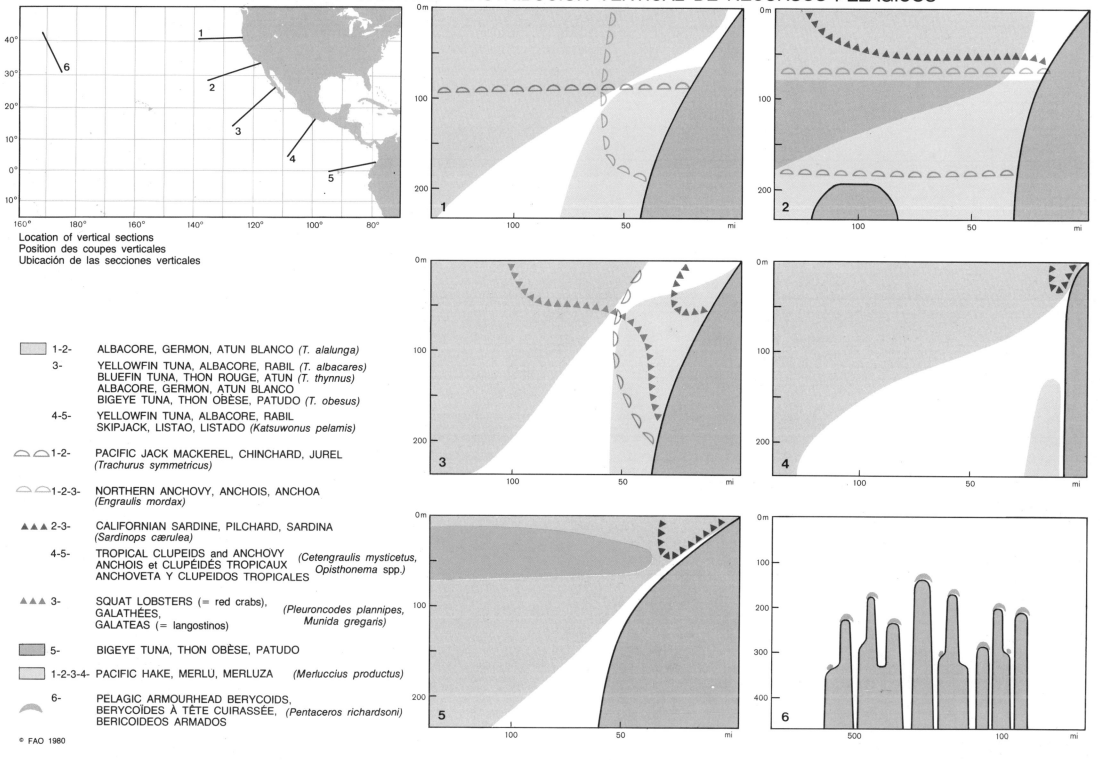

Location of vertical sections
Position des coupes verticales
Ubicación de las secciones verticales

1-2- ALBACORE, GERMON, ATUN BLANCO (T. alalunga)

3- YELLOWFIN TUNA, ALBACORE, RABIL (T. albacares)
BLUEFIN TUNA, THON ROUGE, ATUN (T. thynnus)
ALBACORE, GERMON, ATUN BLANCO
BIGEYE TUNA, THON OBÈSE, PATUDO (T. obesus)

4-5- YELLOWFIN TUNA, ALBACORE, RABIL
SKIPJACK, LISTAO, LISTADO (Katsuwonus pelamis)

1-2- PACIFIC JACK MACKEREL, CHINCHARD, JUREL
(Trachurus symmetricus)

1-2-3- NORTHERN ANCHOVY, ANCHOIS, ANCHOA
(Engraulis mordax)

2-3- CALIFORNIAN SARDINE, PILCHARD, SARDINA
(Sardinops cærulea)

4-5- TROPICAL CLUPEIDS and ANCHOVY (Cetengraulis mysticetus,
ANCHOIS et CLUPÉIDÉS TROPICAUX Opisthonema spp.)
ANCHOVETA Y CLUPEIDOS TROPICALES

3- SQUAT LOBSTERS (= red crabs), (Pleuroncodes plannipes,
GALATHÉES, Munida gregaris)
GALATEAS (= langostinos)

5- BIGEYE TUNA, THON OBÈSE, PATUDO

1-2-3-4- PACIFIC HAKE, MERLU, MERLUZA (Merluccius productus)

6- PELAGIC ARMOURHEAD BERYCOIDS,
BERYCOÏDES À TÊTE CUIRASSÉE, (Pentaceros richardsoni)
BERICOIDEOS ARMADOS

© FAO 1980

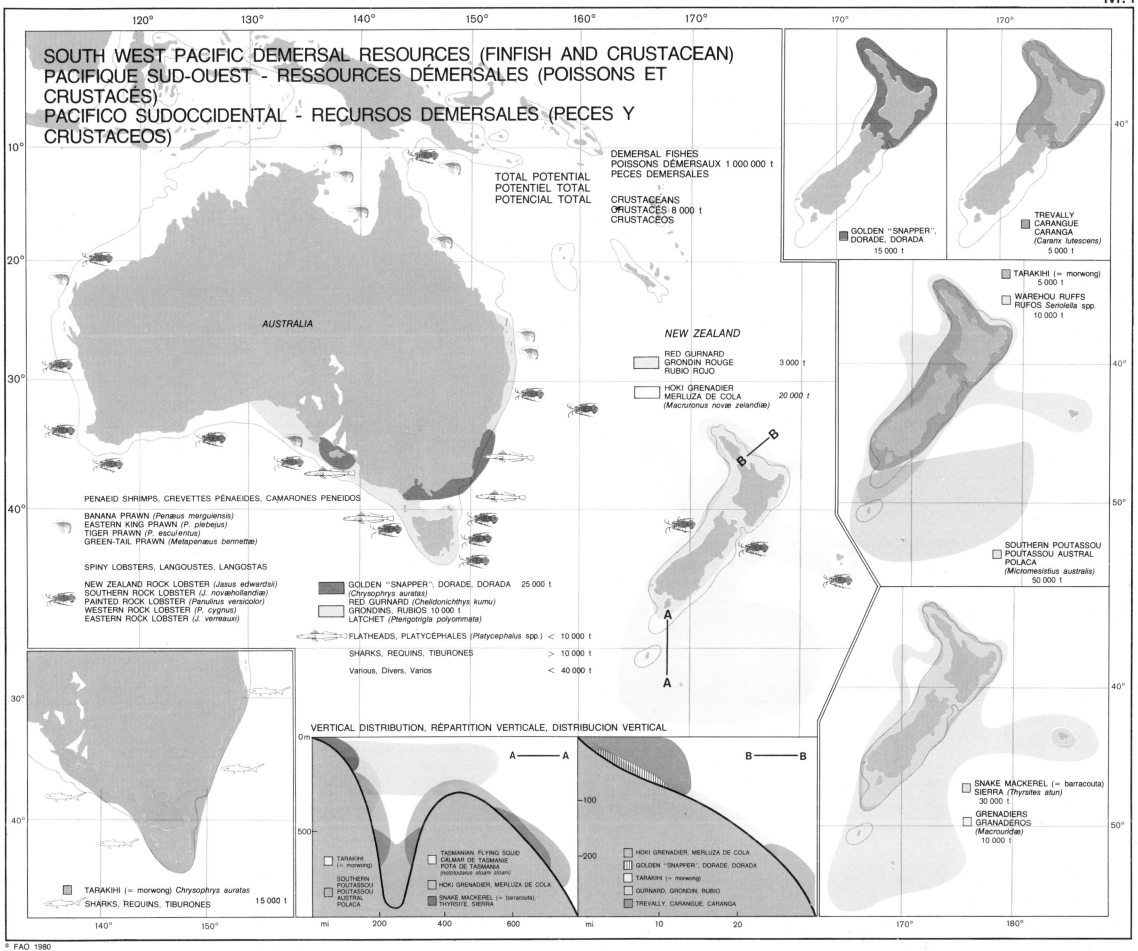

SOUTH WEST PACIFIC DEMERSAL RESOURCES (FINFISH AND CRUSTACEAN)
PACIFIQUE SUD-OUEST - RESSOURCES DÉMERSALES (POISSONS ET CRUSTACÉS)
PACIFICO SUDOCCIDENTAL - RECURSOS DEMERSALES (PECES Y CRUSTACEOS)

DEMERSAL FISHES
POISSONS DÉMERSAUX 1 000 000 t
PECES DEMERSALES

TOTAL POTENTIAL
POTENTIEL TOTAL
POTENCIAL TOTAL

CRUSTACEANS
CRUSTACÉS 8 000 t
CRUSTACEOS

AUSTRALIA

NEW ZEALAND

RED GURNARD
GRONDIN ROUGE   3 000 t
RUBIO ROJO

HOKI GRENADIER
MERLUZA DE COLA   20 000 t
(Macruronus novæ zelandiæ)

PENAEID SHRIMPS, CREVETTES PÉNAEIDES, CAMARONES PENEIDOS

BANANA PRAWN (Penæus merguiensis)
EASTERN KING PRAWN (P. plebejus)
TIGER PRAWN (P. esculentus)
GREEN-TAIL PRAWN (Metapenæus bennettæ)

SPINY LOBSTERS, LANGOUSTES, LANGOSTAS

NEW ZEALAND ROCK LOBSTER (Jasus edwardsii)
SOUTHERN ROCK LOBSTER (J. novæhollandiæ)
PAINTED ROCK LOBSTER (Panulirus versicolor)
WESTERN ROCK LOBSTER (P. cygnus)
EASTERN ROCK LOBSTER (J. verreauxi)

GOLDEN "SNAPPER", DORADE, DORADA   25 000 t
(Chrysophrys auratas)
RED GURNARD (Chelidonichthys kumu)
GRONDINS, RUBIOS 10 000 t
LATCHET (Pterigotrigla polyommata)

FLATHEADS, PLATYCÉPHALES (Platycephalus spp.) < 10 000 t

SHARKS, REQUINS, TIBURONES   > 10 000 t

Various, Divers, Varios   < 40 000 t

GOLDEN "SNAPPER",
DORADE, DORADA
15 000 t

TREVALLY
CARANGUE
CARANGA
(Caranx lutescens)
5 000 t

TARAKIHI (= morwong)
5 000 t

WAREHOU RUFFS
RUFOS Seriolella spp.
10 000 t

SOUTHERN POUTASSOU
POUTASSOU AUSTRAL
POLACA
(Micromesistius australis)
50 000 t

SNAKE MACKEREL (= barracouta)
SIERRA (Thyrsites atun)
30 000 t

GRENADIERS
GRANADEROS
(Macrouridæ)
10 000 t

TARAKIHI (= morwong) Chrysophrys auratas
SHARKS, REQUINS, TIBURONES   15 000 t

VERTICAL DISTRIBUTION, RÉPARTITION VERTICALE, DISTRIBUCION VERTICAL

0 m

A — A

TARAKIHI
(= morwong)

SOUTHERN
POUTASSOU
POUTASSOU
AUSTRAL
POLACA

TASMANIAN FLYING SQUID
CALMAR DE TASMANIE
POTA DE TASMANIA
(nototodarus sloani sloani)

HOKI GRENADIER, MERLUZA DE COLA

SNAKE MACKEREL (= barracouta),
THYRSITE, SIERRA

500

B — B

-100

-200

HOKI GRENADIER, MERLUZA DE COLA

GOLDEN "SNAPPER", DORADE, DORADA

TARAKIHI (= morwong)

GURNARD, GRONDIN, RUBIO

TREVALLY, CARANGUE, CARANGA

mi   200   400   600

mi   10   20

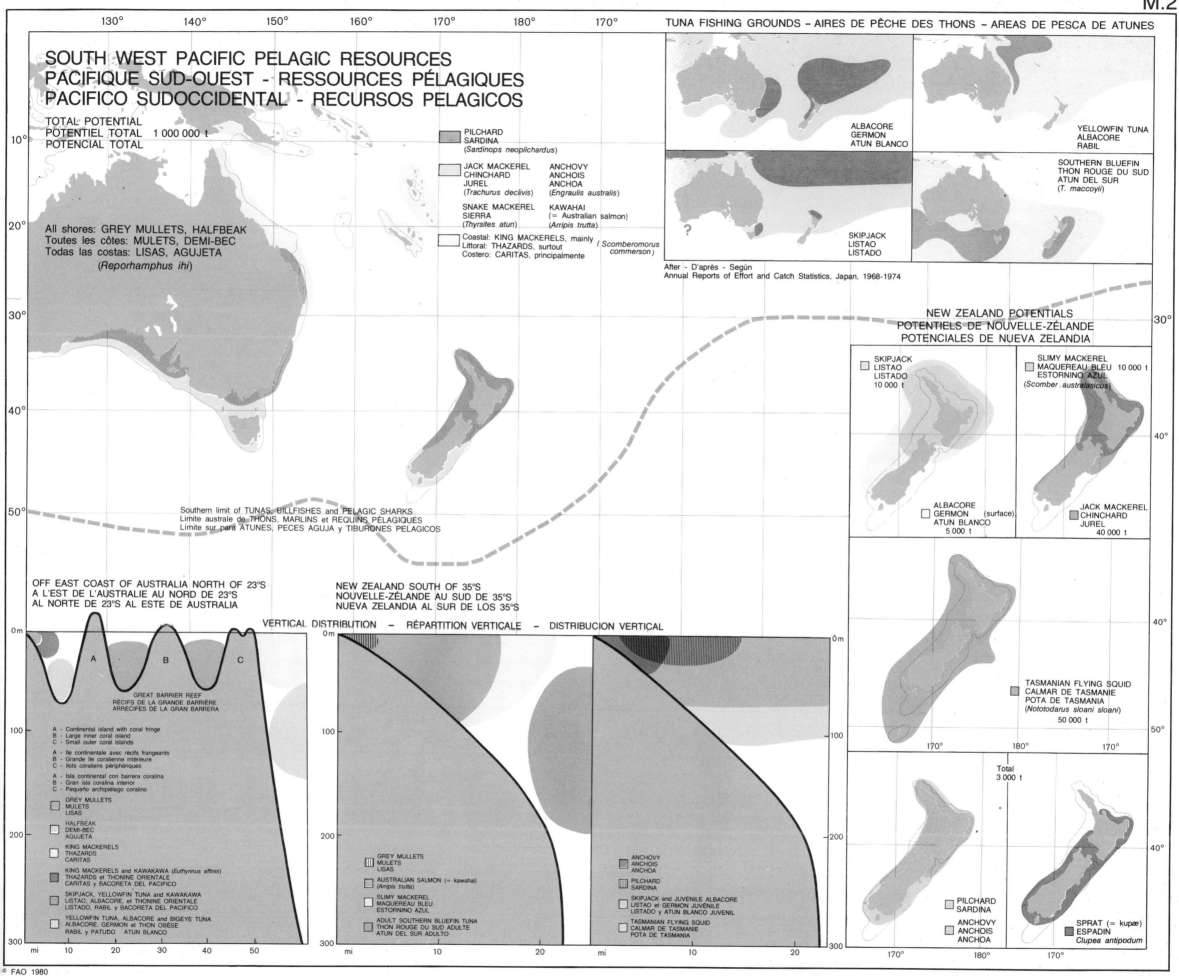

SOUTH WEST PACIFIC PELAGIC RESOURCES
PACIFIQUE SUD-OUEST - RESSOURCES PÉLAGIQUES
PACIFICO SUDOCCIDENTAL - RECURSOS PELAGICOS

TOTAL POTENTIAL
POTENTIEL TOTAL   1 000 000 t
POTENCIAL TOTAL

All shores: GREY MULLETS, HALFBEAK
Toutes les côtes: MULETS, DEMI-BEC
Todas las costas: LISAS, AGUJETA

(Reporhamphus ihi)

PILCHARD
SARDINA
(Sardinops neopilchardus)

JACK MACKEREL   ANCHOVY
CHINCHARD   ANCHOIS
JUREL   ANCHOA
(Trachurus declivis) (Engraulis australis)

SNAKE MACKEREL   KAWAHAI
SIERRA   (= Australian salmon)
(Thyrsites atun) (Arripis trutta)

Coastal: KING MACKERELS, mainly (Scomberomorus
Littoral: THAZARDS, surtout   commerson)
Costero: CARITAS, principalmente

TUNA FISHING GROUNDS - AIRES DE PÊCHE DES THONS - AREAS DE PESCA DE ATUNES

ALBACORE
GERMON
ATUN BLANCO

YELLOWFIN TUNA
ALBACORE
RABIL

SOUTHERN BLUEFIN
THON ROUGE DU SUD
ATUN DEL SUR
(T. maccoyii)

SKIPJACK
LISTAO
LISTADO

After - D'après - Según
Annual Reports of Effort and Catch Statistics, Japan, 1968-1974

NEW ZEALAND POTENTIALS
POTENTIELS DE NOUVELLE-ZÉLANDE
POTENCIALES DE NUEVA ZELANDIA

SKIPJACK
LISTAO
LISTADO
10 000 t

SLIMY MACKEREL
MAQUEREAU BLEU 10 000 t
ESTORNINO AZUL
(Scomber. australasicus)

ALBACORE
GERMON (surface)
ATUN BLANCO
5 000 t

JACK MACKEREL
CHINCHARD
JUREL
40 000 t

Southern limit of TUNAS, BILLFISHES and PELAGIC SHARKS
Limite australe de THONS, MARLINS et REQUINS PÉLAGIQUES
Límite sur para ATUNES, PECES AGUJA y TIBURONES PELAGICOS

TASMANIAN FLYING SQUID
CALMAR DE TASMANIE
POTA DE TASMANIA
(Nototodarus sloani sloani)
50 000 t

OFF EAST COAST OF AUSTRALIA NORTH OF 23°S
A L'EST DE L'AUSTRALIE AU NORD DE 23°S
AL NORTE DE 23°S AL ESTE DE AUSTRALIA

NEW ZEALAND SOUTH OF 35°S
NOUVELLE-ZÉLANDE AU SUD DE 35°S
NUEVA ZELANDIA AL SUR DE LOS 35°S

VERTICAL DISTRIBUTION - RÉPARTITION VERTICALE - DISTRIBUCION VERTICAL

GREAT BARRIER REEF
RÉCIFS DE LA GRANDE BARRIÈRE
ARRECIFES DE LA GRAN BARRERA

A - Continental island with coral fringe
B - Large inner coral island
C - Small outer coral islands

A - Île continentale avec récifs frangeants
B - Grande île coralienne intérieure
C - Ilots coraliens périphériques

A - Isla continental con barrera coralina
B - Gran isla coralina interior
C - Pequeño archipiélago coralino

GREY MULLETS
MULETS
LISAS

HALFBEAK
DEMI-BEC
AGUJETA

KING MACKERELS
THAZARDS
CARITAS

KING MACKERELS and KAWAKAWA (Euthynnus affinis)
THAZARDS et THONINE ORIENTALE
CARITAS y BACORETA DEL PACIFICO

SKIPJACK, YELLOWFIN TUNA and KAWAKAWA
LISTAO, ALBACORE, et THONINE ORIENTALE
LISTADO, RABIL y BACORETA DEL PACIFICO

YELLOWFIN TUNA, ALBACORE and BIGEYE TUNA
ALBACORE, GERMON et THON OBÈSE
RABIL, ATUN BLANCO et ATUN PATUDO

GREY MULLETS
MULETS
LISAS

AUSTRALIAN SALMON (= kawahai)
(Arripis trutta)

SLIMY MACKEREL
MAQUEREAU BLEU
ESTORNINO AZUL

ADULT SOUTHERN BLUEFIN TUNA
THON ROUGE DU SUD ADULTE
ATUN DEL SUR ADULTO

ANCHOVY
ANCHOIS
ANCHOA

PILCHARD
SARDINA

SKIPJACK and JUVENILE ALBACORE
LISTADO et GERMON JUVÉNILE
LISTADO y ATUN BLANCO JUVENIL

TASMANIAN FLYING SQUID
CALMAR DE TASMANIE
POTA DE TASMANIA

Total
3 000 t

PILCHARD
SARDINA

ANCHOVY
ANCHOIS
ANCHOA

SPRAT (= kupœ)
ESPADIN
Clupea antipodum

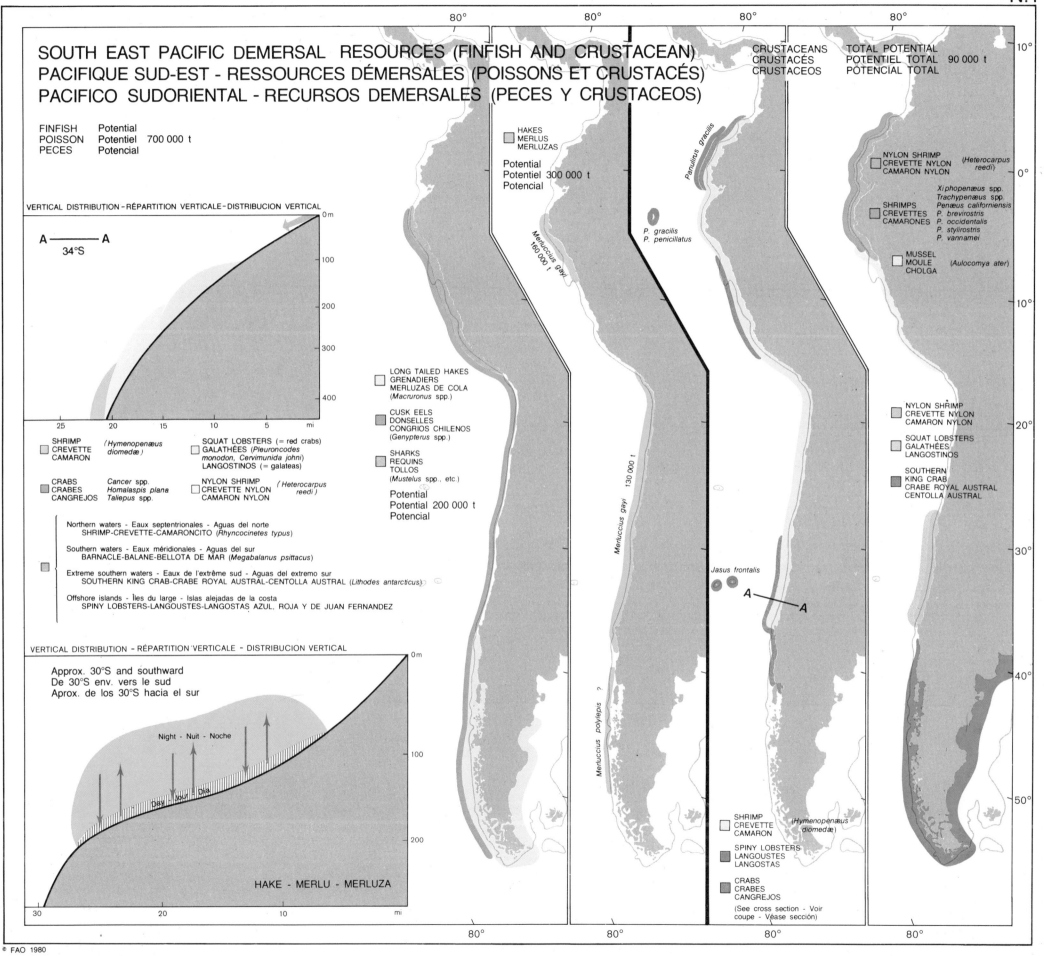

SOUTH EAST PACIFIC DEMERSAL RESOURCES (FINFISH AND CRUSTACEAN)
PACIFIQUE SUD-EST - RESSOURCES DÉMERSALES (POISSONS ET CRUSTACÉS)
PACIFICO SUDORIENTAL - RECURSOS DEMERSALES (PECES Y CRUSTACEOS)

FINFISH   Potential
POISSON   Potentiel 700 000 t
PECES   Potencial

CRUSTACEANS   TOTAL POTENTIAL
CRUSTACÉS   POTENTIEL TOTAL 90 000 t
CRUSTACEOS   POTENCIAL TOTAL

VERTICAL DISTRIBUTION - RÉPARTITION VERTICALE - DISTRIBUCION VERTICAL

A ———— A
34°S

0 m
100
200
300
400

25   20   15   10   5   mi

SHRIMP   (Hymenopenæus
CREVETTE   diomedæ)
CAMARON

SQUAT LOBSTERS (= red crabs)
GALATHÉES (Pleuroncodes
monodon, Cervimunida johni)
LANGOSTINOS (= galateas)

CRABS   Cancer spp.
CRABES   Homalaspis plana
CANGREJOS Taliepus spp.

NYLON SHRIMP   (Heterocarpus
CREVETTE NYLON   reedi)
CAMARON NYLON

Northern waters - Eaux septentrionales - Aguas del norte
SHRIMP-CREVETTE-CAMARONCITO (Rhyncocinetes typus)

Southern waters - Eaux méridionales - Aguas del sur
BARNACLE-BALANE-BELLOTA DE MAR (Megabalanus psittacus)

Extreme southern waters - Eaux de l'extrême sud - Aguas del extremo sur
SOUTHERN KING CRAB-CRABE ROYAL AUSTRAL-CENTOLLA AUSTRAL (Lithodes antarcticus)

Offshore islands - Îles du large - Islas alejadas de la costa
SPINY LOBSTERS-LANGOUSTES-LANGOSTAS AZUL, ROJA Y DE JUAN FERNANDEZ

VERTICAL DISTRIBUTION - RÉPARTITION VERTICALE - DISTRIBUCION VERTICAL

Approx. 30°S and southward
De 30°S env. vers le sud
Aprox. de los 30°S hacia el sur

0 m

Night - Nuit - Noche

Day - Jour - Día

100

200

HAKE - MERLU - MERLUZA

30   20   10   mi

HAKES
MERLUS
MERLUZAS

Potential
Potentiel 300 000 t
Potencial

Panulirus gracilis

P. gracilis
P. penicillatus

LONG TAILED HAKES
GRENADIERS
MERLUZAS DE COLA
(Macruronus spp.)

CUSK EELS
DONSELLES
CONGRIOS CHILENOS
(Genypterus spp.)

SHARKS
REQUINS
TOLLOS
(Mustelus spp., etc.)

Potential
Potentiel 200 000 t
Potencial

Merluccius gayi
160 000 t

Merluccius gayi
130 000 t

Merluccius polylepis

SHRIMP   (Hymenopenæus
CREVETTE   diomedæ)
CAMARON

SPINY LOBSTERS
LANGOUSTES
LANGOSTAS

CRABS
CRABES
CANGREJOS

(See cross section - Voir
coupe - Véase sección)

Jasus frontalis

A

A

NYLON SHRIMP   (Heterocarpus
CREVETTE NYLON   reedi)
CAMARON NYLON

SHRIMPS   Xiphopenæus spp.
CREVETTES   Trachypenæus spp.
CAMARONES   Penæus californiensis
               P. brevirostris
               P. occidentalis
               P. stylirostris
               P. vannamei

MUSSEL
MOULE   (Aulocomya ater)
CHOLGA

NYLON SHRIMP
CREVETTE NYLON
CAMARON NYLON

SQUAT LOBSTERS
GALATHÉES
LANGOSTINOS

SOUTHERN
KING CRAB
CRABE ROYAL AUSTRAL
CENTOLLA AUSTRAL

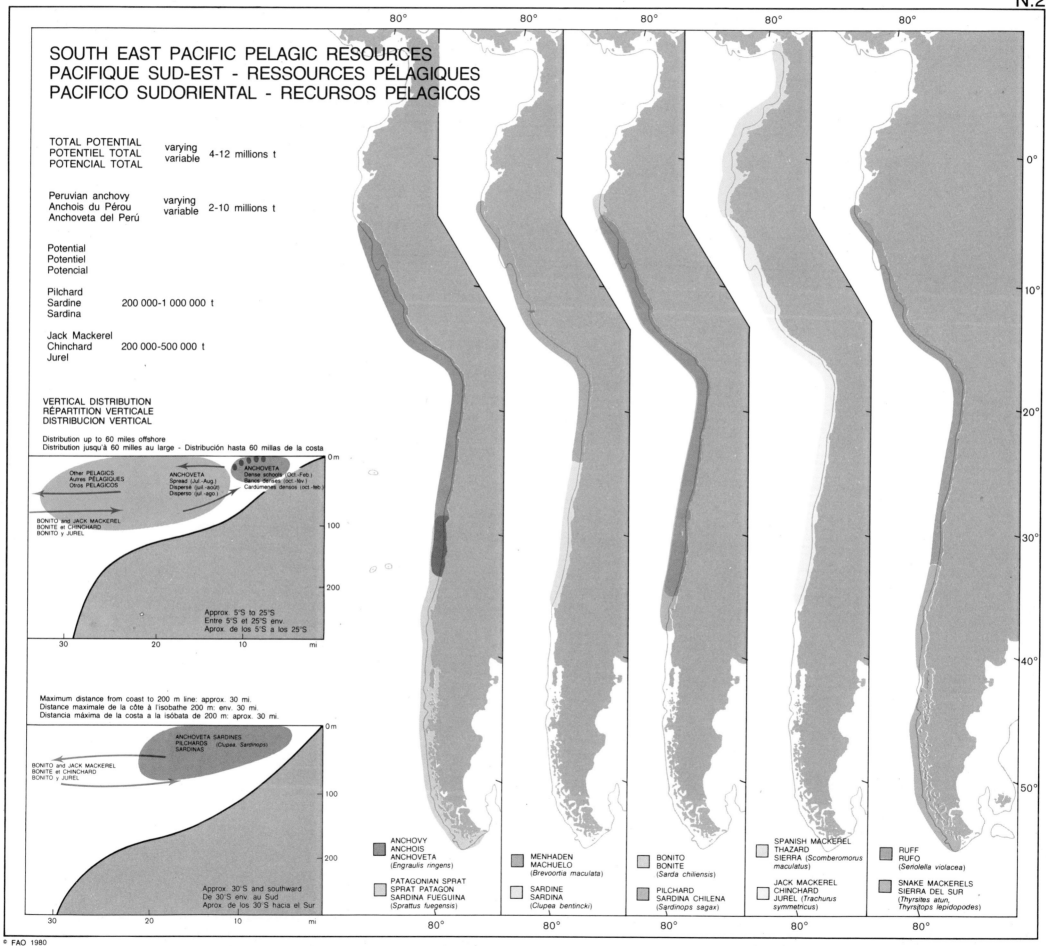

SOUTH EAST PACIFIC PELAGIC RESOURCES
PACIFIQUE SUD-EST - RESSOURCES PÉLAGIQUES
PACIFICO SUDORIENTAL - RECURSOS PELAGICOS

TOTAL POTENTIAL
POTENTIEL TOTAL   varying   4-12 millions t
POTENCIAL TOTAL   variable

Peruvian anchovy
Anchois du Pérou   varying   2-10 millions t
Anchoveta del Perú   variable

Potential
Potentiel
Potencial

Pilchard
Sardine   200 000-1 000 000 t
Sardina

Jack Mackerel
Chinchard   200 000-500 000 t
Jurel

VERTICAL DISTRIBUTION
RÉPARTITION VERTICALE
DISTRIBUCION VERTICAL

Distribution up to 60 miles offshore
Distribution jusqu'à 60 milles au large - Distribución hasta 60 millas de la costa

Other PELAGICS
Autres PÉLAGIQUES
Otros PELAGICOS

ANCHOVETA
Spread (Jul.-Aug.)
Dispersé (juil.-août)
Disperso (jul.-ago.)

ANCHOVETA
Dense schools (Oct.-Feb.)
Bancs denses (oct.-fév.)
Cardúmenes densos (oct.-feb.)

BONITO and JACK MACKEREL
BONITE et CHINCHARD
BONITO y JUREL

Approx. 5°S to 25°S
Entre 5°S et 25°S env.
Aprox. de los 5°S a los 25°S

0 m
100
200

30   20   10   mi

Maximum distance from coast to 200 m line: approx. 30 mi.
Distance maximale de la côte à l'isobathe 200 m: env. 30 mi.
Distancia máxima de la costa a la isóbata de 200 m: aprox. 30 mi.

ANCHOVETA SARDINES
PILCHARDS   (Clupea, Sardinops)
SARDINAS

BONITO and JACK MACKEREL
BONITE et CHINCHARD
BONITO y JUREL

Approx. 30°S and southward
De 30°S env. au Sud
Aprox. de los 30°S hacia el Sur

0 m
100
200

30   20   10   mi

ANCHOVY
ANCHOIS
ANCHOVETA
(Engraulis ringens)

PATAGONIAN SPRAT
SPRAT PATAGON
SARDINA FUEGUINA
(Sprattus fuegensis)

MENHADEN
MACHUELO
(Brevoortia maculata)

SARDINE
SARDINA
(Clupea bentincki)

BONITO
BONITE
(Sarda chiliensis)

PILCHARD
SARDINA CHILENA
(Sardinops sagax)

SPANISH MACKEREL
THAZARD
SIERRA (Scomberomorus
maculatus)

JACK MACKEREL
CHINCHARD
JUREL (Trachurus
symmetricus)

RUFF
RUFO
(Seriolella violacea)

SNAKE MACKERELS
SIERRA DEL SUR
(Thyrsites atun,
Thyrsitops lepidopodes)

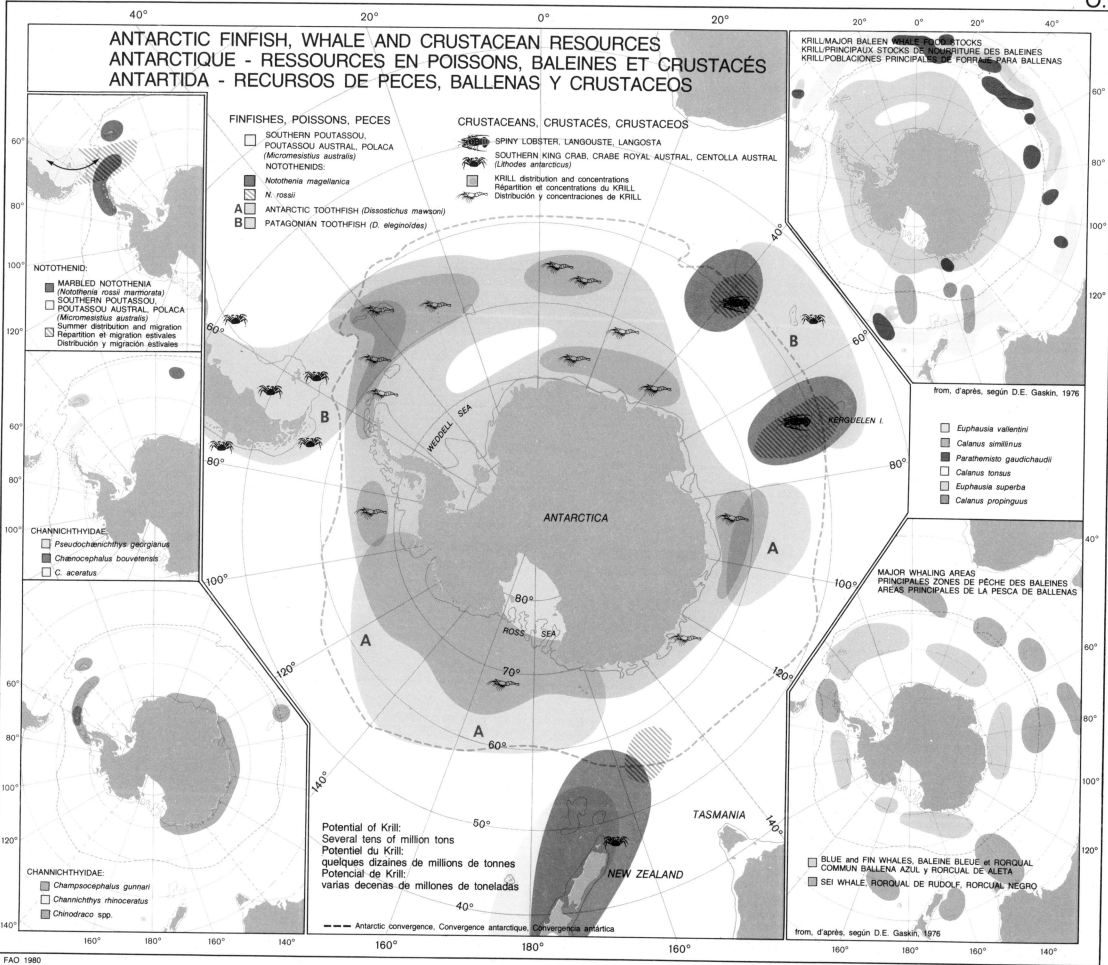

O.1

ANTARCTIC FINFISH, WHALE AND CRUSTACEAN RESOURCES
ANTARCTIQUE - RESSOURCES EN POISSONS, BALEINES ET CRUSTACÉS
ANTARTIDA - RECURSOS DE PECES, BALLENAS Y CRUSTACEOS

FINFISHES, POISSONS, PECES

SOUTHERN POUTASSOU,
POUTASSOU AUSTRAL, POLACA
(*Micromesistius australis*)

NOTOTHENIDS:

Notothenia magellanica

N. rossii

A ANTARCTIC TOOTHFISH (*Dissostichus mawsoni*)

B PATAGONIAN TOOTHFISH (*D. eleginoïdes*)

CRUSTACEANS, CRUSTACÉS, CRUSTACEOS

SPINY LOBSTER, LANGOUSTE, LANGOSTA

SOUTHERN KING CRAB, CRABE ROYAL AUSTRAL, CENTOLLA AUSTRAL
(*Lithodes antarcticus*)

KRILL distribution and concentrations
Répartition et concentrations du KRILL
Distribución y concentraciones de KRILL

NOTOTHENID:

MARBLED NOTOTHENIA
(*Notothenia rossii marmorata*)

SOUTHERN POUTASSOU,
POUTASSOU AUSTRAL, POLACA
(*Micromesistius australis*)
Summer distribution and migration
Répartition et migration estivales
Distribución y migración estivales

CHANNICHTHYIDAE:

Pseudochænichthys georgianus

Chænocephalus bouvetensis

C. aceratus

CHANNICHTHYIDAE:

Champsocephalus gunnari

Channichthys rhinoceratus

Chinodraco spp.

WEDDELL SEA

KERGUELEN I.

ANTARCTICA

ROSS SEA

80°

70°

60°

A

B

TASMANIA

NEW ZEALAND

Potential of Krill:
Several tens of million tons
Potentiel du Krill:
quelques dizaines de millions de tonnes
Potencial de Krill:
varias decenas de millones de toneladas

- - - Antarctic convergence, Convergence antarctique, Convergencia antártica

KRILL/MAJOR BALEEN WHALE FOOD STOCKS
KRILL/PRINCIPAUX STOCKS DE NOURRITURE DES BALEINES
KRILL/POBLACIONES PRINCIPALES DE FORRAJE PARA BALLENAS

from, d'après, según D.E. Gaskin, 1976

Euphausia vallentini

Calanus simillinus

Parathemisto gaudichaudii

Calanus tonsus

Euphausia superba

Calanus propinguus

MAJOR WHALING AREAS
PRINCIPALES ZONES DE PÊCHE DES BALEINES
AREAS PRINCIPALES DE LA PESCA DE BALLENAS

BLUE and FIN WHALES, BALEINE BLEUE et RORQUAL
COMMUN BALLENA AZUL y RORCUAL DE ALETA

SEI WHALE, RORQUAL DE RUDOLF, RORCUAL NEGRO

from, d'après, según D.E. Gaskin, 1976

UNEXPLOITED AND LIGHTLY EXPLOITED RESOURCES
RESSOURCES PEU OU PAS EXPLOITÉES
RECURSOS POCO EXPLOTADOS O INEXPLOTADOS

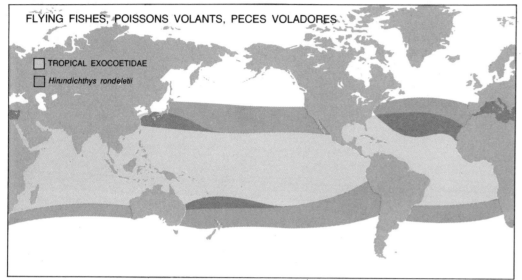

FLYING FISHES, POISSONS VOLANTS, PECES VOLADORES

☐ TROPICAL EXOCOETIDAE

☐ *Hirundichthys rondeletii*

Parin, 1967

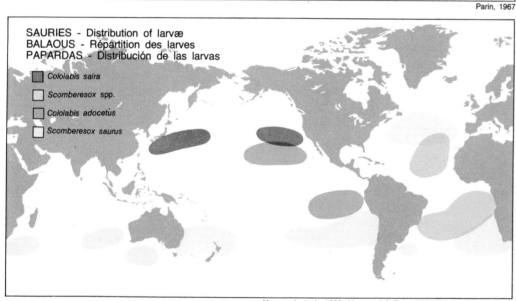

SAURIES - Distribution of larvæ
BALAOUS - Répartition des larves
PAPARDAS - Distribución de las larvas

☐ *Cololabis saira*

☐ *Scomberesox spp.*

☐ *Cololabis adocetus*

☐ *Scomberesox saurus*

Ueyanagi et al., 1969; Ueyanagi & Doi, 1971; Ueyanagi et al., 1972

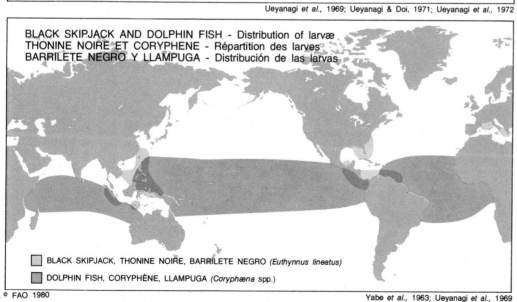

BLACK SKIPJACK AND DOLPHIN FISH - Distribution of larvæ
THONINE NOIRE ET CORYPHENE - Répartition des larves
BARRILETE NEGRO Y LLAMPUGA - Distribución de las larvas

☐ BLACK SKIPJACK, THONINE NOIRE, BARRILETE NEGRO (*Euthynnus lineatus*)

☐ DOLPHIN FISH, CORYPHÈNE, LLAMPUGA (*Coryphæna spp.*)

© FAO 1980

Yabe et al., 1963; Ueyanagi et al., 1969

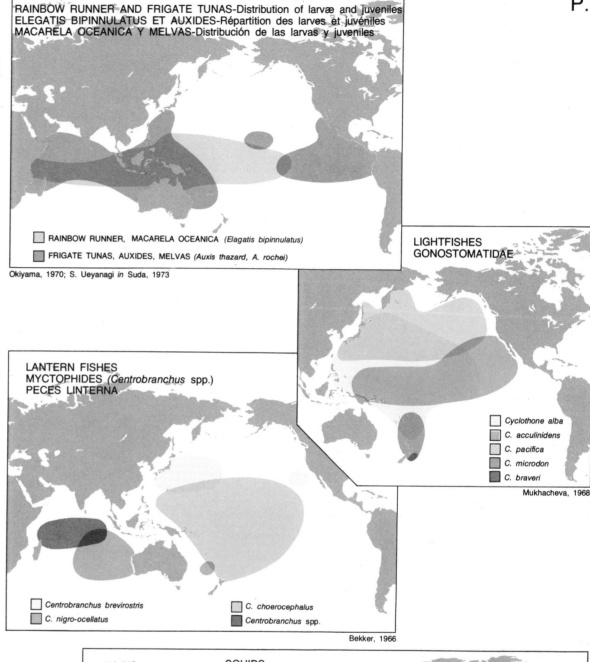

RAINBOW RUNNER AND FRIGATE TUNAS-Distribution of larvæ and juveniles
ELEGATIS BIPINNULATUS ET AUXIDES-Répartition des larves et juvéniles
MACARELA OCEANICA Y MELVAS-Distribución de las larvas y juveniles

☐ RAINBOW RUNNER, MACARELA OCEANICA (*Elagatis bipinnulatus*)

☐ FRIGATE TUNAS, AUXIDES, MELVAS (*Auxis thazard, A. rochei*)

Okiyama, 1970; S. Ueyanagi in Suda, 1973

LIGHTFISHES
GONOSTOMATIDAE

☐ *Cyclothone alba*

☐ *C. acculinidens*

☐ *C. pacifica*

☐ *C. microdon*

☐ *C. braveri*

Mukhacheva, 1968

LANTERN FISHES
MYCTOPHIDES (*Centrobranchus* spp.)
PECES LINTERNA

☐ *Centrobranchus brevirostris*   ☐ *C. choerocephalus*

☐ *C. nigro-ocellatus*   ☐ *Centrobranchus* spp.

Bekker, 1966

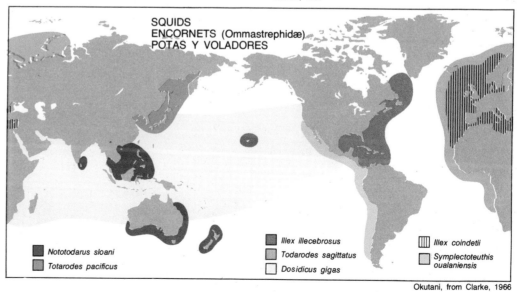

SQUIDS
ENCORNETS (Ommastrephidæ)
POTAS Y VOLADORES

☐ *Nototodarus sloani*   ☐ *Illex illecebrosus*   ☐ *Illex coindetii*

☐ *Totarodes pacificus*   ☐ *Todarodes sagittatus*   ☐ *Symplectoteuthis oualaniensis*

                                ☐ *Dosidicus gigas*

Okutani, from Clarke, 1966

ALPHABETICAL INDEX OF FISH NAMES

On the maps and vertical sections use has been made as far as possible of the common or vernacular names, in particular those appearing in the *Yearbook of fishery statistics* published by FAO or officially adopted by bodies like the International Commission for the Conservation of Atlantic Tunas, etc. When there is no sufficiently explicit common name in English, French or Spanish, the local name of common use in the area where the stock is exploited has been given. In some cases, when there is no common name (for instance, for a resource not yet exploited) or when it has to be clearly indicated, the scientific name is used or added.

The alphabetic index lists over 700 common and scientific fish names used in the Atlas, with cross references to the sheets upon which they occur on the map and/or in the vertical sections. In some cases the common name is identical in two languages; for instance *bonito* is used both in English and in Spanish. In other cases the same common name is employed for different fish in two languages; for example, the English *albacore* is called *germon* in French, whereas the French *albacore* is *yellowfin tuna* in English. Where confusion might arise, the language is indicated in the index after the name by the abbreviation *Eng., Fr.* or *Esp.* In the same language identical stocks may have different common names in different areas, for example, on the west coast of South America *barrilete* is used instead of the official Spanish name *listado (oceanic skipjack)*; important synonyms are given in parentheses in the index. Again, the same common name may be used for several stocks in one language while different names are used in other languages; for instance, *cusk eel* is used in English for both *Brotula* spp. and *Genypterus* spp., while in French and Spanish the former is *brotule* and *brótula*, and the latter is *donselle* and *abadejo*. The Afrikaans name *kingklip* is also often employed for some stocks of the second species.

INDEX ALPHABÉTIQUE DES NOMS DE POISSONS

Sur les cartes et dans les coupes verticales, on a utilisé autant que possible les noms communs ou vernaculaires, en particulier ceux qui figurent dans l'*Annuaire statistique des pêches* publié par la FAO, ou ceux qui sont officiellement adoptés par des organismes tels que la Commission internationale pour la conservation des thonidés de l'Atlantique. En l'absence de nom commun suffisamment explicite en anglais, espagnol ou français, le nom local couramment en usage dans la zone où le stock est exploité est alors donné. Dans certains cas, en l'absence de nom commun (par exemple, pour une ressource encore inexploitée), ou lorsqu'il est nécessaire de le préciser, le nom scientifique a été utilisé ou ajouté.

L'index alphabétique énumère plus de 700 noms de poissons communs et scientifiques utilisés dans l'Atlas, avec renvoi aux planches où ils figurent sur la carte et/ou dans les coupes verticales. Dans certains cas, le nom commun est identique dans deux langues; par exemple, *bonito* est utilisé en anglais et en espagnol. Dans d'autres cas, on utilise le même nom commun pour des poissons différents dans deux langues; par exemple, le nom français *albacore* correspond à *yellowfin tuna* en anglais, alors que le nom anglais *albacore* correspond à *germon* en français. Pour éviter toute confusion, la langue est indiquée dans l'index par l'abréviation *Fr., Eng.* ou *Esp.* à la suite du nom. Des stocks identiques peuvent avoir des noms communs différents dans la même langue selon les diverses zones; par exemple en Méditerranée le *loup (de mer)* est souvent désigné par le terme *bar* et dans le golfe de Guinée ce terme désigne en fait un sciaenidé; sur la côte ouest de l'Amérique du Sud, on utilise *barrilete* au lieu du nom espagnol officiel *listado (bonite à ventre rayé)*; les synonymes importants sont indiqués entre parenthèses dans l'index. Par ailleurs, le même nom commun peut servir à désigner plusieurs stocks dans une langue, alors qu'ils portent différents noms dans d'autres langues; par exemple, *cusk eel* est utilisé en anglais à la fois pour *Brotula* spp. et *Genypterus* spp., alors qu'en français on emploie *brotule* pour le premier et *donselle* pour le second.

NOMENCLATURA ICTIOLOGICA ALFABETICA

En los mapas y perfiles se han utilizado en la medida de lo posible los nombres comunes, en particular los que figuran en el *Anuario estadístico de pesca* publicado por la FAO, o los adoptados oficialmente por organismos como la Comisión Internacional para la Conservación del Atún del Atlántico. A falta de un nombre común suficientemente explícito en español, francés o inglés, se da el nombre local utilizado corrientemente en la zona donde se explota esa población. En algunos casos, en ausencia de un nombre común (por ejemplo, de un recurso todavía no explotado), o cuando es necesario precisarlo, se ha utilizado o añadido el nombre científico.

El índice alfabético incluye más de 700 nombres comunes y científicos utilizados en el Atlas, remitiendo en cada caso a las páginas en que dichos nombres aparecen en el mapa y/o en las secciones. En algunos casos, el nombre común es idéntico en dos idiomas: por ejemplo, *bonito* se usa tanto en español como en inglés. En otros casos, un mismo nombre común se aplica a diversos peces en dos idiomas: por ejemplo, el pez denominado en inglés *albacore* se llama en francés *germon*, mientras que el pez que los franceses llaman *albacore* se conoce en inglés por *yellowfin*. Cuando puede haber lugar a confusión se indica en el índice con una abreviatura, *Esp., Fr.* o *Eng.*, el idioma de que se trata. Una misma población puede tener diversos nombres comunes en un mismo idioma, según las diversas zonas; por ejemplo, en el Mediterráneo se utiliza frecuentemente *boquerón* en lugar de *anchoa*, y en la costa occidental de Sudamérica se utiliza *barrilete* en lugar del nombre oficial *listado*; los sinónimos importantes se incluyen en el índice entre paréntesis. Puede suceder también que en un idioma se utilice un mismo nombre común para diversas poblaciones, mientras en otros idiomas se utilizan nombres diversos para cada una de ellas; por ejemplo, *cusk eel* designa en inglés tanto los peces *Brotula* spp. como *Genypterus* spp., mientras en español los primeros se denominan *brótulas* y los segundos *abadejos*.

Anchois argentin 2.6
Anchois du Cap F.2
Anchois du Pérou 2.5, L.2, N.2
Anchois japonais I.2
Anchois tropical L.4
Anchoíta E.2
Anchoíta argentina 2.6
Anchoveta L.2, N.2
Anchoveta del Perú 2.5, L.2, N.2
Anchoveta tropical L.4
Anchovy B.2, C.2, D.2, E.2, G.2, H.2, I.2, K.2, M.2, N.2
Angolan dentex F.1
Anguila G.1
Anguille G.1
Anjova E.2
Anoli de mer I.1, K.1
Anoplopoma fimbria J.1, L.1
Antarctic toothfish O.1
Arenque A.2, B.2, I.2, J.2
Arenque Atlántico-escandinavo 2.10, B.2
Arenque de Dunmore B.2
Arenque de la plataforma B.2
Arenque del Mar Báltico B.2
Arenque del Mar de Irlanda B.2
Arenque del Mar del Norte 2.9, B.2
Arenque redondo I.2
Argentine anchovy 2.6
Argentine shrimp E.3
Ariidae K.1
Aristeomorpha foliacea D.3, G.3
Aristeus antennatus G.3
Aristeus varidens D.3, F.3
Arripis trutta M.2
Arrowtooth flounder J.1
Artemesia longilinearis E.3
Asian salmon 2.12
Atherestes stomias J.1
Atka mackerel I.1
Atlantic bonito 1.8
Atlanto-Scandian herring 2.10, B.2
Atún 1.9, 1.11, B.2, G.2, H.2, K.2, L.3, L.4, M.2
Atún aleta amarilla C.2, L.3, L.4
Atún blanco 1.8, B.2, C.2, E.2, G.2, L.3, L.4, M.2
Atún blanco del Pacífico Norte 2.13
Atún del sur 1.8, 2.16, H.2, M.2
Aulocomya ater N.1
Australian salmon M.2
Austroglossus spp. F.1

Auxide 1.8, P.1
Auxis rochei P.1
Auxis thazard P.1
Axillary bream D.1
Aya E.1

B

Bacaladilla B.2, G.1
Bacalao A.1, B.1, I.1
Bacalao del Atlántico Norte 2.2
Bacalao del Pacífico J.1
Bacalao polar B.1
Bacoreta 1.8, C.2
Bacoreta del Pacífico M.2
Bagre marino D.1, E.1, H.1, K.1
Balaena mysticetus 1.13
Balaenoptera acutorostra 1.13
Balaenoptera borealis 1.13
Balaenoptera musculus 1.13
Balaenoptera musculus brevicauda 1.13
Balaenoptera physalus 1.13
Balai japonais J.1
Balane N.1
Balaou L.2, P.1
Balaou du Pacifique 2.3
Baleine 1.13, O.1
Baleine américaine 1.13
Baleine bleue 1.13, O.1
Baleine bleue pygmée 1.13
Baleine franche 1.13
Baleine grise 1.13
Baleine japonaise 1.13
Ballena 1.13, O.1
Ballena azul 1.13, O.1
Ballena azul pigmea 1.13
Ballena de aleta 1.13, 2.18
Ballena enana 1.13
Ballena gris 1.13
Ballena jorobada 1.13, 2.18
Baltic herring B.2
Banana prawn K.3, M.1
Barbudo D.1, F.1, H.1
Barnacle N.1
Barracouta M.1
Barrilete (*nombre oficial* Listado) C.2, D.2, H.2, L.3, L.4, M.2
Barrilete negro P.1

Bass F.1, G.1
Bécasse de mer D.2
Bellota de mar N.1
Berberecho A.3
Bericoídeo armado L.4
Berycoïde à tête cuirassée L.4
Besugo E.1
Bígaro A.3
Bigeye C.2, D.2, E.2, K.1
Bigeye tuna 1.8, B.2, C.2, D.2, E.2, H.2, L.3, L.4, M.2
Bigorneau A.3
Billfish M.2
Bivalve E.3, G.3
Bivalvo E.3, G.3
Black cod J.1
Black croaker D.1, F.1
Black skipjack P.1
Blackbelly rosefish E.1
Blackfin tuna C.2, E.2, G.2
Blue crab C.3
Blue mussel A.3
Blue spiny lobster L.1
Blue whale 1.13, O.1
Blue whiting B.2
Bluefin tuna B.2, G.2, L.3, L.4
Bluefish E.2
Bocina A.3
Boga G.1
Bogavante 1.9, 1.12, A.3, D.3, G.3
Bogavante americano A.3
Bogavante europeo A.3
Bogue G.1
Bonefish D.1
Bonga D.2
Bonite E.2, G.2, N.2
Bonite du Pacifique est 1.8
Bonito E.2, G.2, N.2
Bonito atlántico 1.8
Bonito del Pacífico Este 1.8
Boquerón G.2
Boreogadus saida B.1
Bouquet A.3
Bowhead whale 1.13
Brazilian lobster E.3
Brazilian sardine E.2
Brazilian spiny lobster E.3
Bream G.1
Brevoortia spp. C.2

Brevoortia maculata N.2
Brevoortia tyrannus A.2
Broadbill swordfish G.2
Brótula D.1, F.1
Brotula barbata D.1, F.1
Brotule D.1, F.1
Brown shrimp 2.1, C.3, E.3
Buccin A.3
Buccinum undatum A.3
Buey A.3, J.3, L.1
Buey del Pacífico J.3
Bullet tuna 1.8
Butterfish K.1

C

Caballa A.2, B.2, G.2
Caballa azul K.2
Caballa del Indo-Pacífico H.2, K.2
Cachalot 1.13
Cachalote 1.13
Cachucho F.1
Cachucho de Angola F.1
Calamar A.3, D.3, E.3, G.3, I.3, J.2, J.3
Calamar común L.3
Calamar gonátido J.3
Calamarete E.3
Calanus propinguus O.1
Calanus simillinus O.1
Calanus tonsus O.1
Californian sardine L.2, L.4
Callinectes spp. C.3, E.3
Callinectes sapidus C.3
Callinectes toxotes L.1
Calmar d'Hawaï L.3
Calmar de Tasmanie M.1, M.2
Calmar géant L.3
Calmar japonais I.2, I.3
Camarón 1.9, 1.12, C.3, E.3, G.3, I.1, I.3, J.3, N.1
Camarón argentino E.3
Camarón blanco 2.1, C.3, E.3
Camarón café 2.1, C.3, E.3
Camarón común A.3
Camarón costero F.3, G.3
Camarón de agua dulce E.3
Camarón de profundidad D.3, F.3, G.3, H.3
Camarón fidel L.1

Camarón legítimo E.3
Camarón no peneido H.3
Camarón nylon N.1
Camarón pandálido L.1
Camarón peneido C.3, H.3, K.3, L.1, M.1
Camarón real rojo C.3
Camarón rojo con manchas C.3, E.3
Camarón rosado 2.1, C.3, D.3, E.3
Camarón siete barbas E.3
Camaroncito N.1
Cancer spp. N.1
Cancer antennarius L.1
Cancer anthonyi L.1
Cancer magister J.3, L.1
Cancer pagurus A.3
Cancer productus L.1
Cangrejo 1.9, 1.12, A.3, C.3, E.3, H.3, I.3, J.3, L.1, N.1
Cangrejo azul C.3
Cangrejo ruso I.3, J.3
Cangrejo Tanner I.3, J.3
Cape anchovy F.2
Cape hake F.1
Capelan A.2, B.2
Capelin A.2, B.2
Capellán A.2, B.2
Capitaine D.1
Carabinero A.3, D.3, F.3, G.3
Caranga C.2, H.2, M.1
Carangidae K.1
Carangue C.2, H.2, M.1
Caranx lutescens M.1
Caranx ronchus D.2
Cardium edule A.3
Caribbean spiny lobster C.3, E.3
Carita M.2
Carite 1.8
Carite oriental 1.8
Carite pintado 1.8
Castagnole J.2
Castañeta E.1, J.2
Castanha E.1
Catalugo K.1
Cefalópodo 1.11, D.3, E.3, G.3, I.3, J.3, L.3
Centolla austral E.3, N.1, O.1
Central Atlantic sardinella 2.11
Central Pacific anchovy L.2
Centrobranchus spp. P.1
Centrobranchus brevirostris P.1

Centrobranchus choerocephalus P.1
Centrobranchus nigro-ocellatus P.1
Cephalopod 1.11, D.3, E.3, G.3, I.3, J.3, L.3
Céphalopode 1.11, D.3, E.3, G.3, I.3, J.3, L.3
Cervimunida johni N.1
Cetengraulis mysticetus L.2, L.4
Chachito E.1
Chaenocephalus aceratus O.1
Chaenocephalus bouvetensis O.1
Champsocephalus gunnari O.1
Channichthyidae O.1
Channichthys rhinoceratus O.1
Cheilodactylus spp. E.1
Cheilodactylus macropterus M.1
Chelidonichthys kumu M.1
Chicharra D.2
Chinchard D.1, D.2, F.1, G.2, H.2, I.2, L.2, L.4, M.2, N.2
Chinchard de Cunene F.1, F.2
Chinchard du Cap F.2
Chinchard japonais I.2
Chinchard jaune D.2
Chinchard noir D.2
Chinodraco spp. O.1
Chinook salmon of North American origin J.2
Chionocetes spp. I.3, J.3
Chionocetes opilio A.3
Chlamys islandicus A.3
Cholga N.1
Chrysophrys auratas M.1
Chub mackerel C.2, D.2, F.2, I.2, L.2
Chum salmon of North American origin J.2
Cigala 1.9, A.3, D.3, G.3
Cigarras G.3
Cioba E.1
Clupea N.2
Clupea antipodum M.2
Clupea bentincki N.2
Clupea harengus A.2, B.2
Clupea pallasi I.2, J.2
Clupeid C.2, H.2, L.2
Clupéidé C.2, H.2, L.2
Clupéidé tropical L.4
Clupeido C.2, H.2, L.2
Clupeido tropical L.4
Coastal shrimp F.3, G.3
Cockle A.3
Cod A.1, B.1, I.1
Coho salmon of North American origin J.2

15

Cojinova I.2
Colín B.1
Colin d'Alaska 2.3, I.1, J.1
Colín de Alaska 2.3, I.1, J.1
Cololabis adocetus P.1
Cololabis saira L.2, P.1
Common Pacific squid L.3
Common prawn A.3
Common scallop A.3
Common shrimp A.3
Common sole B.1
Common squid E.3
Conger D.1
Congre D.1
Congrio D.1
Congrio chileno N.1
Coque A.3
Coquillage G.3
Coquille St Jacques A.3, E.3
Corvina C.1, D.1, E.1, F.1, H.1, I.1, K.1
Corvina blanca E.1
Corvina grande D.1
Corvina negra D.1, F.1
Coryphaena spp. P.1
Coryphène P.1
Courbine D.1
Courbine blanche E.1
Coutelas F.2
Crab 1.9, 1.12, C.3, E.3, H.3, I.3, J.3, L.1, N.1
Crabe 1.9, 1.12, A.3, C.3, E.3, H.3, I.3, J.3, L.1, N.1
Crabe bleu C.3
Crabe royal austral E.3, N.1, O.1
Crabe royal boréal I.3, J.3
Crabe Tanner I.3, J.3
Crangon crangon A.3, G.3
Crassostrea angulata A.3
Crassostrea virginica A.3
Crevette 1.9, 1.12, C.3, E.3, G.3, I.1, I.3, J.3, K.2, N.1
Crevette argentine E.3
Crevette blanche 2.1, C.3, E.3
Crevette brésilienne C.3, E.3
Crevette brune 2.1, C.3, E.3
Crevette côtière F.3, G.3
Crevette d'eau douce E.3
Crevette fidel L.1
Crevette grise A.3
Crevette non pénaéide H.3
Crevette nordique A.3, J.3

Crevette nylon N.1
Crevette pandalide L.1
Crevette pénaéide C.3, H.3, K.3, L.1, M.1
Crevette profonde A.3, D.3, F.3, G.3, H.3
Crevette rose C.3, E.3, G.3
Crevette rose du large D.3, F.3
Crevette royale rouge C.3
Croaker C.1, D.1, E.1, F.1, H.1, I.1, K.1
Crustacé 1.9, 1.12, A.3, C.3, D.3, E.3, F.3, G.3, H.3, I.3, J.3, L.1, M.1, N.1, O.1
Crustacean 1.9, 1.12, A.3, C.3, D.3, E.3, F.3, G.3, H.3, I.3, J.3, L.1, M1, N.1, O.1
Crustáceo 1.9, 1.12, A.3, C.3, D.3, E.3, F.3, G.3, H.3, I.3, J.3, L.1, M.1, N.1, O.1
Cunene jack mackerel F.1, F.2
Cusk eel D.1, E.1, F.1, N.1
Cutlassfish D.1
Cuttlefish D.3, G.3, I.1, I.3
Cyclothone acculinidens P.1
Cyclothone alba P.1
Cyclothone braveri P.1
Cyclothone microdon P.1
Cyclothone pacifica P.1
Cynoglosse D.1, F.1
Cynoscion striatus E.1

D

Décaptère D.2, H.2, K.2
Decapterus spp. D.2, H.2, K.2
Deepsea lobster H.3
Deepwater pink shrimp D.3, F.3
Deepwater prawn D.3
Deepwater shrimp A.3, F.3, G.3, H.3
Deepwater snapper H.1
Demersal fishes 1.6, 1.10, A.1, B.1, C.1, D.1, E.1, F.1, G.1, H.1, I.1, J.1, K.1, K.2, L.1, M.1, N.1
Demi-bec M.2
Denté aux gros yeux F.1
Denté d'Angola F.1
Dentex angolensis F.1
Dentex macrophthalmus F.1
Dhoma H.1
Dissostichus eleginoïdes O.1
Dissostichus mawsoni O.1
Dosidiscus gigas L.3, P.1
Dolphin fish P.1

Donselle E.1, N.1
Dorada B.1, M.1
Dorade B.1, D.1, F.1, G.1, K.1, M.1
Dormeur L.1
Dormeur du Pacifique J.3
Dover sole J.1
Drum C.1
Dungeness crab J.3
Dunmore herring B.2
Dussumieria acuta H.2

E

East coast rock lobster F.3
Eastern king prawn M.1
Eastern Pacific bonito 1.8
Eastern rock lobster M.1
Edible crab A.3
Eel G.1
Eelpout E.1
Eglefin A.1, B.1
Eglefino A.1, B.1
Elagatis bipinnulatus P.1
Eledone spp. G.3
Elops lacerta D.1
Encornet D.3, G.3, I.3, J.2, J.3, P.1
Encornet commun E.3, L.3
Encornet gonatide J.3
Endeavour prawn K.3
Engraulis anchoita E.2
Engraulis australis M.2
Engraulis capensis F.2
Engraulis encrasicolus B.2, D.2, G.2
Engraulis japonicus I.2
Engraulis mordax L.2, L.4
Engraulis ringens L.2, N.2
Eschrichtius robustus 1.13
Espadín B.2, G.2, M.2
Espadon A.2, G.2
Espárido D.1, F.1, G.1, I.1, K.1
Estornino C.2, D.2, F.2, I.2, L.2
Estornino azul M.2
Ethmalosa fimbriata D.2
Ethmalose D.2
Etrumeus teres F.2
Eubalaena glacialis 1.13
Euphausia superba O.1

Euphausia vallentini O.1
European hake D.1
European lobster A.3
European pilchard D.2
European spiny lobster A.3
Euthynnus affinis M.2
Euthynnus alleteratus C.2
Euthynnus lineatus P.1

F

Faneca D.1
Faneca noruega B.1
Faux encornet A.3, E.3
Faux hareng L.2
Fidel shrimp L.1
Fin whale 1.13, 2.18, O.1
Flat oyster A.3
Flat sardinella 2.11, D.2, F.2
Flatfish A.1, D.1, E.1, G.1, H.1, I.1, J.1, L.1
Flathead E.1, M.1
Flathead sole J.1
Flet G.1, I.1
Flet arrowtooth J.1
Flétan J.1
Flounder F.1, G.1, I.1
Flying fish I.2, P.1
Flying squid I.2, I.3
Freshwater prawn E.3
Frigate tuna 1.8, P.1

G

Gadoid G.1
Gadoidé G.1
Gadoídeo G.1
Gadus macrocephalus I.1, J.1
Gadus morhua A.1, B.1
Galatea L.1, L.4, N.1
Galathée 1.9, L.1, L.4, N.1
Gallineta A.1, B.1
Gamba J.3, K.2
Gamba boreal A.3, J.3
Gamba de altura D.3, G.3
Gamba rosada F.3, G.3
Gasparot A.2

Gastéropode G.3
Gastropod mollusc G.3
Gastrópodo G.3
Genypterus spp. E.1
Genypterus capensis F.1
Germon 1.8, B.2, C.2, D.2, E.2, G.2, L.3, L.4, M.2
Germon du Pacifique nord 2.13
Ghol H.1
Gilthead sea bream B.1
Glyptocephalus cynoglossus A.1
Goat fishes D.1, G.1, K.1
Golden " snapper " M.1
Gonatid squid J.3
Gonostomatidae P.1
Granadero A.1, M.1
Green spiny lobster F.3
Green-tail prawn M.1
Grenadier E.1, M.1, N.1
Grey mullet C.2, G.1, M.2
Grey whale 1.13
Grondin D.1, G.1, I.1, M.1
Grondin rouge M.1
Grosse crevette rose 2.1, D.3
Grouper C.1, D.1, E.1, H.1, K.1
Grunt D.1, F.1, H.1
Gulf of Mexico penaeid 2.1
Gurnard D.1, G.1, I.1, M.1

H

Haddock A.1, B.1
Hake B.1, C.1, D.1, E.1, G.1, J.1, L.1, N.1
Halfbeak M.2
Halibut J.1
Hard clam A.3
Hareng A.2, B.2, I.2, J.2
Hareng atlantico-scandinave 2.10, B.2
Hareng de Dunmore B.2
Hareng de la Baltique B.2
Hareng de la mer d'Irlande B.2
Hareng de la mer du Nord 2.9, B.2
Hareng du plateau B.2
Hawaiian flying squid L.3
Hawkfish E.1
Helicolenus spp. E.1
Herring A.2, B.2, I.2, J.2
Heterocarpus reedi N.1

Hipogloso J.1
Hipogloso japonés J.1
Hippoglossoides elassodon J.1
Hippoglossoides platessoides A.1
Hippoglossus stenolepis J.1
Hirundichthys rondeletii P.1
Hoki grenadier M.1
Homalaspis plana N.1
Homard 1.9, 1.12, A.3, D.3, G.3
Homard américain A.3
Homard européen A.3
Homarus americanus A.3
Homarus gammarus A.3, G.3
Homarus vulgaris D.3
Horse mackerel D.2
Huître A.3
Huître plate A.3
Huître portugaise A.3, G.3
Humpback 2.18
Humpback whale 1.13
Hymenopenaeus diomedae N.1
Hymenopenaeus mulleri E.3
Hymenopenaeus robustus C.3
Hymenopenaeus triarthrus F.3

I

Illex coindetii G.3, P.1
Illex illecebrosus A.3, P.1
Illex illecebrosus argentinus E.3
Indian eel H.1
Indian mackerel H.2, K.2
Indian oil sardine H.2
Irish Sea herring B.2

J

Jack C.2, D.2, H.2, K.1
Jack mackerel D.1, D.2, F.1, G.2, H.2, I.2, L.2, M.2, N.2
Japanese anchovy I.2
Japanese jack mackerel I.2
Japanese pilchard I.2
Japanese Spanish mackerel 1.8
Jasus edwardsii M.1
Jasus frontalis N.1
Jasus lalandii F.3

Jasus novaehollandiae M.1
Jasus tristani F.3
Jasus verreauxi M.1
Jibia D.3, G.3, I.1, I.3
John Dory F.1
Jubarte 2.18
Jumbo squid L.3
Jurel D.1, D.2, F.1, G.2, H.2, I.2, K.1, L.2, L.4, M.2, N.2
Jurel de Cunene F.1, F.2
Jurel del Cabo F.2
Jurel japonés I.2

K

Karkara H.1
Katsuwonus pelamis C.2, L.3, L.4
Kawahai M.2
Kawakawa 1.8, M.2
King mackerel 1.8, M.2
King prawn K.3
King weakfish E.1
Kingklip E.1, F.1
Koth H.1
Krill O.1
Kupae M.2

L

Lacha C.2
Ladyfish D.1
Lagarto I.1, K.1
Lançon A.2, B.1, I.1
Langosta 1.9, 1.12, A.3, C.3, D.3, E.3, F.3, G.3, H.3, K.3, L.1, M.1, N.1, O.1
Langosta austral F.3
Langosta azul L.1, N.1
Langosta Cabo Verde E.3
Langosta común E.3
Langosta de Natal F.3
Langosta de profundidad H.3
Langosta de Tristán F.3
Langosta espinosa C.3
Langosta europea A.3
Langosta roja L.1, N.1
Langosta verde F.3
Langostino 1.9, E.3, L.1, L.4, N.1

Langouste 1.9, 1.12, A.3, C.3, D.3, E.3, F.3, G.3, H.3, K.3, L.1, M.1, N.1, O.1
Langouste bleue L.1
Langouste brésilienne E.3
Langouste de la côte sud F.3
Langouste de Natal F.3
Langouste de Tristan F.3
Langouste des Caraïbes C.3, E.3
Langouste du Cap F.3
Langouste européenne A.3
Langouste profonde H.3
Langouste rouge L.1
Langouste verte F.3
Langoustine 1.9, A.3, D.3, G.3
Lantern fish F.2, P.1
Lanzón A.2, B.1, I.1
Large croaker D.1
Large eye dentex F.1
Latchet M.1
Layang scad K.2
Legítimo E.3
Leiognathus spp. K.1
Lenguado A.1, D.1, E.1, G.1, H.1, I.1, J.1, L.1
Lenguado común B.1
Lenguado del Cabo F.1
Lengüeta D.1, F.1
Lepidopsetta bilineata J.1
Lepidopus caudatus F.2
Lieu noir B.1
Lightfish P.1
Limanda aspera I.1, J.1
Limanda ferruginea A.1
Limanda japonesa I.1, J.1
Limanda nórdica A.1
Limande à queue jaune A.1
Limande japonaise I.1, J.1
Lisa C.2, G.1, M.2
Listado 1.8, C.2, D.2, H.2, L.3, L.4, M.2
Listado del Pacífico 2.15
Listao 1.8, C.2, D.2, H.2, L.3, L.4, M.2
Listao du Pacifique 2.15
Lithodes antarcticus E.3, N.1, O.1
Litorina littorea A.3
Little tunny C.2
Lizard fish I.1, K.1
Llampuga P.1
Lobster 1.9, 1.12, A.3, D.3, E.3, G.3
Locust lobster G.3

Loliginidae D.3, I.3
Loligo spp. E.3
Loligo opalescens J.3, L.3
Loligo vulgaris G.3
Long tailed hake E.1, N.1
Lorca de Atka I.1
Loup G.1
Lubina F.1, G.1
Lutjanidae K.1
Lutjanidé C.1, D.1, E.1, H.1, K.1
Lutjanidé de profondeur H.1
Lutjanus purpureus (aya) E.1

M

Maasbanker F.2
Maasbanker mackerel F.2
Macarela D.2, H.2, K.1, K.2
Macarela oceánica P.1
Machete D.1
Mâchoiron D.1, K.1
Machuelo 2.11, D.2, F.2, G.2, L.2, N.2
Mackerel A.2, B.2, D.2, G.2
Macrobrachium spp. E.3
Macrodon ancylodon E.1
Macropetasma spp. F.3
Macrorhamphosus spp. D.2
Macroure de roche A.1
Macrouridae M.1
Macrourus rupestris A.1
Macruronus spp. N.1
Macruronus magellanicus E.1
Macruronus novae zelandiae M.1
Mactre solide A.3
Makaire rayé du Pacifique 2.17
Mallotus villosus A.2, B.2
Maquereau A.2, B.2, D.2, G.2
Maquereau bleu K.2, M.2
Maquereau de l'Indo-Pacifique H.2, K.2
Maquereau espagnol C.2, D.2, F.2, I.2, L.2
Marbled notothenia O.1
Marine catfish D.1, E.1, H.1
Marisco G.3
Marlín M.2
Marlín rayado del Pacífico 2.17
Mauritanian hake D.1
Meagre D.1

Pacific skipjack tuna 2.15
Pacific striped marlin 2.17
Pagellus acarne D.1
Pageot D.1
Pagre rouge E.1
Painted rock lobster M.1
Palaemon serratus G.3
Palinurus spp. F.3
Palinurus charlestonei D.3
Palinurus elephas A.3, D.3, G.3
Palinurus gilchristi F.3
Palinurus mauritanicus D.3
Palometa J.2, K.1
Pámpano E.1
Panamanian blue crab L.1
Pandalid shrimp L.1
Pandalopsis dispar J.3
Pandalus borealis A.3, J.3
Pandalus jordani J.3, L.1
Pandalus platyceros J.3, L.1
Panga F.1
Panulirus argus C.3, E.3
Panulirus cygnus M.1
Panulirus delagoae F.3
Panulirus gracilis L.1, N.1
Panulirus inflatus L.1
Panulirus interruptus L.1
Panulirus laevicauda C.3, E.3
Panulirus ornatus K.3
Panulirus penicillatus L.1, N.1
Panulirus regius D.3, F.3
Panulirus versicolor M.1
Paparda L.2, P.1
Paparda del Pacífico 2.3
Paracubiceps spp. D.1
Paralithodes kamtschatica I.3, J.3
Parapenaeopsis spp. K.3
Parapenaeopsis atlantica D.3
Parapenaeus longirostris D.3, F.3, G.3
Parathemisto gaudichaudii O.1
Pardete C.2
Pargo C.1, D.1, E.1, H.1, K.1
Pargo colorado E.1
Pargo de profundidad H.1
Paroctopus appollyon J.3
Patagonian hake 2.7, E.1
Patagonian sprat E.2, N.2
Patagonian toothfish O.1

Patudo 1.8, B.2, C.2, D.2, E.2, H.2, L.3, L.4, M.2
Patudo del Pacífico 2.14
Peces demersales 1.6, 1.10, A.1, B.1, C.1, D.1, E.1, F.1, G.1, H.1, I.1, J.1, K.1, L.1, M.1, N.1
Peces pelágicos 1.7, 1.10, A.2, B.2, C.2, D.1, D.2, E.2, F.2, G.2, H.2, I.2, J.2, K.2, L.2, L.4, M.2, N.2
Pecten d'Amérique A.3
Pecten maximus A.3
Pecten tehneleus E.3
Pelagic armourhead berycoids L.4
Pelagic fishes 1.7, 1.10, A.2, B.2, C.2, D.1, D.2, E.2, F.2, G.2, H.2, I.2, J.2, K.2, L.2, L.4, M.2, N.2
Pelagic shark M.2
Pélamide 1.8
Penaeid E.3, I.3, K.3
Penaeid shrimp C.3, H.3, K.3, L.1, M.1
Pénaéide E.3, I.3, K.3
Pénaéide du golfe du Mexique 2.1
Penaeus aztecus 2.1, C.3, E.3
Penaeus brasiliensis C.3, E.3
Penaeus brevirostris L.1, N.1
Penaeus californiensis L.1, N.1
Penaeus duorarum 2.1, C.3, D.3, E.3
Penaeus esculentus M.1
Penaeus indicus K.3
Penaeus kerathurus G.3
Penaeus latisulcatus K.3
Penaeus merguiensis K.3, M.1
Penaeus monodon K.3
Penaeus occidentalis L.1, N.1
Penaeus paulensis E.3
Penaeus plebejus M.1
Penaeus schmitti C.3, E.3
Penaeus semisulcatus K.3
Penaeus setiferus 2.1, C.3
Penaeus stylirostris L.1, N.1
Penaeus vannamei L.1, N.1
Peneido E.3, I.3, K.3
Peneido del Golfo de México 2.1
Pentaceros richardsoni L.4
Pentheroscion m'bizi D.1, F.1
Pequeño camarón costero D.3
Percophis brasiliensis E.1
Peruvian anchovy 2.5, L.2, N.2
Pescadilla E.1
Pescadilla real E.1
Petit rorqual 1.13
Petite crevette côtière D.3

Pétoncle A.3
Pez aguja M.2
Pez cinto F.2
Pez espada A.2, G.2
Pez linterna F.2, P.1
Pez mesopelágico H.2
Pez palo E.1
Pez sable D.1
Pez sable común I.1
Pez volador I.2, Q.1
Pilchard (*Eng.*) B.2, D.2, F.2, G.2, I.2, M.2, N.2
Pilchard (*Fr.*) I.2, L.2, L.4, N.2
Pilchard du Japon I.2
Pinchagua A.2
Pinguipe E.1
Pink knife prawn F.3
Pink salmon of North American origin J.2
Pink shrimp 2.1, C.3, D.3, E.3, G.3
Placopecten magellanicus A.3
Plaice B.1
Platija B.1, G.1, I.1
Platija arrowtooth J.1
Platija canadiense A.1
Platycéphale M.1
Platycephalus spp. M.1
Plesionika spp. G.3
Plesionika martia D.3
Plesiopenaeus edwardsianus D.3, F.3
Pleurogrammus azonus I.1
Pleuroncodes monodon N.1
Pleuroncodes plannipes L.1, L.4
Pleuronectes platessa B.1
Plie B.1
Plie canadienne A.1
Plie de la mer du Nord 2.8
Plie grise A.1
Poisson chat E.1, H.1
Poisson mésopélagique H.2
Poisson plat A.1, D.1, E.1, G.1, H.1, I.1, J.1, L.1
Poisson-sabre D.1, I.1
Poisson volant I.2, P.1
Poissons démersaux 1.6, 1.10, A.1, B.1, C.1, D.1, E.1, F.1, G.1, H.1, I.1, J.1, K.1, K.2, L.1, M.1, N.1
Poissons pélagiques 1.7, 1.10, A.2, B.2, C.2, D.2, E.2, F.2, G.2, H.2, I.2, J.2, K.2, L.2, L.4, M.2, N.2
Polaca E.1, M.1, O.1
Polar cod B.1
Pollachius virens B.1

Polynémidé F.1, H.1
Pomadasydé D.1, F.1, H.1
Pomatomus saltatrix E.2
Pomfret J.2
Pompano E.1
Portuguese cupped oyster A.3, G.3
Portuguese oyster A.3
Pota P.1
Pota de Hawaii L.3
Pota de Tasmania M.1, M.2
Pota gigante L.3
Pota japonesa I.2, I.3
Poulpe D.3, G.3, I.1, I.3, J.3
Poutassou B.2, G.1
Poutassou austral E.1, M.1, O.1
Pouting D.1
Praire A.3
Priacanthidae K.1
Pseudochaenichthys georgianus O.1
Pterigotrigla polyommata M.1
Pterogymnus laniarus F.1
Pulpo D.3, G.3, I.1, I.3, J.3
Pygmy blue whale 1.13

Q

Queen crab A.3
Quisquilla A.3

R

Rabil 1.8, C.2, D.2, E.2, H.2, L.3, L.4, M.2
Raie D.1, F.1, G.1, H.1
Rainbow runner P.1
Rainbow sardine H.2
Rascacio F.1, I.1, J.1, L.1
Rascasse E.1, F.1, L.1
Rastrelliger spp. H.2, K.2
Ray D.1, F.1, G.1
Raya D.1, F.1, G.1, H.1
Red crab 1.9, L.1, L.4, N.1
Red gurnard M.1
Red porgy E.1
Red snapper E.1

Red spiny lobster L.1
Redeye round herring I.2
Redeye sardine F.2
Redfish A.1, B.1, F.1
Reporhamphus ihi M.2
Requin E.1, G.1, H.1, I.2, L.1, M.1, N.1
Requin pélagique M.2
Rhyncocinetes typus N.1
Ribbon fish I.1
Right whale 1.13
Rock crab L.1
Rock sole J.1
Rockfish L.1
Rodaballo de roca J.1
Roncador D.1, F.1, H.1
Rorcual de aleta O.1
Rorcual negro 1.13, O.1
Rorqual commun 2.18, O.1
Rorqual de Rudolf 1.13, O.1
Rosada del Cabo F.1
Rossia macrosoma G.3
Rouget D.1, G.1, K.1
Round herring F.2
Round sardinella 2.11, D.2, F.2
Round scad K.2
Roundnose grenadier A.1
Royal red shrimp C.3
Rubio D.1, E.1, G.1, I.1, M.1
Rubio rojo M.1
Ruff N.2
Rufo M.1, N.2

S

Sable fish J.1, L.1
Saint-Pierre F.1
Saithe B.1
Salema G.1
Salmon 2.12
Salmón 2.12
Salmón de Alaska 2.12
Salmón de Asia 2.12
Salmón de origen norteamericano J.2
Salmón del Pacífico Norte 2.12
Salmonete D.1, G.1, K.1
San Pedro F.1

Sand lance I.1
Sand perch E.1
Sandeel A.2, B.1
Sarda chiliensis N.2
Sarda sarda E.2, G.2
Sardina B.2, D,2, F.2, G.2, H.2, I.2, K.2, L.2, L.4, M.2, N.2
Sardina chilena N.2
Sardina del Indo-Pacífico H.2
Sardina fueguina E.2, N.2
Sardina japonesa I.2
Sardina pilchardus B.2, D.2, G.2
Sardina redonda F.2
Sardine B.2, D.2, E.2, G.2, N.2
Sardineau D.1
Sardinela D.2, E.2
Sardinella 2.11, D,2, G.2, H.2, K.2
Sardinella spp. H.2, K.2
Sardinella aurita D.2, F.2, G.2
Sardinella brasiliensis E.2
Sardinella dayi H.2
Sardinella eba D.2, F.2
Sardinella fimbriata H.2
Sardinella longiceps H.2
Sardinella maderensis G.2
Sardinella sindensis H.2
Sardinelle 2.11, D.2, E.2, G.2, H.2, K.2
Sardinelle brésilienne E.2
Sardinelle de l'Atlantique centre-est 2.11
Sardinelle de l'Indo-Pacifique H.2
Sardinelle plate 2.11, D.2, F.2
Sardinelle ronde 2.11, D.2, F.2
Sardinops F.2, N.2
Sardinops caerulea L.2, L.4
Sardinops melanosticta I.2
Sardinops neopilchardus M.2
Sardinops ocellata F.2
Sardinops sagax N.2
Saumon 2.12
Saumon asiatique 2.12
Saumon d'Alaska 2.12
Saumon d'origine nord-américaine J.2
Saumon du Pacifique nord 2.12
Saupe G.1
Saurida undosquamis I.1
Saury P.1
Scabbardfish F.2
Scad D.2, H.2, K.1, K.2
Scallop A.3, E.3

Sciaenidae K.1
Sciaenidé C.1, E.1, H.1, I.1
Scomber spp. G.2
Scomber australasicus K.2, M.2
Scomber japonicus C.2, D.2, F.2, I.2, L.2
Scomber scombrus A.2, B.2
Scomberesox spp. P.1
Scomberesox saurus P.1
Scomberomorus commerson M.2
Scomberomorus maculatus N.2
Scyllarides elizabethae F.3
Scyllarides latus G.3
Scyllarus aretus G.3
Sea bob E.3
Sea bream D.1, F.1, G.1, I.1, K.1
Sea catfish K.1
Sea scallop A.3
Sébaste A.1, B.1, I.1, J.1
Sebastes spp. B.1
Sebastes alutus I.1, J.1
Sebastes marinus A.1
Sebastes mentella A.1
Sei whale 1.13, O.1
Seiche D.3, G.3, I.1, I.3
Selar crumenophthalmus D.2
Senegalese hake D.1
Sepia officinalis D.3, G.3
Sepiola rondeleti G.3
Sergestidae K.3
Sergestidé K.3
Sergéstido K.3
Seriola quinqueradiata I.2
Sériole I.2
Seriolella spp. M.1
Seriolella violacea N.2
Serranidé C.1, F.1
Serránido C.1
Shadine F.2, I.2
Shark E.1, G.1, H.1, I.2, L.1, M.1, N.1
Sharptoothed eel I.1
Shelf herring B.2
Shellfish G.3
Short-finned squid A.3, E.3
Shrimp 1.9, 1.12, A.3, C.3, E.3, G.3, I.1, I.3, J.3, K.2, N.1
Side striped shrimp J.3
Sierra M.1, M.2, N.2
Sierra del Sur N.2
Silver hake A.1

Skate D.1, H.1
Skipjack 1.8, C.2, D.2, H.2, L.3, L.4, M.2
Slimy mackerel K.2, M.2
Slipmouth K.1
Small coastal shrimp D.3
Snake mackerel M.1, M.2, N.2
Snapper C.1, D.1, E.1, H.1, K.1
Snow crab J.3
Sockeye 2.12
Sockeye salmon of North American origin J.2
Soft clam A.3
Sole G.1, I.1
Sole commune B.1
Sole Dover J.1
Sole du Cap F.1
Solea solea B.1
Solenocera spp. K.3
Solenocera agassizi L.1
Solenocera membranacea G.3
Solla I.1
Solla del Mar del Norte 2.8
Solla Dover J.1
South coast rock lobster F.3
Southern blue whiting E.1
Southern bluefin 2.16, M.2
Southern bluefin tuna 1.8, H.2, M.2
Southern king crab E.3, N.1, O.1
Southern poutassou M.1, O.1
Southern rock lobster M.1
Spanish mackerel N.2
Sparidé F.1, G.1, I.1
Sparus auratus B.1
Sperm whale 1.13
Spiny lobster 1.9, 1.12, A.3, C.3, D.3, F.3, H.3, L.1, M.1, N.1, O.1
Spisula solidissima A.3
Spot prawn J.3
Spotted red shrimp C.3, E.3
Spotted Spanish mackerel 1.8
Sprat B.2, G.2, M.2
Sprat patagon E.2, N.2
Sprattus fuegensis E.2, N.2
Sprattus sprattus B.2, G.2
Squat lobster 1.9, L.1, L.4, N.1
Squid D.3, G.3, I.3, J.2, J.3, P.1
Stolephorus spp. K.2
Striped mullet C.2
Striped weakfish E.1

Stromatée J.2
Stromateidae K.1
Suela G.1
Surf clam A.3
Swordfish A.2
Symplectoteuthis oualaniensis P.1
Synodontidae K.1

T

Tacaud D.1
Tacaud norvégien B.1
Taliepus spp. N.1
Tanner crab I.3, J.3
Tarakihi M.1
Tasmanian flying squid M.1, M.2
Tassergal E.2
Thazard 1.8, M.2, N.2
Thazard oriental 1.8
Thazard tacheté 1.8
Theragra chalcogramma I.1, J.1
Thon 1.8, 1.11, H.2, K.2, L.3, M.2
Thon albacore 1.8
Thon noir C.2, E.2
Thon obèse 1.8, B.2, C.2, D.2, E.2, H.2, L.3, L.4, M.2
Thon obèse du Pacifique 2.14
Thon rouge 1.8, B.2, G.2, L.3, L.4
Thon rouge du Sud 1.8, 2.16, H.2, M.2
Thonine C.2
Thonine noire P.1
Thonine orientale 1.8, M.2
Threadfin D.1, F.1, H.1
Threadfin bream K.1
Threadherring L.2
Thunnus alalunga B.2, C.2, L.3, L.4
Thunnus albacares C.2, L.3, L.4
Thunnus atlanticus C.2, E.2
Thunnus maccoyii M.2
Thunnus obesus B.2, C.2, L.3, L.4
Thunnus thynnus B.2, L.3, L.4
Thyrsite M.1
Thyrsites atun M.1, M.2, N.2
Thyrsitops lepidopodes N.2
Tiburón E.1, G.1, H.1, I.2, L.1, M.1
Tiburón pelágico M.2
Tiger prawn K.3, M.1

Todarodes pacificus I.2, I.3, P.1
Todarodes sagittatus G.3, P.1
Tollo N.1
Tonguesole D.1, F.1
Tourteau A.3
Trachinote E.1
Trachurus spp. D.2
Trachurus declivis M.2
Trachurus japonicus I.2
Trachurus mediterraneus G.2
Trachurus symmetricus L.2, L.4, N.2
Trachurus trecae D.2
Trachurus trachurus D.2, G.1
Trachypenaeus spp. N.1
Trevally M.1
Trichiurus lepturus I.1
Trisopterus esmarkii B.1
Trisopterus luscus D.1
Tristan rock lobster F.3
Trompetero D.2
Tropical anchovy L.4
Tropical clupeid L.4
Tropical Exocetidae P.1
Trumpet fish D.2
Turbot de roche J.1
Tuna 1.8, 1.11, H.2, K.2, L.3, M.2

U

Umbrina canosai E.1
Univalve G.3

V

Vermelho E.1
Vieira A.3, E.3
Vieira americana A.3
Viuda E.1
Volador A.3, E.3, I.2, P.1

W

Wam H.1
Warehou ruff M.1
Weakfish E.1
West coast rock lobster F.3
Western rock lobster M.1
Whale 1.13, O.1
Whelk A.3
White croaker E.1

White shrimp 2.1, C.3, E.3
Whiting B.1
Winkle A.3
Witch A.1

X

Xiphias gladius A.2, G.2
Xiphopenaeus spp. N.1
Xiphopenaeus kroyeri E.3
Xiphopenaeus riveti L.1

Y

Yellowfin C.2, D.2, E.2
Yellowfin sole I.1, J.1
Yellowfin tuna 1.8, H.2, L.3, L.4, M.2
Yellowtail I.2
Yellowtail flounder A.1

Z

Zoarcidé E.1

FAO SALES AGENTS AND BOOKSELLERS · AGENTS ET DÉPOSITAIRES DE LA FAO · LIBRERIAS Y AGENTES DE VENTAS DE LA FAO

Algeria — Société nationale d'édition et de diffusion, 3, boulevard Zirout-Youcef, Algiers.

Antilles, Netherlands — St. Augustinus Boekhandel, Abraham de Veerstraat 12, Willemstad, Curaçao.

Argentina — Editorial Hemisferio Sur S.R.L., Librería Agropecuaria, Pasteur 743, Buenos Aires.

Australia — Hunter Publications, 58A Gipps Street, Collingwood, Vic. 3066; The Assistant Director, Sales and Distribution, Australian Government Publishing Service, P.O. Box 84, Canberra, A.C.T. 2600, and Australian Government Publications and Inquiry Centres in Canberra, Melbourne, Sydney, Perth, Adelaide and Hobart.

Austria — Gerold & Co., Buchhandlung und Verlag, Graben 31, 1011 Vienna.

Bangladesh — Agricultural Development Agencies in Bangladesh, P.O. Box 5045, Dacca 5.

Belgium — Service des publications de la FAO, M.J. De Lannoy, 202, avenue du Roi, 1060 Brussels. CCP 000-0608993-13.

Belize — The Belize Bookshop, P.O. Box 147, Belize.

Bolivia — Los Amigos del Libro, Perú 3712, Casilla 450, Cochabamba; Mercado 1315, La Paz; René Moreno 26, Santa Cruz; Junín esq. 6 de Octubre, Oruro.

Brazil — Livraria Mestre Jou, Rua Guaipá 518, São Paulo 10; Rua Senador Dantas 19-S205/206, Rio de Janeiro; PRODIL, Promoção e Dist. de Livros Ltda., Av. Venâncio Aires 196, Caixa Postal 4005, Porto Alegre, RS; Livraria Dom Bosco, Rua 14 de Julho 2818, Caixa Postal 962, Campo Grande, MT; A NOSSA LIVRARIA, CLS 103, Bloco C, Lojas 2/6, Brasilia, D.F.; FIMAC, Distribuidora de Livros Ltda., Rua de Bahia 478, Loja 10, Belo Horizonte, ME; METRO CUBICO, Livros e Revistas Técnicas Ltda., Praça São Sebastião, Rua 10 de Julho 613, Caixa Postal 199, Manaus, Amazonas; Distribuidora Luso Mercantil, Rua 13 de Maio 524, Caixa Postal 1124, Belém, Pará; G. Lisbóa Livros Ltda., Rua Princesa Isabel 129, Recife, PE; Livraria Cometa Distribuidora Ltda., Rua da Independencia 46, Salvador, Bahia.

Canada — Renouf Publishing Co. Ltd., 2182 Catherine St. West, Montreal, Que. H3H 1M7.

Chile — Tecnolibro S.A., Merced 753, entrepiso 15, Santiago.

China — China National Publications Import Corporation, P.O. Box 88, Peking.

Colombia — Litexsa Colombiana Ltda., Calle 55, Nº 16-44, Apartado Aéreo 51340, Bogotá.

Costa Rica — Librería, Imprenta y Litografía Lehmann S.A., Apartado 10011, San José.

Cuba — Empresa de Comercio Exterior de Publicaciones, O'Reiley 407, Havana.

Cyprus — MAM, P.O. Box 1722, Nicosia.

Denmark — Ejnar Munksgaard, Norregade 6, Copenhagen S.

Dominican Rep. — Fundación Dominicana de Desarrollo, Casa de las Gárgolas, Mercedes 4, Santo Domingo.

Ecuador — Su Librería Cía. Ltda., García Moreno 1172, Apartado 2556, Quito; Calle Chimborazo 416, Guayaquil.

El Salvador — Librería Cultural Salvadoreña S.A., Calle Arce 423, Apartado Postal 2296, San Salvador.

Finland — Akateeminen Kirjakauppa, 1 Keskuskatu, Helsinki.

France — Editions A. Pedone, 13, rue Soufflot, 75005 Paris.

Germany, F.R. — Alexander Horn Internationale Buchhandlung, Spiegelgasse 9, Postfach 3340, Wiesbaden.

Ghana — Fides Enterprises, P.O. Box 1628, Accra; Ghana Publishing Corporation, P.O. Box 3632, Accra.

Greece — " Eleftheroudakis ", 4 Nikis Street, Athens.

Guatemala — Distribuciones Culturales y Técnicas « Artemis », Quinta Avenida 12-11, Zona 1, Guatemala City.

Guinea-Bissau — Conselho Nacional da Cultura, Avenida da Unidade Africana, C.P. 294, Bissau.

Guyana — Guyana National Trading Corporation Ltd., 45-47 Water Street, Georgetown.

Haiti — Max Bouchereau, Librairie « A la Caravelle », B.P. 111, Port-au-Prince.

Honduras — The Bookstore, Apartado Postal 167-C, Tegucigalpa.

Hong Kong — Swindon Book Co., 13-15 Lock Road, Kowloon.

Iceland — Snaebjörn Jónsson and Co. h.f., Hafnarstraeti 9, P.O. Box 1131, Reykjavik.

India — Oxford Book and Stationery Co., Scindia House, New Delhi; 17 Park Street, Calcutta.

Indonesia — P.T. Gunung Agung, 6 Kwitang, Djakarta.

Iran — Iran Book Co. Ltd., 127 Nadershah Avenue, P.O. Box 14-1532, Tehran.

Iraq — National House for Publishing, Distributing and Advertising, Rashid Street, Baghdad.

Ireland — The Controller, Stationery Office, Dublin.

Israel — Emanuel Brown, P.O. Box 4101, 35 Allenby Road and Nachlat Benyamin Street, Tel Aviv; 9 Shlomzion Hamalka Street, Jerusalem.

Italy — Distribution and Sales Section, Food and Agriculture Organization of the United Nations, Via delle Terme di Caracalla, 00100 Rome; Libreria Scientifica Dott. L. De Biasio " Aeiou ", Via Meravigli 16, 20123 Milan; Libreria Commissionaria Sansoni " Licosa ", Via Lamarmora 45, C.P. 552, 50121 Florence.

Jamaica — Teacher Book Centre Ltd., 95 Church Street, Kingston.

Japan — Maruzen Company Ltd., P.O. Box 5050, Tokyo Central 100-31.

Kenya — Text Book Centre Ltd., P.O. Box 47540, Nairobi.

Korea, Rep. of — The Eul-Yoo Publishing Co. Ltd., 5 2-Ka, Chong-ro, Seoul.

Kuwait — Saeed & Samir Bookstore Co. Ltd., P.O. Box 5445, Kuwait.

Luxembourg — Service des publications de la FAO, M.J. De Lannoy, 202, avenue du Roi, 1060 Brussels (Belgium).

Mauritius — Nalanda Company Limited, 30 Bourbon Street, Port Louis.

Mexico — Dilitsa S.A., Puebla 182-D, Apartado 24-448, Mexico City 7, D.F.

Morocco — Librairie « Aux Belles Images », 281, avenue Mohammed V, Rabat.

Netherlands — N.V. Martinus Nijhoff, Lange Voorhout 9, The Hague.

New Zealand — Government Printing Office: Government Bookshops at Rutland Street, P.O. Box 5344, Auckland; Alma Street, P.O. Box 857, Hamilton; Mulgrave Street, Private Bag, Wellington; 130 Oxford Terrace, P.O. Box 1721, Christchurch; Princes Street, P.O. Box 1104, Dunedin.

Nicaragua — Librería Interamericana Nicaragüense S.A., Apartado 2206, Managua.

Nigeria — University Bookshop (Nigeria) Ltd., University of Ibadan, Ibadan.

Norway — Johan Grundt Tanum Bokhandel, Karl Johansgt. GT 41-43, Oslo 1.

Pakistan — Mirza Book Agency, 65 The Mall, Lahore 3.

Panama — Distribuidora Lewis S.A., Edificio Dorasol, Calle 25 y Avenida Balboa, Apartado 1634, Panama 1.

Paraguay — Agencia de Librerías Nizza S.A., Paraguarí 144, Asunción.

Peru — Librería Distribuidora Santa Rosa, Jirón Apurímac 375, Casilla 4937, Lima.

Philippines — The Modern Book Company, 928 Rizal Avenue, Manila.

Poland — Ars Polona-Ruch, Krakowskie Przedmiescie 7, Warsaw.

Portugal — Livraria Bertrand, S.A.R.L., Apartado 37, Amadora; Livraria Portugal, Dias y Andrade Ltda., Apartado 2681, Rua do Carmo 70-74, Lisbon-2; Edições ITAU, Avda. República 46A c/v-E, Lisbon-1.

Romania — Ilexim, Calea Grivitei Nº 64-66, B.P. 2001, Bucarest.

Saudi Arabia — University Bookshop, Airport Road, P.O. Box 394, Riyadh.

Senegal — Librairie Africa, 58, avenue Georges Pompidou, B.P. 1240, Dakar.

Somalia — " Samater's ", P.O. Box 936, Mogadishu.

Spain — Mundi Prensa Libros S.A., Castelló 37, Madrid-1; Librería Agrícola, Fernando VI 2, Madrid-4.

Sri Lanka — M.D. Gunasena and Co. Ltd., 217 Norris Road, Colombo 11.

Switzerland — Librairie Payot S.A., Lausanne et Genève; Buchhandlung und Antiquariat, Heinimann & Co., Kirchgasse 17, 8001 Zurich.

Suriname — VACO nv in Suriname, P.O. Box 1841, Domineenstraat 26/32, Paramaribo.

Sweden — C.E. Fritzes Kungl. Hovbokhandel, Fredsgatan 2, 103 27 Stockholm 16.

Tanzania — Dar es-Salaam Bookshop, P.O. Box 9030, Dar es-Salaam.

Thailand — Suksapan Panit, Mansion 9, Rajadamnern Avenue, Bangkok.

Togo — Librairie du Bon Pasteur, B.P. 1164, Lomé.

Trinidad and Tobago — The Book Shop, 111 Frederick Street, Port of Spain.

Tunisia — Société tunisienne de diffusion, 5, avenue de Carthage, Tunis.

Turkey — Güven Bookstores, Güven Bldg., P.O. Box 145, Müdafaa Cad. 12/5, Kizilay-Ankara; Güven Ari Bookstores, Ankara Cad. No. 45, Cağaloğlu-Istanbul; Güven Bookstore, S.S.K. Konak Tesisleri P-18, Konak-Izmir.

United Kingdom — Her Majesty's Stationery Office, 49 High Holborn, London WC1V 6HB (callers only); P.O. Box 569, London SE1 9NH (trade and London area mail orders); 13a Castle Street, Edinburgh EH2 3AR; 41 The Hayes, Cardiff CF1 1JW; 80 Chichester Street, Belfast BT1 4JY; Brazennose Street, Manchester M60 8AS; 258 Broad Street, Birmingham B1 2HE; Southey House, Wine Street, Bristol BS1 2BQ.

United States of America — UNIPUB, 345 Park Avenue South, New York, N.Y. 10010; mailing address: P.O. Box 433, Murray Hill Station, New York, N.Y. 10016.

Uruguay — Librería Editorial Juan Angel Peri, Alzaibar 1328, Casilla de Correos 1755, Montevideo.

Venezuela — Blume Distribuidora S.A., Av. Rómulo Gallegos esq. 2a. Avenida, Centro Residencial « Los Almendros », Torre 3, Mezzanina, Ofc. 6, Urbanización Montecristo, Caracas.

Yugoslavia — Jugoslovenska Knjiga, Terazije 27/11, Belgrade; Cankarjeva Zalozba, P.O. Box 201-IV, Ljubljana; Prosveta Terazije 16, P.O. Box 555, 11001 Belgrade.

Other countries — Requests from countries where sales agents have not yet been appointed may be sent to: Distribution and Sales Section, Food and Agriculture Organization of the United Nations, Via delle Terme di Caracalla, 00100 Rome, Italy.

Foto-Tipo-lito SAGRAF - Napoli

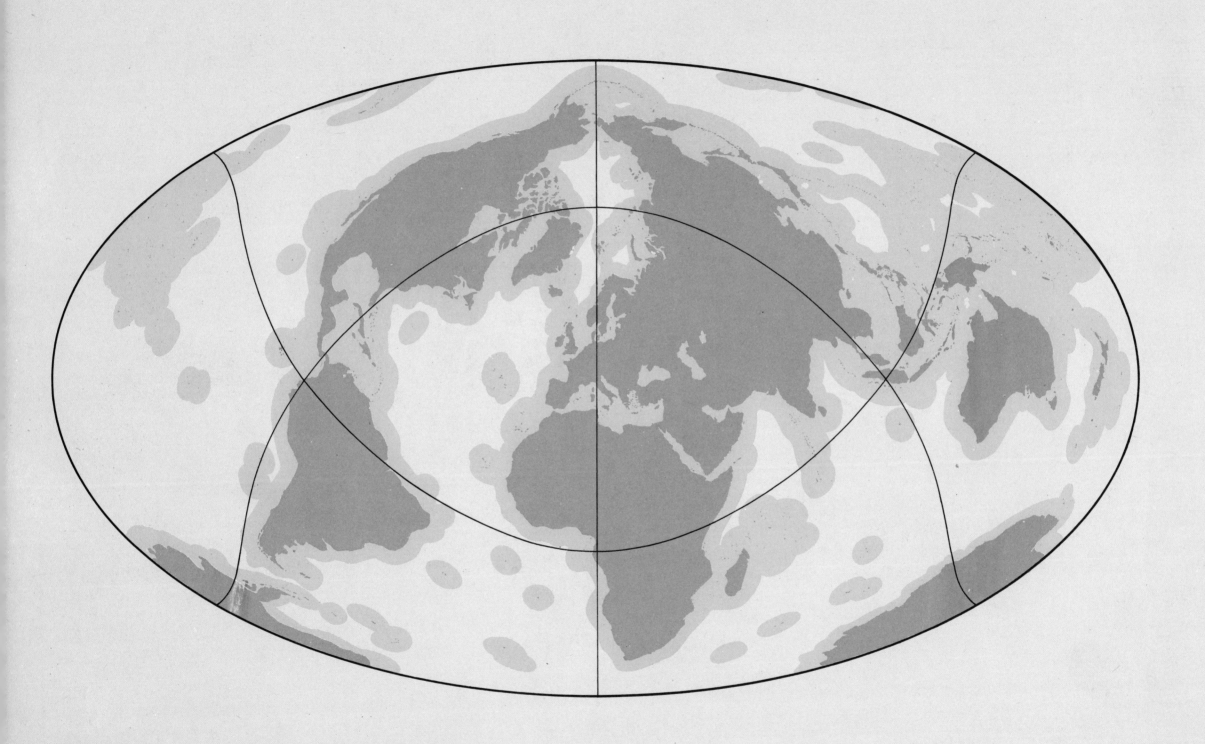